James Griffin

The catechetical reading-book in two parts

I. Outlines of sacred history, II. Lessons on doctrinal subjects

James Griffin

The catechetical reading-book in two parts
I. Outlines of sacred history, II. Lessons on doctrinal subjects

ISBN/EAN: 9783742861917

Manufactured in Europe, USA, Canada, Australia, Japa

Cover: Foto ©Lupo / pixelio.de

Manufactured and distributed by brebook publishing software (www.brebook.com)

James Griffin

The catechetical reading-book in two parts

THE

Catechetical Reading-Book.

IN TWO PARTS.

I.

OUTLINES OF SACRED HISTORY,
PRECEDED BY A LESSON ON SCRIPTURAL GEOGRAPHY.

II.

LESSONS ON DOCTRINAL SUBJECTS,
FOLLOWING THE ORDER AND ARRANGEMENT OF THE CATECHISM.

BY

THE VERY REV. JAMES GRIFFIN,

CANON THEOLOGIAN OF NOTTINGHAM,
AND FORMERLY PROFESSOR AT ST. MARY'S COLLEGE, OSCOTT.

LONDON:
BURNS & LAMBERT, 17 & 18 PORTMAN STREET,
PORTMAN SQUARE.

NIHIL OBSTAT,

Joan. Can. Poen. Morris,

Cens. Syn.

Imprimatur.

N. CARD. WISEMAN.

WESTMON. *April 23, 1864.*

PREFACE.

THE Compiler of the following pages has for many years been seeking for a suitable book to put in the hands of Day and Sunday Scholars, by the help of which they might, by their *own reading*, get a fair knowledge of religion. The only book with which the Compiler is acquainted, as having been written for a school religious reading-book, and which he has very much made use of for want of a better, is Curr's "Familiar Instructions." But this contains too many difficult words, which require a master or a dictionary, and perhaps, in other respects, might be improved; at any rate, a new edition of it was required. Other excellent books exist, but they were not written for the object which the Compiler has had in view, and they were, besides, too large and expensive.

After children have learnt by heart the Elementary

Catechism, or while they are learning it, this book may be put into their hands. They should be required to master its contents, chapter after chapter, and be expected to give answers to the teacher, who, by a question or two, will be able to extract from the pupils the substance of each sentence. It has been written in such a manner, that each sentence shall contain one or two ideas, on which a teacher can easily put questions, and to which a scholar who has carefully read the chapter will easily find an answer. Words requiring the use of a dictionary have, as far as possible, been avoided. Questions at the end of each chapter have not been given, in order to save expense in printing. One great object has been to have a book as cheap as possible, with the hope that it may be more extensively used.

If this book is useful for *Day* Scholars, it is hoped that it may be still more useful for *Sunday* Scholars. Sunday Scholars especially find learning by heart very irksome, and an easy book to read and to learn the substance of, by a little exercise of the *understanding*, and not such an effort of the *memory* as is required in learning by heart, may probably interest them. They can prepare a lesson of this by themselves, in school or at home; and a teacher of ordinary intelligence will be able to question them on the lesson without difficulty, and without having to draw upon any store of catechetical knowledge of his own.

It has also been written in the hope that it may be found of some use, not merely in elementary schools, but also in the junior classes of other Catholic schools, for whom it is often difficult to find a suitable book for school use, and who frequently do not study anything but a small catechism which is committed to memory.

Perhaps, also, this may be found a book suitable to put into the hands of persons who desire to become Catholics, or of adult Catholics who are a little backward in their religious knowledge.

In all the above cases, it is hoped that it may diminish the labour of the clergy, by saving the necessity of so many repetitions and explanations which they are obliged to give to children and others. If this little Manual should, in this way, be found to be of some help to the clergy in the laborious duty of conveying religious ideas to the thousands of children intrusted to their care, it will be a great satisfaction to the Compiler; and, in any case, the defects, which will no doubt be soon discovered in the present attempt, may be a help and a caution to any one whose zeal may prompt him to a similar undertaking.

On the plan of Fleury, in his lesser and greater Catechisms, the first part treats of the history, and the second part of the doctrines of religion; and both have been written that the substance of them may be *learnt*, and not merely superficially read through. They have been written in such a manner, that they may serve as a well-defined historical and doctrinal outline, which will enable the youthful student to derive more profit from, and to classify more easily, the ideas he will acquire by future reading and instruction.

The Compiler of these pages has taken freely from any works which answered his purpose. It would be needless to quote the writers he may have consulted. The poetical extracts are from the works of the late Father Faber, who kindly granted permission to make free use of his volume of hymns.

J. G.

St. Barnabas, Nottingham,
March 25th, 1864.

CONTENTS.

	PAGE
Introductory Lesson on Scriptural Geography	1
Names of the Land, Mountains, Streams	1
Galilee	4
Samaria	5
Judæa	5
Philistia	8
Phœnicia	9
Asia Minor	10
A Few Words on Chronology	12

Part the First.

OUTLINES OF SACRED HISTORY.

CHAPTER I.
Angels, good and bad 17

CHAPTER II.
Adam and Eve 18

CHAPTER III.
Fall from Grace to Sin—A Redeemer promised—Original Sin—Spiritual Condition of Men before Christ 20

CHAPTER IV.
Cain—Abel—Noe 22

CHAPTER V.
Abraham—Isaac—Jacob—Joseph—Holy Job 25

CHAPTER VI.
Israel in Egypt—Moses—The Departure 29

CHAPTER VII.
The Israelites in the Wilderness 31

CHAPTER VIII.
The Israelites in the Wilderness (*continued*)—Moses dies .. 33

CHAPTER IX.
Settlement in the Holy Land under Josue 37

CHAPTER X.
Government of Judges—Book of Ruth 39

CHAPTER XI.
The Kings—Saul—David—Solomon 40

CHAPTER XII.
The Kingdoms of Israel and Juda—Their End 43

CHAPTER XIII.
The Prophets 46

CHAPTER XIV.
The Captivity—End of the Babylonian Empire—Return from Captivity 47

CHAPTER XV.
Jews under the Persians—Esther—Esdras—Nehemias .. 51

CHAPTER XVI.
State of the Jews under Alexander the Great and his Successors—The Maccabees—Herod, the Idumean 55

CHAPTER XVII.
St. John the Baptist—Early Life of Christ 59

CONTENTS.   ix

CHAPTER XVIII.

PAGE

Christ's Public Ministry—Feeds the Multitude—The Transfiguration—Institution of Blessed Eucharist   64

CHAPTER XIX.

Foundation of the Church—Conversion of the Samaritans—Conversion and Labours of St. Paul—Apostolic Labours of St. Peter—Books of the New Testament   72

CHAPTER XX.

History of the Church (*continued*)—Jerusalem destroyed—St. Cletus, the Third Pope—St. Clement, the Fourth Pope—End of the Jewish Nation—Julian's Attempt to rebuild the Temple   78

Part the Second.

LESSONS ON DOCTRINAL SUBJECTS.

CHAPTER I.

Why God made Man, and how Man is to worship God, and to save his Soul   85

CHAPTER II.

FAITH—THE APOSTLES' CREED.

1st Article, "God the Father"   88
2nd Article, "Jesus Christ"   90
3rd Article, "Who was conceived by the Holy Ghost"—"Born of the Virgin Mary"   92
4th Article—Sufferings of Christ—The Way of the Cross and the Seven Last Words—The Sign of the Cross .. 95
5th Article—Descent into Hell and Resurrection   105
6th Article—Ascension into Heaven   107
7th Article—Particular Judgment—General Judgment   .. 109
8th Article—The Holy Ghost—Foundation of the Church .. 112
9th Article—The Church is One, Holy, Catholic, Apostolic, Infallible—Communion of Saints (threefold)   115
10th Article—Forgiveness of Sins   123
11th Article—Resurrection of the Body   127
12th Article—Life Everlasting   128

CHAPTER III.

HOPE—THE LORD'S PRAYER.

	PAGE
Prayer	129
Seven Petitions of the Lord's Prayer	131
Prayer to the Saints	134
The Hail Mary	135

CHAPTER IV.

CHARITY.

Commandments in General	137
1st Commandment	139
2nd Commandment	142
3rd Commandment	144
4th Commandment	148
5th Commandment	152
6th Commandment	155
7th Commandment	157
8th Commandment	159
9th and 10th Commandments	161

CHAPTER V.

Commandments of the Church	163
1st and 2nd Commandments—Resting from Servile Work and hearing Mass	164
3rd Commandment—Fasting and Abstinence	165
4th Commandment—Yearly Confession	169
5th Commandment—Easter Communion	170
6th Commandment—Forbidden Degrees of Kindred—Forbidden Times	173

CHAPTER VI.

The Sacraments in General	174
Baptism, its Necessity, Ceremonies, &c.	176
Confirmation, Scriptural Evidence, Effects, Directions, Preparation for Ceremonies	180
Holy Eucharist—Communion under one Kind—Effects of Holy Communion—Preparation, &c.	185
Sacrifice of the Mass—Ceremonies of the Mass—Latin Language—Parts of the Mass	189
Penance—Scriptural Evidence on Confession—Examination of Conscience—Contrition—Firm Purpose of Amendment—" The Confession "—" The Penance "—Indulgences	197
Extreme Unction—Ceremonies—Directions for Time of Sickness	208

CHAPTER VI. (*continued*.)

	PAGE
Holy Orders—Various Orders—Celibacy	211
Matrimony—Indissoluble—Impediments—Mixed Marriages—Ceremonies of Marriage — Holiness of Marriage — Bad Marriages—Cautions and Directions for a Good Marriage	213

CHAPTER VII.
OF VIRTUES AND VICES.

Theological Virtues	220
Cardinal Virtues	223
Seven Corporal and Spiritual Works of Mercy	225
The Eight Beatitudes	228
The Seven Deadly Sins	230
Sins against the Holy Ghost — The Four Sins crying to Heaven for Vengeance	234
Partaking in the Sins of Others	235
The Three Eminent Good Works—Evangelical Counsels—Four Last Things	236
The Conclusion — The Christian's Rule of Life — The Christian's Daily Exercise	239

THE

Catechetical Reading-Book.

INTRODUCTORY LESSON.

SCRIPTURE GEOGRAPHY.

IT will be very useful in learning the history of religion to know a little of the geography of places named in Scripture, and also some of the dates, when the chief events took place. Geography and chronology (which last tells us of times and dates) have been called the two eyes of history.

The scholar, therefore, should study carefully the present chapter on the geography of the chief places in Palestine and find them on the map, or should have them pointed out by the teacher.

NAMES OF THE LAND, MOUNTAINS, STREAMS.

The land promised for an inheritance to Abraham and his seed, and the scene of the principal events recorded in Scripture, has been known by the following names.

1. *The Land of Chanaan*, from Chanaan, the youngest son of Cham, among whose sons the country was divided.

2. *The Land of the Hebrews*, as the possession of the descendants of Abraham. To Abraham and his posterity, was given the name of Hebrews (passers over),

B

because Abraham had dwelt on the other side of the Euphrates and had passed over it, on his journey to the land of Chanaan.

3. *The Land of Israel*, from the posterity of Jacob, who is also called Israel.

4. *The Land of Juda.*—This name had reference, originally, to that division of the country belonging to the tribe of Juda, but was afterwards applied to the kingdom formed by the tribes of Benjamin and Juda. When the remnant of the two tribes returned from captivity, that of Juda was so pre-eminent, that the name "Land of Juda" or "Judea" was by degrees extended to the whole country.

5. *Palestine*, so called from the Philistines, who obtained possession of a large tract of land in the southwest part of the country along the coast of the Mediterranean Sea. It is now more generally known by this, than by any of its other names.

Palestine had Lebanon on the north, the Mediterranean on the west, the Arabian desert on the east and south. Its length from north to south is about 190 miles, the average width, about 70 miles. This gives an extent of territory equal to about one-fifth of England and Wales. The countries in Europe to which it can be compared in extent are Belgium, Holland, and Switzerland. They each contain about the same number of square miles, that is about eleven thousand. In the time of David the population of Palestine was five millions: Belgium has about four millions; Holland nearly three millions; and Switzerland about two and a quarter millions.

There is scarcely a mountain, valley, plain, or river which has not some historical interest.

Palestine is a *mountainous* country, a land of hills and valleys. The hills in general are not in ranges, but are more or less apart. A mountain chain extends from north to south, on both sides of the Jordan. In its different directions and individual parts it bears various names.

Lebanon or Libanus on the north, which means "white mountain," was so called, because its highest peaks were covered with snow, even in summer. It was famed for its cedars, of which were built the temple of Jerusalem and the palace of Solomon.

Standing in a plain, at the foot of Mount Lebanon, in Syria, is *Damascus*, the city near which St. Paul was struck down by a light from heaven, when he was on his way to persecute the Christians; and *Antioch*, once a seaport, and the place where the disciples were first called Christians.

Mount Carmel is the headland or promontory by the sea, at the extremity of the bay of Acre. " Carmel," means a country of gardens and vineyards. The whole of this mountain is full of caverns, and among them are shown those which the prophets Elias and Eliseus made their place of resort. To Mount Carmel all Israel were gathered on the occasion when fire came from heaven to consume the sacrifice of Elias; and, then, at the foot of the mountain, the priests of Baal were put to death; and on its summit Elias was praying when the long-wished-for rain fell after a long drought.

None of the *streams* in Palestine deserve the name of a river except the *Jordan;* the others are brooks whose beds are dry in summer. The Jordan rises north of the lake of Gennesareth, flows through it, without mingling its waters with those of the lake; on leaving the lake it flows for about sixty miles through a beautiful plain, and empties itself into the Dead Sea. Its course is from north to south, through the whole extent of Palestine, dividing it into two unequal parts, the much smaller being east of the Jordan. The Jews considered it sacred on account of the many miracles connected with it. Christ was baptized in it by St. John the Baptist; its waters turned back to let the Israelites pass through on dry land to Jericho; twice were its waters divided by Elias and Eliseus. It was visited at Easter every year, by thousands of pilgrims.

In the time of Christ, that part of Palestine between the Jordan and the Mediterranean, was divided into three provinces; Judea in the south, Samaria in the centre, and Galilee in the north.

GALILEE.

The most northern point of Galilee is the town called Dan. Here Jeroboam, after the revolt of the ten tribes, set up one of his golden calves.

The Sea of Galilee, or the Lake of Tiberias, is twelve miles in length, and five or six miles wide. In ancient times, boats and fishermen were continually employed on its waters. It was subject, like other lakes surrounded by hills, to sudden and violent gusts of wind. From its shores the Apostles were called to be fishers of men. Here was the scene of the miraculous draught of fishes, and the calming of the raging winds. Here Christ walked on the waters, and on its shores, after His resurrection, He manifested Himself to His Apostles (St. John xxi.). To the north of the lake is the hill of the Beatitudes, where Christ preached His Sermon on the Mount.

Mount Thabor, the scene of the transfiguration, lies west, at the south extremity of the lake, and its top, one thousand feet high, commands a wide view of the Mediterranean, the Jordan, and Lake Tiberias.

The Dead Sea, Salt Sea, or Sea of Sodom, lies furthest to the south. No living things are seen about it, or found in its waters. It is the site of the cities destroyed by fire from heaven. It is forty miles in length, and about ten in breadth. All around has a sterile and dismal appearance. The waters are bitter, salt, and sulphureous.

Capharnaum is on the west coast of the Sea of Galilee. Our Saviour most frequently resided here after the commencement of His public ministry. It was called "His own city." He often taught in the synagogues here, and worked miracles. It did not profit by His preaching; hence the woe pronounced against it. Its site is now utterly unknown. Bethsaida and Corozaïn, near the same lake, shared the same woe, and for the same reason.

Nazareth was built on a hill-side, nearly surrounded by mountains. Our Saviour, on one occasion, was led by His fellow-townsmen to the brow of the hill on which the city was built, that they might cast Him down headlong. The valley of Nazareth is about two miles and a half long. Nazareth was the residence of Christ before His public ministry; hence, He was called "Jesus of Nazareth." *Cana*, the scene of the first miracle of Christ, is near Nazareth. *Naim*, at whose gates Christ raised the widow's son, lies seven miles south-east of Nazareth.

Samaria.

Samaria was the central province of Judæa.

Samaria, was the name of the chief town, the capital of the ten tribes that formed the kingdom of Israel, or the kingdom of Samaria. When the Jews began to rebuild Jerusalem and the temple, they refused the assistance of the Samaritans; hence, the hatred that arose between them. The Samaritans built a temple on Mount Garizim, in opposition to the one in Jerusalem. The former was destroyed about one hundred and twenty-nine years before Christ. The Samaritans believed the Gospel on the preaching of Philip the Deacon. Our Saviour praised the Samaritans in the parable of the good Samaritan, and in the miracle of the ten lepers; by the Samaritans our Saviour was welcomed with more willingness than by the Jews. Churches were soon founded, and were at peace after the conversion of Saul.

Bethel was the border town between Israel and Judæa. An idol was set up there by Jeroboam.

Judæa.

Judæa was the southern province, and the name given to the whole country after the captivity, because the tribe of Juda formed the principal part of those who returned.

Joppa was the seaport town of Jerusalem, forty miles north-west of Jerusalem. The cedars for Solomon's temple were sent to this port, by the King of Tyre, and thence by land to Jerusalem. Jonas embarked here to escape going to Nineveh, where he was sent to preach repentance.

Jerusalem was called the Holy City, also the City of David, for David conquered the Jebusites who before possessed it.

For 500 years before Christ it suffered continually from the wars waged by the Syrians, Egyptians, and Romans, to get possession of it. It was finally destroyed by Titus in the seventy-ninth year of the Christian era. The ground on which the city and temple stood, was ploughed up by order of Titus. Two millions of the inhabitants either perished, or were made prisoners. Thus was our Saviour's word fulfilled, "that not one stone should be left upon another."

On the east of Jerusalem, and separated from it by the narrow valley of Josaphat, is the *Mount of Olives*, so called from the olive-trees with which it was covered. It consists of four mountains; and from the highest of them, Christ went up into heaven. This one rises up from the garden of Gethsemani, the place of His agony, and is about 2,530 feet in height. This mountain was the favourite resort of our blessed Saviour from the noise and distractions of the city. In the daytime, He was teaching in the temple. On this mountain He sat and told His disciples the signs of His coming, and of the end of the world. Here He led forth His Apostles, gave them His last commission, and, blessing them, departed from them into Heaven.

The Valley of Josaphat lies between Jerusalem and the Mount of Olives. It is very narrow, and about a mile long. *The Brook Cedron* runs through it, and empties itself into the Dead Sea. Here was the general burying-place for the population of the Holy City. The tomb of Josaphat, and others of note, were there. From a passage of the prophet Joel (iii. 2.) there is a belief, that this valley is to be the scene of the resurrection, and of the general judgment. David crossed the Brook Cedron with his attendants, when he fled from his son Absalom; and weeping as he went, ascended the Mount of Olives: and our blessed Saviour crossed this brook to enter into the Garden of Gethsemani, on that night when he was betrayed into the hands of His enemies.

At Jerusalem, we read of the *Pool of Siloë*, where the blind man was directed by Christ to go and wash. Also the *Pool of Bethsaida*, which had miraculous powers (St. John v. 4), where Christ cured the man afflicted for thirty-eight years.

Water had to be artificially collected in cisterns, or pools, as it often could not be obtained by sinking wells. Some of immense extent were filled with water, during the rainy season. The early and the latter rain fell at two stated times in the year; one at the end of October, the other in April; at other times, rain was not known, but the want of it was supplied by the abundant dews.

Bethania, nearly two miles distant from Jerusalem, was the residence of Lazarus, who was raised to life. Here, during the last days of His life, Christ retired every evening from Jerusalem. It was on the other side of the Mount of Olives.

Bethphage is on the east of Bethania. From this village Christ sent two of His disciples to bring an ass and her colt, that He might ride thereon to Jerusalem; thus fulfilling a prophecy.

Emmaus, eight miles north-west of Jerusalem, is noted for the interview which took place between our Lord and the two disciples on the day of His resurrection.

Jericho, the city of Palms, lies north-east of Jerusalem, and six miles from the Jordan. It was the first place that fell into the hands of the Israelites. Afterwards it was the seat of one of the schools of the prophets, and was next in importance to Jerusalem. It is often mentioned in the Gospels. Near this, at *Galgal*, were the head-quarters of the Israelites, while engaged in conquering the country. The tabernacle also remained here till it was removed to Siloh. The tabernacle and ark remained in Siloh until the close of the life of Heli, the high-priest, when they were taken by the Philistines, and the sons of Heli slain. Samuel spent his youth at Siloh in the service of the sanctuary. North-east, between Jerusalem and Jericho, is a mountainous tract of country, stern and wild in its appearance, probably *the wilderness,* where, after His baptism, Jesus was led by the Spirit to be tempted by the devil. The highest of those mountains is the scene of the forty days fast; and from this, Satan showed our Lord all the kingdoms of the earth.

Bethlehem was distant six miles from Jerusalem, towards the south. It was the birthplace of Christ. It was called the "City of David," as it was the place of David's birth. It was about ninety miles direct from Nazareth; but, considering the hilly nature of the country, a journey between the two places must be considered much greater. The Blessed Virgin had to journey from Nazareth to Bethlehem, on occasion of the general registration ordered by the Emperor Augustus.

The three celebrated Pools of Solomon at Bethlehem, were built to supply Jerusalem with water. The waters were thrown into a cistern and conveyed to Jerusalem.

Hebron is sixteen miles south of Bethlehem. Here was Abraham's burying-place, which he had bought for himself. When David became king, he made Hebron his capital, and continued to reside in it until Jerusalem was taken from the Jebusites.

Bersabee lay twenty-seven miles south of Hebron. It was at the southern extremity of Chanaan; hence the expression "from Dan to Bersabee" meant the whole length of the kingdom of Juda. Bersabee means, *the well of the oath,* from the treaty sworn to, there, between Abimelech and Abraham. It is often spoken of in sacred history.

The east of the Jordan, has not so many places worthy of being remembered.

Philistia.

The country of the Philistines lay on the coast of the Mediterranean, west and south-west of Judæa. In the time of Josue it had five lordships, called from the chief town of each.

Accaron was the northernmost of the five cities; the Ark when taken was sent from Geth to Accaron, and thence sent back, drawn by two milch cows on a new cart; they took the way to Bethsames.

Geth was celebrated as the residence of Goliath, the champion of the Philistines. David, to save his life from Saul, fled to the King of Geth.

Azotus had a famous temple of Dagon; the image fell down when the Ark was brought into it. It was taken after a siege of twenty-nine years by Psammetticus, king of Egypt. This is the longest siege on record. Azotus is mentioned in the history of Philip the Deacon.

Ascalon, ten miles south-west of Azotus, was the principal maritime town of Philistia.

Gaza, fifteen miles from Ascalon, was the most southern of the five townships. Gaza is renowned as the scene of some of Samson's mighty deeds, and of his death. Here he drew down the temple of Dagon on his own head and on the assembled multitude. Near Gaza, Philip baptized the officer of Candace, queen of the Ethiopians.

Phœnicia.

This country lay along the seacoast, on the north-west of Palestine; and is often referred to in sacred history.

Sidon was a famous commercial town on the seacoast; none were skilled in hewing timber like the Sidonians; they assisted in the first and second temples. It brought on itself, the threats of the prophets.

Sarephtha, south of Sidon, was the residence of the prophet Elias; here he multiplied the oil and meal, and raised the widow's son.

Tyre, south of Sarephtha and twenty-two miles from Sidon (called the daughter of Sidon), was founded by a colony from that city. It soon surpassed the parent city; its merchants were princes. It was besieged for five years without success by Salmanasar, king of Assyria. It was taken after thirteen years' siege by Nabuchodonosor. New Tyre, built after the destruction of Old Tyre, was taken by Alexander the Great.

Asia Minor.

Asia Minor is a peninsula, nine hundred miles in length from east to west, and four hundred miles from north to south. It is the most western part of Asia, bounded on the south by the Mediterranean, on the east by the Euphrates, on the north by the Black Sea, and on the west by the Ægean Sea.

It contained, anciently, twelve provinces. Many of them are mentioned in the New Testament, and were the scenes of important events in the history of the early Christian churches. The seven churches of the Apocalypse were in Asia Minor.

St. Peter addressed his first letter to the Christians scattered through Pontus, Bithynia, &c., provinces lying along the Black Sea.

In Mysia, at *Troas*, St. Paul saw the vision of the man of Macedonia, and raised the young man Eutychus.

Pergamus was one of the "seven churches" of Asia, named in the Apocalypse (Rev. ii. 12). In Lydia, was *Smyrna*, one of the "seven churches" (Rev. ii. 8), the scene of the labours of the martyr Polycarp, the disciple of St. John. *Sardis*, the chief town of Lydia, was also one of the "seven churches."

Philadelphia, twenty-eight miles east of Sardis, was one of the "seven churches."

Ephesus, once the first and greatest metropolis of Asia, was famous for the temple of Diana, which, from its size, beauty, and magnificence, was one of the seven wonders of the world.

The preaching of St. Paul was very successful here, and created a tumult among the sellers of the silver shrines of Diana. It was one of the "seven churches." The first bishop was St. Timothy. St. John lived and laboured here; and the Blessed Virgin lived and died here under the care of St. John. The great general council against Nestorius was held at Ephesus.

At *Antioch of Pisidia*, St. Paul and St. Barnabas preached and delivered that memorable discourse recorded in the thirteenth chapter of the Acts; but the envy of the Jews caused them to be expelled, and they went to Iconium.

Tarsus, the chief town of Cilicia, was the birthplace of St. Paul. In learning and refinement, it ranked by the side of Athens and Alexandria.

The Cappadocians are addressed in St. Peter's first epistle, and are mentioned as being at Jerusalem on the day of Pentecost, and some were probably converted.

In Galatia, the Gospel was soon preached, and St. Paul addressed to them one of his epistles.

Of Phrygia, *Laodicea* was the capital, and was one of the "seven churches" (Rev. iii. 14—19). It was not safe to live here, through the frequent earthquakes.

To the people of *Colosse*, the Apostle addressed one of his epistles. Two years after it was destroyed by an earthquake.

St. Paul and St. Barnabas had fled to *Iconium*, from Antioch of Pisidia, but being driven from there also, they fled to Lystra and Derbe, cities of Lycaonia. At Lystra the people would have worshipped the two Apostles as Jupiter and Mercury; but soon after St. Paul was stoned and left as dead.

In reading the sacred histories, there is brought before us, in regular succession, the sovereignties established on the banks of the Tigris and Euphrates, and the States that rose to eminence on the eastern shore of the Mediterranean Sea; the kingdoms of Egypt, Ethiopia, Syria, Assyria, Babylon, and Persia, and the influence which they possessed in the affairs of men in different ages of the world. It would be well, therefore, for every student to see now and then, on some map of the ancient world, how those countries were situated in regard to one another.

A FEW WORDS ON CHRONOLOGY.

As in going a journey it is pleasant to know how many miles you have travelled and how many yet remain, so, in passing through the forty centuries between Adam and our Saviour's coming, it is pleasant to know where you are, how many centuries have passed, and how many yet remain.

The Hebrews were the only ancient people who had a regular chronological history. In the Sacred Scriptures there is a chain of such history beginning at the Creation, and ending at the time when genuine profane history begins. The Scriptural dates are marked by the registered succession of first-born sons; then by the time during which a succession of judges and kings are recorded to have held office.

The duration of the world from the creation of the first man recorded in Genesis, till the birth of Christ, is computed to be about 4,000 years. At the middle of this period, or two thousand years before Christ, and two thousand years after the creation of man, Abraham was born. The call of Abraham to leave his own country and to go and settle in another, was the beginning of that important arrangement of Providence, by which one family was separated from the rest of the world, and in time increased to a nation. That nation was planted in a central place of the earth, that they might keep up among them the knowledge of the one true God, which was almost lost, and afterwards teach it to the rest of mankind. In the middle of the period between the birth of Abraham and the birth of Christ, or about the year B.C. (before Christ) 1000, Solomon's temple was finished. At this era or period of time, the promises made to Abraham were fulfilled, for then, and not till then, did his seed reign in peace and prosperity from the great river Euphrates to the shores of the Mediterranean Sea.

From the Creation to the time of the Deluge, little is known, but the time from the Deluge till Christ may, for the sake of memory, be arranged in periods of five hundred years each, as in the following table :—

	Anno Mundi. A.M. Years after Creation.	Years before Christ. B.C.
Creation		4000
Noah	1500	2500
Abraham ..	2000	2000
Moses	2500	1500
Solomon	3000	1000
Esdras	3500	500
Jesus Christ	4000	Anno Domini. A.D. Year of our Lord, 1.

Part the First.

OUTLINES OF SACRED HISTORY.

Outlines of Sacred History.

CHAPTER I.

ANGELS, GOOD AND BAD.

"In the beginning God created heaven and earth."

GOD had been from all eternity infinitely happy and perfect in Himself. He was at length pleased to create a great multitude of beings who might share with Him in His happiness. They are called angels, which word means messengers. They are so called because one of their chief employments is to carry God's messages to men; and it was in this employment that men first came to know them. God made them spirits without bodies. It was not intended that they should be placed in eternal happiness till they had passed through some trial, and had given some proof of their faithfulness to God. We cannot well understand, how, or what that trial was. In knowledge and all spiritual gifts they were far more excellent than men ever were. They therefore must have known, in the first moment of their creation, who God was, and that they were His creatures. Yet many of those spirits thought so much of themselves and of the beauty with which God had clothed them, that they looked on themselves as equal to God, and refused to serve Him. This first sin was the sin of pride. The chief of them was called Satan, or Lucifer (that is, Morning Star), from his brightness; his followers and companions are called the evil spirits and devils. In driven out of heaven, and were cast into hell, which was there and then made to be their prison. There they have been ever since, and will for ever be. Hell is a place of fire and torments, and of everything dreadful, beyond all that man can imagine. Out of hell there is no release. Hell was not created in the beginning for wicked men, but only for the devil and his angels.

The other spirits, the good angels, remained faithful to God. They knew Him, loved, and worshipped Him, their Creator. St. Michael is their chief. They were soon put in possession of never-ending happiness.

CHAPTER II.

ADAM AND EVE.

It is not against Scripture to believe that this world was created, and had lasted many ages before man was made. Religion begins with man, and does not require us to know what might have been before man was created.

God created the world,— that is, made it out of nothing. He spoke the word, and all things were made. He commanded, and they were created. He made all things in six days. He furnished the earth that it might be a worthy dwelling-place for the being that was to live in it. He made the light, and set up the sun and moon and stars in heaven. He clothed the earth with verdure, planted it with trees and flowers, and filled it with living creatures. When all was ready, then on the sixth day, man was made to be the master of this newly-fashioned pare himself for that eternal rest, for which God had made him.

When God was about to make man, He said, "Let us make man to our own image and likeness." He then made for him a body from the dust of the earth, and breathed into his face the breath of life — that is, He created a spiritual and immortal soul, and united it to the body. It is the soul, not the body of man, which has some likeness to God; for God has no body, but is a pure spirit. After this, God made woman to be the companion of man. Her name was Eve; she was made from one of the ribs of Adam, to show that man and wife should love each other, and be as one body. It was then that God appointed marriage. He blessed them, and bade them increase, and multiply, and fill the earth, and rule over it. They had the fruits of trees and plants permitted them for their food; but not the flesh of animals. They were placed in a delightful garden (somewhere in the neighbourhood of the rivers Tigris and Euphrates), called the garden of Eden, or Paradise, which they had to keep in order (Gen. ii. 14). They had no want nor trouble. They suffered no sickness or diseases which lead to death, for they were not to have died. They could eat of all the trees in Paradise but one; the fruit of that one, was forbidden to them. This was the only proof of obedience required from them. They conversed with God as friend with friend, and lived happily. After their time of easy trial was over, they were to have been taken into heaven, to join the good angels, and to have seen God for ever. Man was made for this end, and thus was to have filled the places left empty by the fallen angels.

CHAPTER III.

THE FALL FROM GRACE TO SIN.

ADAM AND EVE remained probably but a short time in this happy state. Satan beheld their happiness with envy. The evil spirits have power from God to tempt man, to try his obedience, and to seek his utter ruin. We always, therefore, have reason to fear and be on our guard against their cunning. The devil is one of our great enemies. One of those evil spirits, in the form of a serpent, by lying and false promises, deceived Eve into eating the forbidden fruit. She gave to her husband, and he also ate of it. This act in them was a sin of grievous disobedience to God, which stripped them of grace, made them worthy of eternal death in hell, and at once shut heaven against them. Besides this death of the soul, they brought upon themselves a sad change even in this world. Man had now to till the earth by the labour and sweat of his brow, and then he was to return to the dust from which he came. Moreover, woman was to bring forth her children in pain. Both were driven out of Paradise into the wide world, now to them become a wilderness. The seasons became changeable and severe; heat and cold, hunger and thirst, began to trouble them. Long sicknesses and diseases were sent in punishment, yet in mercy, to prepare man for the grave. All the powers of his soul, which had been poisoned by sin, became so weak and helpless and disordered, that all manner of wickedness took possession of the heart which had little or no power to resist. Ignorance took the place of knowledge, and passion disturbed or drove away reason. Such was the fall of our first parents from holiness to sin! What a miserable fall it was!

A Redeemer promised.—Yet, miserable as was their condition, God did not leave them without hope. At the very time that God pronounced His judgment against them, He gave them promise (Gen. iii.15) of a Redeemer. By virtue and merits of that promised Saviour, God took pity on them, gave them time to repent, though after death neither they nor their children could enter heaven till Christ had actually come. As the ransom money promised, but not yet paid down, often at once improves the condition of the prisoner, so a Saviour promised, but not yet sent, began to bring blessings to fallen man.

Original Sin.—God had created man, not for a *natural*, but for a *supernatural* end. *Supernatural*, means something beyond what is natural. The happiness promised to man in heaven is *supernatural*. God need not have created man for such happiness at all. Adam by his sin missed in obtaining what was intended for him. As he was the head of the human family, he lost his title-deeds to heaven for his children, as well as for himself. Thus, a nobleman guilty of disloyalty to his king, loses his estate and honours, and is banished from his country. By the father's crime his children also, and his descendants for generations, may have to live in poverty and exile, until perhaps, at last, they are restored by an act of royal grace. This was done for fallen, banished man.

As we are the children of Adam, we are born deprived of the privileges which he once had. This blemish of our birth is called "original sin." We are conceived and born in original sin. This means that the soul of man at its creation is no longer clothed with that supernatural grace in which Adam's soul was created, and which, if not lost, would have made us fit for heaven.

Spiritual condition of men before Christ.—But man *was* to be restored, and in the meanwhile, before Christ actually came on earth, sufficient graces were given to all men to be saved; but more abundantly to the Jews. This was through the merits of the promised Saviour. Christ, therefore, has been the salvation of men in all times. He is the Lamb that was slain from the beginning of the world.

The spiritual condition of man before Christ came, on many accounts, was inferior to what it has been since. Still, it was not so bad, as many, under a mistake, have thought. St. Leo, on this subject, says, "Let men cease from their complaints against Providence, as having so long delayed the birth of a Saviour, as though the former ages had not received the fruit of the mysteries realized in the latter ages of the world. The incarnation of the Word produced *before* its accomplishment what it has produced since; and never in the remotest antiquity was the mystery of man's salvation without effect." Again, St. Leo says, " It is not by a new design, nor by a slow act of compassion, that God has provided for human things; but from the beginning of the world, He has established for all men one and the same cause of salvation. The grace of God, by which the saints of all time were justified, has *increased* without doubt by the birth of Christ; but it was not *begun* at His birth."

CHAPTER IV.

CAIN—ABEL—NOE.

THE first children of Adam and Eve were Cain and Abel. They worshipped God by sacrifice and offerings. Cain offered of the fruits of the earth; but Abel, who was a shepherd, offered of the firstlings of his flock. God, who knows the heart, showed more favour to the offering of Abel than to that of Cain. Cain, being filled with envy, slew his brother.

Murder became a common crime among the descendants of Cain, and soon, other frightful disorders were committed, which violated the sanctity and unity of marriage.

Meanwhile Adam and Eve had given birth to Seth, who was destined to be the father of a race of just and religious men like Abel. It was among his descendants, that there appear those virtuous men who were called *patriarchs* or heads of families. There are reckoned *ten* before the Deluge, beginning with Adam and ending with

Noe. One of these, Henoch, was miraculously taken out of the world. The holy life of these patriarchs bore a singular contrast, during many long years, to the wicked life of other men, and for this reason the Holy Scriptures call them "*the children of God*," whilst they call the descendants of Cain, "*the children of men.*"

But at last the *children of God* intermarried with the *children of men*, and allowed themselves to be corrupted, so that the whole human race became corrupt. God even repented that He had made man, and resolved to destroy him. But with all their wickedness, we do not read of any idolatry before the Deluge. It was easy for them in those times, to keep up the belief in one true God, for Noe lived with Mathusalem, and Mathusalem with Adam.

In this general wickedness, only Noe, a descendant of Seth, found favour with God. God warned him that He was about to send a deluge of water on the earth. Noe was ordered to build an ark, a large square vessel to float upon the waters. It was to be large enough to hold beasts of each species, male and female, and birds, and food enough for a year. Noe was one hundred and twenty years building this vessel, and during that time, kept warning the people to repent. They did not heed his warnings. At last Noe entered the ark with the living creatures, and his family, in all eight persons. The floodgates of heaven were opened, the sea burst over its boundary, and the waters rose far higher than the top of the highest mountain. Thus all flesh was destroyed except those whom God saved in the ark. When this wonderful event took place the world had lasted about 1,500 years. It now had to begin again.

Noe, at length, came out of the ark, at the command of God, and built an altar, and taking of the cattle and fowls that were with him, offered upon it a sacrifice of thanksgiving. After the Deluge, men were permitted to kill animals and to eat their flesh. The three sons of Noe again peopled the world, so that all men are brethren. Men now became weaker in body, and instead of living from eight hundred to a thousand years, their lives soon dwindled down to eighty or a hundred. The Deluge did not make them better; they soon became worse than before. They knew their wickedness, and feared that another deluge might be sent upon the world. So to make themselves famous, or in hopes of making themselves safe, against what they thought might happen, about one hundred years after Noe came out of the ark, they foolishly and impiously began to build a high tower of many stories, into which they might escape. The tower of Babel or confusion, was never finished, for God sent upon them a confusion of tongues, and they could not understand each other's language. Then they separated from one another, and became the founders of nations, each having its own language, as it is now.

The three sons of Noe were Sem, Cham, and Japhet. The descendants of Sem settled in Asia, those of Cham chiefly peopled Africa, and the posterity of Japhet peopled Europe. Soon after the Deluge, cities began to be built, which afterwards rose to great eminence. Assur, a descendant of Sem, built Nineve on the Tigris, the future capital of the Assyrian empire, and Nimrod erected a kingdom on the banks of the Euphrates. Babel seems to have been the capital of his kingdom; this was probably the germ of the city of Babylon, that, many ages afterwards, rose to great power and splendour.

Then they began to make war upon each other, the strong to oppress the weak, and to commit every sort of crime. They forgot God, and worshipped all manner of creatures instead of Him. In all this, they acted against conscience and the light of reason, which then, as now, teaches us the chief, plain duties we owe to God and to one another. We must always reverence the voice of conscience, as the voice of God within us. We must observe well what reason and conscience command, but especially what they forbid.

CHAPTER V.

ABRAHAM—ISAAC—JACOB—JOSEPH—HOLY JOB.

As the descendants of Noah increased, and were dispersed over the earth, they gradually forsook the worship of the only true God. They began to adore the sun, the moon, and men like themselves, and animals, and even statues of gold and silver, of wood and stone. Thus they became idolaters. The true religion, that is, the knowledge of one God and of the law of Nature, was now preserved only by a few holy persons, the descendants of Sem, Noah's eldest son. Idolatry was beginning to make its way even amongst them, when God chose one out of the number, to save him from being corrupted. God told him to leave his country and friends, and go away to another land that should be shown him. This was Abraham; and this event is often spoken of, as *the vocation or calling of Abraham*. It took place about four hundred and fifty years after the Deluge. Abraham may be remembered as having lived about midway between Adam and Christ; that is, about two thousand years after Adam and two thousand years before Christ. Abraham has always been celebrated all over the East. It is not the Hebrews alone, who look on him as their head and founder. Abraham was born two years after Noah's death, A.M. 2008, and may have lived many years with Sem, Noah's eldest son.

Abraham obeyed the call of God, and passing the river Euphrates, came from Mesopotamia to the land of Chanaan. This land was occupied by different families descended from Chanaan, the son of Cham; to a great extent open and uncultivated, yet with some towns or cities scattered over it. The seacoast to the southward was in possession of the Philistines, from whom the whole country afterwards derived the name of Palestine. The valley of the Jordan seems to have been more thickly peopled, having in it several cities, in the midst of a luxuriant country, of which Sodom and Gomorrha were the chief. The inhabitants of these cities, had become wicked in the extreme. They were governed by kings, each city having its own king. But these kings were tributary to an empire, the centre of which was on the eastern bank of the Tigris. It is probable that the kingdom erected by Nimrod, had by this time extended itself to the Jordan.

God made a covenant with Abraham. A covenant is an agreement between two or more persons. God declared to Abraham that He would be his God, that He would be his protector, and that Abraham was to serve Him as the only God, Creator of heaven and earth. Abraham was remarkable for his faith and obedience. In calling Abraham, God's design was to make him the head and founder of a new nation, which was to rule from the Euphrates to the shore of the Mediterranean Sea. This nation was to be God's own people, to preserve the tradition of the true religion, to keep the ancient revelations, and to have many favours bestowed on them not given to other nations. More especially, the promised Saviour was to come from this race. The other nations of the earth, called the Gentiles, were to be left under God's ordinary Providence, and were to receive sufficient, but not extraordinary graces.

Abraham's life was remarkable for many visions, wonders, and communications with God. All these things may be read in the first book of Scripture called Genesis (chap. xii. to chap. xxv.). In Abraham's time, the Lord rained upon Sodom and Gomorrha, brimstone and fire from heaven. And He destroyed those cities and all the country round about, and all things that spring from the earth. And Lot's wife (though warned by an angel to the contrary), looking behind her, with foolish curiosity, to see the burning cities, was turned into a pillar of salt. The site of those cities to this day, is covered by a pestilential lake, called the Dead Sea. This lake never loses its bitterness, notwithstanding it receives the fresh waters of the Jordan and other rivers. Lot was Abraham's nephew. God would have spared those cities at the prayers of Abraham if only ten just men could have been found in them; but they were not.

After Abraham's death, God repeated the promises He had made, to Isaac his son. Isaac had two sons, Esau and Jacob; the blessings and promises which seemed to belong to Esau, the elder of the twin brothers, came upon Jacob the younger. Jacob's life was full of visions and wonders (Genesis, chap. xxvii. to chap. xxxv.). Jacob's name was changed by an angel into Israel. The country was afterwards from him, called Israel, and his descendants, Israelites. Jacob was the father of twelve sons, who in after-times were considered as the heads of the twelve tribes of Israel. These are called the twelve *patriarchs*, and this name is also given to all the saints who had lived under the law of Nature, from this time up to Adam. Those ages are called the *patriarchal ages*.

Joseph was the favourite son of Jacob. His brothers were filled with envy on this account. They were determined to get rid of him. At first they thought of killing him; but they sold him as a slave to some merchants, who were passing by, on their way into Egypt. Joseph was sold in Egypt to Putiphar, an officer of King Pharaoh. Joseph came in time to be second in Egypt, next to the king himself. His wonderful and touching history is given in Genesis at great length (Genesis, chap. xxxix. to chap. xlviii.). The family of Jacob, in all seventy in number, went and settled in Egypt, in the land of Gessen, the extremity of Egypt, between the Red Sea and the Nile. This happened *two hundred and fifteen years* after the covenant with Abraham; and *two hundred and fifteen years* after Jacob had come into Egypt, his descendants departed—that is, in all *four hundred and thirty years* since the covenant with Abraham, according to St. Paul. The Israelites were placed in a fruitful part of the country, and increased with amazing rapidity.

When Jacob was about to die, he called together his sons, and blessed them, and uttered wonderful prophecies about each of them, especially about Juda (Genesis, xlix.). He declared that Juda should rule over his brethren, and that the Saviour should come from him. Joseph promised his dying father that he should be buried in the burial-place of his forefathers in Chanaan. Joseph, by the leave of Pharaoh (Genesis l.), took the body of his father which had been embalmed, and with the ancients of Pharaoh's house, and all the elders of the land of Egypt, and his brethren, and a train of chariots and horsemen, a great multitude, buried him with great lamentations in the double cave which Abraham had bought, together with a field, for a burying-place. Joseph in time also died; but before his death he said to his brethren, "God will visit you after my death, and will make you go up out of this land, to the land which He swore to Abraham, Isaac, and Jacob." And he made them swear to him, saying, "God will visit you, carry my bones with you out of this place." Thus, with the death of Joseph, ends the Book of Genesis, the first of the five books written by Moses. Joseph had been *eighty* years governor of Egypt.

JOB.—The history of Holy Job is contained in the book of Scripture called the Book of Job. Job lived, perhaps, about the time of the death of Joseph. He was a model of moderation and charity in prosperity, and of patience in adversity. He possessed immense riches, and his name was celebrated throughout all the East. Messengers brought him tidings, one after another, that the Sabeans had carried away his oxen and she-asses, that the fire of heaven had consumed his sheep and their keepers, that the Chaldeans had carried off his camels, and that a violent wind had blown down one of his houses, and had buried all his sons beneath its ruins. The holy patriarch was overwhelmed with grief; but still bowed in submission to the will of God, and never ceased to bless His holy name.

After this, Job was afflicted with horrible ulcers from head to foot. An outcast from amongst men, he sat down, outside the city, upon a dunghill. His wife ridiculed his piety, and his friends came as if to comfort him; but they only increased his sorrows, for their words only tended to make him blaspheme God and His providence.

Job answered and refuted all their irreligion and pretended wisdom. However, some expression of doubt and impatience *did* escape him in the midst of his sufferings. He immediately repented, and obtained pardon of God. The Almighty at length rewarded him for all his past losses. Job blessed God in his latter state, even more than in the former.

The Book of Job is full of the noblest and sublimest poetry that ever was written. If the Book of Job was written by Moses, as is believed by many; astronomy, mineralogy, and natural history, must have been cultivated to a considerable extent. There can be no doubt that in the knowledge which Moses displays of a great variety of subjects, we have a clear indication of the advancement of the Egyptians of that age, in science and art. Moses was skilled in the wisdom of the Egyptians.

CHAPTER VI.

ISRAEL IN EGYPT—MOSES—THE DEPARTURE.

The rapid increase of the Israelites made them, in process of time, objects of alarm to the Egyptians. A king arising who knew not Joseph; he began to adopt the most severe measures, to lessen their number. He reduced them to the lowest slavery, employed them in building cities, oppressing them with the hardest labour. But finding that they still continued to increase, he commanded that all their male children should be thrown into the river as soon as they were born, and only females preserved alive. At this time, Moses was born, and was preserved from the effects of this edict in consequence of having been taken under the protection of the king's daughter. His parents had placed him in a basket of bulrushes, and laid him among the reeds by the brink of the river, and Pharaoh's daughter finding him, adopted him as her own son. Thus, Moses received an education, which fitted him for the important office to which he was destined, as leader and governor of the Israelites.

When Moses came of age, having been made acquainted with his descent from Abraham, Isaac, and Jacob, and having been instructed by his parents in the privileges bestowed upon their nation by the God of Heaven, he gave up his fair hopes and prospects, as an Egyptian of high, even of royal rank, and claimed his connection with the despised and persecuted Israelites. He saw an Egyptian striking, probably putting to death, an Israelite, and taking the part of the Israelite, he killed the Egyptian. This being discovered, he fled across the Red Sea, to the mountains which lie between the gulfs into which the Red Sea divides itself at its northern extremity, which was then called the land of Madian. Moses was then forty years of age. He thus obtained an opportunity of becoming acquainted with that district of country, and with the whole of the desert that lies between it and the land of Chanaan.

When Moses had dwelt in Madian for the space of forty years, the Almighty appeared to him, and told him to return to Egypt, there to call together the heads of the Israelites, and then to go to Pharaoh, and demand liberty for the people to leave the land of Egypt. Moses did so. The demand was, of course, refused; but by a number of plagues, which Moses was commissioned to inflict on the land of Egypt, the last of which was the destruction, in one night, of all the first-born sons in Egypt, Pharaoh was compelled to yield to the demand, and to let the people go.

Moses led them towards the Red Sea, as if he intended going round the northern extremity of the western gulf of it; but by direction of God he turned, and encamped close by the gulf on the western side. Pharaoh, seeing the immense body of the Israelites, consisting of 600,000 men, with their wives and children, entangled in the land, and apparently within his reach; pursued them with his whole army, and came up with them as they lay encamped, unable to go forward (for the sea was in their front), or to turn either to the north or the south. In this extremity, the Almighty caused the sea to divide, and directed Moses to lead the people through the bed of it. The Israelites thus passed in safety into the Arabian desert, while the Egyptian army, in attempting to follow them, were caught by the return of the sea to its usual bed, and were drowned.

The account of this journey of the Israelites out of Egypt, about fifteen hundred years before Christ, is found in the second book of Scripture called Exodus, which word means, *departure*.

CHAPTER VII.

THE ISRAELITES IN THE WILDERNESS.

WHEN the waters of the Red Sea closed over Pharaoh and his Egyptian hosts, the Israelites, after so great a deliverance, must have set forth on their way full of joy and confidence. The land of bondage was behind them, the land of promise was before them, a vast desert lay between them; but He who had saved them in the sea, intended to save them in the desert sands. Moses then conducted the people to the mountainous district, where he himself had found refuge, for he wished to avoid the Philistines, who were a warlike people, through whose country he must have gone, had he taken another and the more direct road. By taking this route, he seemed to be exposing the multitudes with him to perish of hunger and thirst in the desert. But God provided for them.

They marched forward for three days without finding water. A month after their departure from Egypt, all their provisions were consumed. They were then miraculously fed with manna from heaven. Every morning they gathered enough for the day, and on the sixth, enough for two days, that they might not have to gather any on the Sabbath. This miracle continued during their forty years in the desert. They were first attacked by the Amalekites, who were defeated by the hands of Moses uplifted in prayer, on the top of Mount Horeb. It was fifty days after they left Egypt that the Israelites reached the wilderness of Sinai, one of the mountains of the Horeb chain. Here they encamped, and Jethro, father-in-law of Moses, who lived near their encampment, brought to him his wife and two sons, and assisted him by his advice and experience.

God having freed His people from the tyranny of the Egyptians, before settling them in the promised land, gave them the laws by which they were to live there. The time of *revealed religion* and the *written law* begins now; for before this, men lived under the *law of nature*—that is, according to natural reason and the religious tradition of their forefathers. It was now designed to raise stronger barriers against idolatry, which was spreading everywhere; for ignorance and blindness had wonderfully increased since the time of Abraham. God wished to trust no longer to the memory of men the history of religion and of His covenant, but to have it written.

After solemn preparations, Moses was called to the top of Sinai to receive, amidst terrible thunders and lightnings, the commandments of God. The Almighty wrote with His own hand upon two tablets of stone, which He gave to Moses on the top of Mount Sinai, the ten commandments, which contain the great first principles of duty to God and our neighbour. He dictated to Moses many other regulations, concerning the setting up of the tabernacle, the making of the ark, the appointing of Aaron (the brother of Moses) and his sons to the high priesthood. The Almighty settled the ceremony of their consecration, the form and material of their robes, the office of the priests and Levites, with other religious observances. He appointed laws to regulate their feasts, ceremonies, sacrifices, contracts, marriages, funerals, and many other lesser points of daily observance in social life. Besides all this, He made the laws for the political regulation and government of the country, so that God Himself was their only lawgiver. The object of these numerous laws was to separate the Hebrew people as much as possible from other nations, lest they also, should be corrupted by idolatry. To put the laws into vigorous execution, Moses appointed an assembly of seventy counsellors, who became, as it were, the senate of the people of God. Besides the habitual private reading of the law, it had every seven years to be publicly read to the people assembled for eight days, at the Feast of Tabernacles.

As a wandering people could only have a moveable tent, instructions were given to erect a tabernacle, or tent, which could be taken down and put up again at pleasure. The tabernacle, with its rich furniture, was completed by skilful artificers, whom God filled with knowledge to execute the work which He had ordered. When all was finished, it was set up, the first day of the second year, after their leaving Egypt. A cloud rested over the tabernacle by day, and shone like fire by night. When the cloud was taken up, then the people knew that they had to go forward on their journeys. Yet, notwithstanding this constant sign of God's presence among them, the people were continually disobedient, or ungrateful and forgetful of Him.

The Book of Leviticus, the third Book of Moses, contains the laws regarding the Levites, and the priests and their various duties, and hence its name.

CHAPTER VIII.

THE ISRAELITES IN THE WILDERNESS—*continued*.

THE Lord ordered Moses to number the children of Israel. This census gave upwards of 600,000 men. The Book of Numbers is so called from its beginning with the account of this numbering of the people. Fourteen months after the Israelites had left Egypt, the cloud lifted itself up from the tabernacle, and thus gave the signal for the Israelites to begin their march. The children of Israel knew and obeyed the sign which told them to depart out of the wilderness of Sinai, where they had dwelt eleven months. They marched in a prescribed order, each tribe under its own leader and its own standard. The tabernacle borne by Levites, the miraculous cloud floating over it, led the way. They were accompanied by Hobab, the brother-in-law of Moses, and son of Jethro, and they profited by his experience and knowledge of the desert country.

This multitude of men, women, and children, moved through the desert and wilderness of Arabia, which extends from Sinai northwards to the land of Chanaan. Moses was sadly troubled with the discontent of the people, as well as with the ill-will of his brother Aaron and his sister Mary. And now the Hebrew people approached the land of promise; their wanderings seemed nearly over, and they encamped at Cades, on the border of Chanaan. Twelve spies were sent, one from each tribe, to examine the country. They returned at the end of forty days, with good news of the great fertility and richness of the country, but added that the people were powerful, and some of giant race. The Israelites were filled with terror, wept all night, and in the morning were for going back to Egypt, under a new leader. The Almighty was angry with the unbelief of the people, and would have destroyed them, but for the prayer of Moses. But a sentence had gone forth against this people that had tried God's patience by their sins, already ten times; that they were to turn back from the promised land, and to live and die in the desert. Only their children under twenty, who had not partaken of their sin were to enter it, with Caleb and Josue, when their fathers should be no more. The Hebrews heard the sentence with grief, and then by a strange perversity, resolved to go in and possess the land by their own strength, though Moses with the ark, and those faithful to their duty, remained in the camp. They were, of course, defeated by their enemies, and pursued with slaughter. After their defeat the children of Israel

THE ISRAELITES IN THE WILDERNESS. 35

prayed the Almighty, but in vain, to recall the sentence He had passed against them.

Then the nation returned to their life in the desert. At length, after thirty-eight years spent in wandering and encamping, they were permitted to approach the land of Chanaan, and encamped once more at Cades. As there was no water in this place the people again murmured. Moses, at the command of God, struck the rock, and it yielded a plentiful supply. Nevertheless, Moses and Aaron for some sin, perhaps a want of confidence, on this occasion, were not permitted to lead the people into the promised land.

Aaron died shortly after on Mount Hor, and was succeeded by his son Eleazar. The king of Edom having refused to allow Moses to pass through his territory, the Israelites had to fall back into the desert, and to go as far as the top of the eastern gulf of the Red Sea, in order to get round the land of Edom. They murmured through this disappointment, and were punished by venomous serpents that came from the burning sands, and whose bite was mortal. They at length finished this long and wearisome march round the mountainous country of Edom, and having conquered and taken possession of the country of the Ammonites and of the king of Basan, they found themselves on the plains of Moab, separated from the land of promise only by the river Jordan. Here they encamped, to the dismay of the surrounding nations, especially the Moabites and the Madianites.

Balac, the king of Moab, believed that the Israelites had more than mortal strength to aid them, therefore he did not attempt to do battle with them, but looked for other means to destroy them. He hoped that the curse of Balaam, a prophet and a worshipper of the true God, would have this effect. Balaam seduced by promises and presents, tried to curse the people of God, but could only utter blessings. Then he advised the king to corrupt them, and invite them to their idol feasts. A great number were thus seduced by the Moabites and Madianites, and 24,000 were carried off by a plague in punishment of their sins. After this the Moabites and Madianites were destroyed, and the wicked prophet Balaam slain. Two of the tribes had permission to settle in the country lately conquered on the east of the Jordan, on condition that the fighting men of those tribes should continue to help their brethren in conquering the rest of the country.

Moses Dies.—And now the long and anxious life of Moses was drawing to a close. Moses made a third numbering of the people of Israel, and found that the generation that had come out of Egypt had passed away. Moses knew that his end was drawing near. He appointed Josue his successor. He repeated to the people a clear and lively history of their past lives, from their leaving the wilderness of Sinai, until the day he stood before them on the borders of the land of promise. He reminded them of the awful giving of the law, and repeated all its most solemn commands. This history is contained in a Book of the Bible called Deuteronomy, which means a repetition of the Law. It was written by desire of Moses, and delivered by himself to the priests to lay up in the ark.

He afterwards gave a blessing to each tribe as he departed. For Moses went up from the plains of Moab to Mount Nebo, and from one of its heights God showed him the land of Chanaan, the land promised to Abraham, and which the children of Abraham were about to possess. When he died he was one hundred and twenty years old. The children of Israel mourned for him in the plains of Moab for thirty days. To this day, the Jews mourn every year the death of their lawgiver. No monument marked the place of his last repose, for the Israelites, though they were often rebellious to him in life, might, with their idolatrous tendency, have begun to worship him in death.

CHAPTER IX.

SETTLEMENT IN THE HOLY LAND UNDER JOSUE.

On the death of Moses, Josue his successor received from the people a promise of obedience. He sent spies across the Jordan to Jericho, a fortified town on the other side of the river, and the first they would have to besiege. He then prepared to cross the river with all his people. A miracle marked the opening of his mission. Forty years ago the waters of the Red Sea had been divided for Moses and the Israelites to pass over into the wilderness, and now the Jordan divided, and left a dry channel for them to cross over into the promised land. Though the Jordan was at that time the fullest, and accustomed to overflow its banks, yet as soon as the priests who bore the ark touched its waters, they divided and stood in a heap on either side. They encamped at Galgal on the other side of the river, and celebrated the passover for the first time, in their new land. But the Israelites could not take quiet possession. Many nations, abominable for their wickedness, had to be rooted out. Jericho, the first city of which they got possession, fell at the sound of the trumpets. City after city fell into their hands. Josue defeated the kings of the south and east that had united together against him, and then turned to meet the kings of the north, who had leagued also with each other. He exterminated their armies, burnt their cities, and found that in six years he had defeated thirty-one kings or princes, and conquered their kingdoms from the confines of Egypt and Idumea, to Lebanon and Sidon.

Thus the land was possessed by the children of Israel, excepting that portion near the Mediterranean, which they unwisely left in the possession of the Philistines, who afterwards were a constant source of trouble to them. But they were, no doubt, desirous to settle down in peace in their new possessions. Josue removed his camp into the land allotted to his tribe, and he set up the tabernacle there, at a place called Silo, where it continued to the days of David. The bones of Joseph, which they had carried with them out of Egypt, and through their wanderings, were now buried at Sichem, in the burying-place of Jacob.

Having set up the tabernacle, Josue set himself to finish the division of the land. The division was made according to the numbers in each tribe. The tribes of Reuben and Gad, who had come along with their brethren, and faithfully helped them during six years to conquer the country, were dismissed in honour by Josue, to their homes on the east side of the Jordan, with an exhortation to be true to the Lord their God. Each tribe had its own separate division or province; and each family had its own lot of land which could not be sold, except for a limited number of years; as it had to return into the family of the original possessor in the year of Jubilee, which was every fiftieth year. Each tribe had its chief or prince, and each tribe had to furnish a band of soldiers for the common defence, commanded by its own chiefs, while the whole army was led by one of those heads of tribes, often divinely appointed. The tribe of Levi had no lands, but dwelt in forty-eight cities in various parts of the country, and were supported by the tithes and contributions of the other tribes. As they were the teachers and expounders of the law, and were thus distributed through the whole nation, this must have very much helped to keep up a knowledge of religion, and to prevent the people from falling into barbarism.

So the Israelites rested from their wanderings and wars with their enemies, and the land had peace many years. Josue died at the age of one hundred and ten years. The actions of his life, as the successor of Moses, are written in the Book of Josue.

CHAPTER X.

GOVERNMENT OF JUDGES. BOOK OF RUTH.

The next period of Jewish history includes a space of about four hundred years. During this time, the government of the Hebrew people is called a Theocracy, that is a divine government, because God was pleased to allow them to look to Him as their supreme Ruler or King, and to consult Him in all their difficulties, through the high priest. Immediately after the death of Josue, they seem to have gone on well, and to have served God faithfully; the great works God had done for them being still fresh in their minds. In course of time they often fell into idolatry, and, in punishment of their sin, they were attacked and subdued by their enemies, who were either the Chanaanites whom, contrary to God's commands they had suffered to remain in the land, or the Madianites, Moabites, Philistines, or some other neighbouring nation, and who were never thoroughly subdued till the time of David. Suffering and oppression brought them to repentance; they sought once more their God and King, and He raised up deliverers for them, who are called Judges and whose deeds are written in the Book of Judges.

The Judges are twelve in number. Of these the most remarkable are Deborah the prophetess, Gideon who subdued the Madianites, Jephte who conquered the Ammonites, and the mighty Samson who drove back the Philistines. Eli was the eleventh judge, but he governed too feebly, to check either the boldness of the enemies of Israel, or the misconduct of his own sons.

Samuel the twelfth judge succeeded Eli. But when Samuel was old he made his sons judges over Israel, and they walked not in his ways. Then the Israelites asked for a king to rule them like other nations. And the Lord said to Samuel, "Hearken unto their voice and make them a king."

Book of Ruth.—The general history of the Israelites under the judges is nothing more than an account of the idolatrous tyrants into whose hands God gave them in punishment of their sins, and of the exploits of the chosen deliverers, who from time to time were raised up, to set them free, on their repentance. But one story is related and forms the Book of Ruth, which regards the family from which Christ Himself was afterwards born; which shows in a beautiful way, both the customs of the time, and the piety which reigned in the heart of many of those Israelites, who lived too private a life to be mentioned in the history of the nation itself. King David was the great grandson of Booz and Ruth. Ruth was a Gentile, a woman of Moab, who having married Booz, an Israelite of the town of Bethlehem, became a worshipper of the true God. It is well to notice King David's family, because our Lord Jesus Christ was (according to the flesh) descended from him. Christ who was to be the Saviour of both Jew and Gentile, was descended from a Jew and a Gentile, from Booz and Ruth.

CHAPTER XI.

THE KINGS.—SAUL—DAVID—SOLOMON.

Saul.—SAMUEL anointed Saul, the first king of Israel. But God, though He had permitted His people to choose a supreme governor, did not leave them to their kings, and Saul, though a brave warrior, soon showed how little he was able to set before his people, the example of obedience to God and of self-command.

From this time the nation was never left without a prophet or inspired teacher, who should reprove both kings and people when they sinned, and should keep them up to their duty, towards their great invisible Ruler. For as the priests confined themselves chiefly to the outward ceremonies of religion, it was the prophets who kept alive the true spirit and practice of it. So thenceforward a king, a high priest, and a prophet were the three most important offices in the Hebrew nation.

Saul reigned forty years. For his repeated disobedience to God's commands, his posterity was excluded from the throne. The histories of Samuel and Saul are to be found in the First Book of Kings.

David.—David, who, in the lifetime of Saul, had been anointed king by Samuel, was continually persecuted, and had to flee to save his life from the jealous fury of Saul. David was mighty and successful in war, and extended the kingdom of Israel as far as the Euphrates. He was a poet and musician, and composed many, perhaps most of the hundred and fifty Psalms, which have, ever since, been used in Divine worship. He brought the ark of the covenant, which had hitherto rested in some obscure place, to Mount Sion in Jerusalem. He made immense preparations to build a fixed temple for the worship of God. Till his time there had been nothing but the moveable tabernacle or tent, which suited a people that wandered from place to place in the desert; but since their settlement in the land, nothing else had been provided. The idolatrous worship of the heathens was carried on, on the high places, that is, on the tops of mountains, not in temples. There was perhaps no fixed building, as a temple, in the world at that time. David was not permitted to build the temple for which he had made such costly preparations, but that honour was reserved for his son.

The Almighty renewed the ancient covenant with this holy king, revealed to him that the Saviour of the world should come from his race, that He should be a King, and rule over all nations, that His kingdom should never end, that He should be a Priest of the order of Melchisedec, that He should be the Son of God and God Himself, that He should suffer before He entered into His glory. From the time of David the expected Saviour was called the Messiah, the Christ, that is, the Anointed One, for kings and priests were consecrated by being anointed with oil. David was a figure of Christ in His sufferings, as Solomon was of Christ in His glory. The history of David is to be found in the Second Book of Kings.

Solomon.—After a glorious reign of forty years, David was succeeded by his son Solomon. This young prince asked of God wisdom to judge his people, and he became the wisest, the greatest, the most powerful king of any age. When he grew old, he fell into sin, and his enemies rose up against him, and God announced to him that his kingdom should be divided after his death.

The name of Solomon has become another term for a wise man. He had all the learning and science of the time, together with supernatural wisdom. He wrote the Book of Proverbs, of Ecclesiastes, and the Canticle of Canticles. The Book of Wisdom also contains his sentiments, though it is not known that he was the actual writer.

Solomon proceeded to execute his father's plans for the building of a temple to the Almighty in Jerusalem. The temple itself was not of great dimensions, for the nature of the Jewish worship did not require the people themselves to be present within the building. Within it, were placed the ark, the altar, the seven-branch candlesticks, and the other furniture for divine service, as in the tabernacle, with a vast number of golden vessels for every purpose that could be needed. It was constructed on the plan of the old tabernacle. The temple, with its two vast courts, were seven years in completion, and 183,300 men were employed in their erection. The whole building was richly ornamented with gold and carved work, and from its lofty situation it must have been seen from afar; while from its courts being always uncovered, the smoke of the daily sacrifice would be visible to the pious worshipper from a distance, as he turned towards the holy place in prayer. There was a magnificent dedication of the temple, and on that occasion, the building was filled with the majesty of God in the form of a cloud; the people fell upon their faces, the trumpets ceased, and the priests were unable to go on with their ministrations. This glorious event happened about one thousand years after Abraham, and one thousand years before the coming of Christ.

The Jewish monarchy reached its highest elevation in the reign of Solomon, and it immediately began to decline. Some have supposed that the combined fleets of Solomon and Hiram, king of Tyre, sent out from Asiongaber in the Red Sea, went round the peninsula of Africa, passing down the Red Sea, doubling the Cape, now called the Cape of Good Hope, and returning by the Mediterranean.

Solomon died, having reigned, as each of the two kings before him, forty years. It is not known whether he repented before his death of the excesses into which he fell, through too great prosperity. It has been thought that in the Book of Ecclesiastes, the penitent monarch expresses his feelings of the vanity of all things, except of loving and serving God. The first part of the Third Book of Kings contains the death of King David, and also the life and death of Solomon.

CHAPTER XII.

THE KINGDOMS OF ISRAEL AND JUDA — THEIR END.

IN punishment of the sins of Solomon, and through the imprudent conduct of his son and successor, Roboam, the kingdom was divided after his death. Only the two tribes of Juda and Benjamin obeyed Roboam; the other ten acknowledged as their king Jeroboam, a man of the tribe of Ephraim. This rebel feared lest the Israelites should return to their allegiance to their lawful king, if, as the law of God required, they should continue to go up to Jerusalem three or four times a year, to pray and to offer sacrifice. To guard against this, he changed the religion of the people, and as they were prone to idolatry, he set up, at Dan and Bethel, the two extreme points of his new kingdom, a golden calf to be worshipped, calling it the God of Israel. He appointed the lowest of the people priests, raised altars, made a religion of his own, in many things still keeping the law of Moses. All the kings who succeeded Jeroboam continued in that false religion. This event is called the schism of Samaria. The seat of the true Church was in Jerusalem, for there, they adored God in the temple which Solomon had built in God's honour; there, was kept the law which God had given to Moses, and the service was performed by the Levites and the priests, the children of Aaron, whom God had chosen. The Jewish Church is often called the synagogue, which word means assembly. The kingdom of the ten tribes, was called the kingdom of Israel, or the kingdom of Samaria, because Samaria was the capital city. The other two tribes were called the kingdom of Juda. The Levites also had left the kingdom of Israel, and had joined the kingdom of Juda, and many others out of the ten tribes remained faithful, and continued to come to Jerusalem. The consequence of this division was almost continual rivalship and warfare between the two kingdoms.

There were in all nineteen kings of Israel, from Jeroboam the first, to Osee the last. Bloodshed, violence, idolatry, marked their short reigns. At last, as had been so continually threatened, the ten tribes were carried captive into Assyria, by the Assyrian king Salmanasar, and the kingdom of Israel, after it had lasted for two hundred and fifty years, came to an end, and was never. again established, B.C. 721. Holy Tobias was, on this occasion, taken captive to Nineveh. Tobias the elder, died prophesying the rebuilding of Jerusalem; his son inherited his virtues. The account of him is given in the book of Scripture, called the Book of Tobias.

Of the kings of Juda, some were good, and others bad. Ezechias was miraculously delivered from the invasion of Sennacherib, son and successor of that Salmanasar, who had destroyed the kingdom of Israel. The mighty army of the invader was smitten by an angel of the Lord, and annihilated in one night. In another invasion by Holofernes, the Assyrian general; we read how the city of Bethulia, was delivered by the courage of the virtuous Judith, as recorded in the Book of Judith. She cut off the head of Holofernes whilst he was asleep, and his army took to flight, and was dispersed. The kingdom of Juda had nineteen kings like the kingdom of Israel, from Roboam the first, to Sedecias the last; but it lasted about one hundred and thirty years after the kingdom of Israel had come to an end. At length, Nabuchodonosor, king of Babylon and Nineveh, took Jerusalem for the first time, and took away part of its inhabitants to Babylon, among others Daniel. The seventy years' captivity is reckoned from this event, B.C. 606. Neither those who remained, nor those who were led away, did penance, though warned; the first by Jeremiah, the second by Ezechiel. They preferred to listen to false prophets. God's avenger again came into Judea; the yoke of Jerusalem was made more galling, though the city was not destroyed. At last, the conqueror came a third time against Jerusalem, destroyed both city and temple, and all the treasures and sacred vessels were carried away to Babylon. All the people were carried away prisoners; only a few husbandmen were left to till the land. B.C. 588.

The history of the kingdoms of Israel and Juda commences in the second half of the Third Book of Kings, and is continued and completed in the Fourth Book of Kings. The two supplementary Books of Chronicles, or Paralipomenon, add a number of facts not given in the four books of Kings—that is, they complete the history of a period of about five hundred years from Saul to the captivity.

CHAPTER XIII.

THE PROPHETS.

It was from the time of the division into the two kingdoms of Juda and Israel, that God sent His prophets more than ever, to console true believers and to convert those that had fallen into idolatry. Jonah was the only prophet sent to preach to Gentiles—namely, to the people of Nineveh. The object of the preaching of the prophets, was to warn the people of Juda and Israel, of the destruction they would bring on themselves by their sins. They also predicted the fate of most of the neighbouring idolatrous nations. To them also as time went on, God continually revealed new particulars, as to the character, actions, and life of the Messiah and of His kingdom.

Those especially are called prophets, who lived after the manner of prophets. They lived often in large and numerous communities, retired from the world. They fasted much, lived sparingly, clothed in the plainest and coarsest manner in sackcloth. They spent their time in prayer, meditation on the law of God, in the instruction of their own disciples, and of the people. They were nearly always hated and ill-treated by the people and the princes. Some were killed, others wandered about in continual affliction. There were also hundreds of impostors and false prophets, who pretended to be inspired, who imitated the dress and manner of the true prophets. This tended to keep the people in delusion. These latter generally said things that were agreeable to their hearers. The event proved, by which, the Spirit of God had spoken; and to make the proof clearer, the prophecies from the time of King Ozias (B.C. 800) were written, and the original copy was kept in the temple.

Isaiah, Ezechiel, Jeremiah, and Daniel were the four greater prophets. They are so called, because their written prophecies are much longer than those of the others, who on that account are called the lesser prophets. There were twelve lesser prophets. Besides those sixteen whose written prophecies remain to us, and which form a large portion of the Old Testament, there were hundreds of others whose prophecies have not come down to us. The last of the prophets was Malachy, about four hundred years before Christ.

CHAPTER XIV.

THE CAPTIVITY—END OF THE BABYLONIAN EMPIRE— RETURN FROM CAPTIVITY.

The Captivity.—DURING the seventy years of the captivity of Babylon, the proud spirit of the rebellious house of Juda was broken, and the thoughts of the people were brought back to the God of their fathers, and they lamented their disobedience and past forgetfulness of God's favours. God gave them prophets in Babylon, as He had done before in their own land, to be guides and comforters to His people during this period of trial.

The Chaldeans had carried away captive the chief of the inhabitants who dwelt at Jerusalem when it was taken, and left none but the poorer people to till the ground. Jeremiah, who was served by his disciple, the prophet Baruch, was especially the prophet of the time of the captivity. He remained at Jerusalem, when all was overwhelmed in ruins, pouring out his lamentations over the fallen city, and comforting the miserable remnant that was left. While he mourned over the woes of the people, he urged upon the few that were left, the duty of repentance, bidding them trust in the Divine mercy, and not fly into Egypt as they desired. They heeded him not, however, and fled to the Egyptians, taking with them Jeremiah; and tradition reports, that after their arrival in Egypt they murdered him. The Jews do not appear to have been harshly treated in captivity. It appears from the history of Susanna that the Jews, notwithstanding their captivity, had the exercise of their own laws, and the power to appoint judges in matters of life and death.

It was impossible that this mingling with strangers, should not cause some change in their manners; since one of their chief maxims heretofore was to separate themselves from all other nations. Many were prevailed upon to worship idols, to eat forbidden food, and to marry wives from among strangers. All conformed to their masters in things which were lawful, one of which was in language. Thus during the seventy years that the captivity lasted, they forgot the Hebrew tongue, and none but the learned among them understood it. Their spoken language was the Syriac or Chaldaic, in which a large portion of the Book of Daniel and Esdras was written.

Daniel, in the first invasion of Nabuchodonosor, was taken captive, and with three other young Hebrews, Ananias, Azarias, and Misael, was brought up at the court of Nabuchodonosor. He became honoured for the wonderful power which God gave him of interpreting the dream of the king, and was made ruler over the whole province of Babylon. His three companions were afterwards cast into a fiery furnace, for refusing to worship a golden image which had been set up by order of the king. The pride of Nabuchodonosor was displeasing to God, who in punishment afflicted him with madness, and he fled from men, and ate grass like an ox. He continued in this state seven years. Then he understood the power of the Most High, and he glorified the God of heaven, and ordered his people to do the same. Nabuchodonosor died B.C. 567.

End of the Babylonian Empire.—About thirty years after this, the empire of the Babylonians passed into other hands, and became the empire of the Medes and Persians. Baltassar, the last king of Babylon, grandson of Nabuchodonosor, was guilty of many crimes, and added to them, that of the profanation of holy things. He made a great feast for a thousand of his nobles; and he had the golden and silver vessels brought forth, which Nabuchodonosor had taken out of the temple in Jerusalem; and the king and his guests drank out of them. In the same hour a hand appeared writing on the wall of the palace, and none of the wise men could read the writing. Daniel was now called, and he read what was written, and this was the interpretation: "God hath numbered thy kingdom and finished it. Thou art weighed in the balance and found wanting. Thy kingdom is divided and given to the Medes and Persians."

The Median and Persian army, under Cyrus, nephew and general of Darius the Mede, had for two years besieged Babylon; and that very night, while the king and the inhabitants were revelling, the great work of turning off the waters of the river which ran through Babylon was finished; and the besieging army marched through the dry bed of the river, and the city was taken in the very way Isaiah had prophesied one hundred and seventy-four years before. Baltassar was surprised at his banquet and slain, B.C. 538. Darius, the Median, took the kingdom. Thus the Babylonian empire came to an end, having lasted eighty-eight years since it had united to itself the Assyrian empire. This was the first of the four great empires seen by Daniel in his vision.

Return from Captivity.—Darius the king came to Babylon, and settled with Cyrus the government of the new empire. They divided it into one hundred and twenty provinces, over each of which a governor was appointed. Over these governors there were three presidents, and the chief of these presidents was the prophet Daniel, who might therefore be regarded as the prime minister of that vast empire. It was in this reign, when Daniel was about eighty years of age, that he was cast into the den of lions, for persevering in the worship of God, in defiance of the foolish decree which Darius had been persuaded by his courtiers to make. In about two years after, Cyrus, by the death of Darius, succeeded to the kingdom. Cyrus, two hundred years before, had been named by Isaiah as the deliverer of Israel. Cyrus was amazed at the prophecies which had announced his victories; he declared that he owed his empire to the God of heaven whom the Jews worshipped, and he signalized the first year of his reign (B.C. 536) by an order for the return of God's people and the rebuilding of the temple, and he even restored the sacred vessels of gold and silver, which the Babylonian kings had plundered in their various inroads. In consequence of that decree, the people assembled from various parts of the empire to the number of about fifty thousand persons and proceeded to Jerusalem. The first care of these restored captives, was to rebuild the city and temple of Jerusalem. The jealousy of the surrounding nations, especially the Samaritans, greatly hindered them. These could not openly oppose them, because Cyrus was their declared friend, and Daniel was at the seat of government to protect them. Soon after this, Daniel died at the age of ninety years. Cyrus died soon after, in the seventh year of the restoration of the Jews and seventieth of his age. He is one of the greatest men of antiquity, and probably became a convert from heathenism to the worship of the true God.

Thus the Jews had been punished for their sins and were now restored. They saw other nations and cities that had been their scourges fall before themselves, or with them, or a little after them, as the prophets had declared. They had seen the fall not only of Samaria, Idumea, Gaza, Ascalon, Damascus, the cities of the Ammonites and Moabites, their perpetual enemies; but also of cities more renowned, such as Tyre, the mistress of the sea; Tanes, Memphis, Thebes with its hundred gates, and Nineveh the seat of the Assyrian kings so long their persecutors, and now of mighty Babylon, the conqueror of all the rest and loaded with the spoils and plunder of the world.

CHAPTER XV.

JEWS UNDER THE PERSIANS—ESTHER—ESDRAS—NEHEMIAS.

B.C. 530 to 336.

WHEN Cyrus gave the Jews their liberty with leave to go back into Judea and rebuild the temple, they did not *all* return, nor at *one* time. A great number remained in Babylon, and some few of the ten tribes joined them that returned. Zorobabel, of royal blood, grandson of Joachim, had brought back the first company, who rebuilt the altar, and laid the foundation of the second temple.

Cambyses, Smerdis, and Darius Hystaspes.—During the two reigns of Cambyses and Smerdis, successors of Cyrus, the enemies of the Jews contrived to prevent them from proceeding with the temple, having poisoned the minds of these princes against them. Then came Darius Hystaspes who must be carefully distinguished from Darius the Mede, and from two others of the name of Darius, who afterwards came to the empire. This Darius being elected king, in consequence of his horse having been the first to neigh, which the nobles had whimsically agreed on as the sign of the person to be chosen, married the daughter of Cyrus and was disposed to fulfil all his intentions. He, therefore, issued a new decree for the rebuilding of the city and temple of Jerusalem, and in the sixth year of his reign the second temple was finished and dedicated (B.C. 516) twenty years after their return home, exactly seventy years after it had been destroyed by Nabuchodonosor. He left his dominions and his quarrel with Greece to his son Xerxes (B.C. 486). During this reign Esdras was born; but his public acts belong to a subsequent reign.

Esther.—Xerxes, unfortunate in his war with Greece, died B.C. 465, and was succeeded by Artaxerxes Longimanus, who is believed to be the Assuerus of the Book of Esther. He repudiated Vasthi, his queen, and Esther, the Jewess, was made queen in her stead. Esther had been brought up by her uncle Mardocheus, and was still aided by his advice. Aman, a favourite of the king, having remarked that Mardocheus did not bow to him, or show him the reverence he received from others, determined to revenge himself, and to bring about a general massacre of the Jews throughout the kingdom. Esther was told of this by Mardocheus, and after having prayed and humbled herself before God, she went to Assuerus to entreat for her own life and that of her people. Assuerus granted all her requests; and the end of it was, that Aman was hanged on the gibbet which he had prepared for Mardocheus, the Jew. The Book of Esther contains the full account of this event. In memory of this signal deliverance, a festival was instituted, which is still kept by the Jews. It is called Purim or Lots, because Aman cast the lot (in Hebrew, *Pur*) to destroy them. The Book of Esther is read in their synagogue, and the name of Aman is execrated with clapping of hands and stamping of feet.

Esdras.—In the seventh year of Artaxerxes (B.C. 458), seventy-eight years from the first edict of Cyrus, Esdras, the Jewish priest and prophet, who was still in Babylon, obtained, probably through the influence of Esther, an ample commission to return to Jerusalem with as many Jews as chose to accompany him. Esdras immediately set to work to bring into order the little community over which he presided. He revived the rites and ceremonies of the Jewish church, according to the prescribed order. He also arranged, or as some think, established the synagogue service. Esdras transcribed the Old Testament from the old Hebrew character which had fallen into disuse, into the present Hebrew or Chaldaic character. He also set in order the sacred books, of which he made a careful revision, and he collected the ancient traditions and records of the people of God, and from them composed the two books which are as a supplement to the Books of Kings, called the Books of Paralipomenon (that is, of things left out), or Chronicles. To these he added the history of his own time, which was finished by Nehemias, the governor. These books completed the long course of history begun by Moses, and which was continued by succeeding authors without interruption up to the re-establishment of Jerusalem ending B.C. 430. The two Books of Maccabees do not take up the history where these books finish, but commence after a silence of about two hundred and fifty years. Whilst Esdras and Nehemias were closing this great work of history, Herodotus, called the father of history, that is of profane history, began to write. Thus, the last writer of sacred history lived with the first of profane history, and when this only began, the people of God beginning as late as Abraham, could narrate the history of fifteen hundred years.

Nehemias.—While Esdras was engaged in these important works, Nehemias was serving as cupbearer to Artaxerxes, B.C. 445, and ninety years after the return from the captivity, when intelligence having reached him that the walls and gates of Jerusalem were still in ruins, he was deeply affected and procured, probably through the influence of Queen Esther, liberty to repair to Jerusalem and to do whatever was necessary for completing the defence of the city. He arrived about thirteen years after Esdras (B.C. 445). Having made considerable progress in restoring the city and polity of the Jews, and having been governor twelve years, he returned to Persia (B.C. 433), but in a few years (B.C. 428) he came back to Jerusalem a second time, when he found that abuses had again begun to appear. The Sabbath was openly violated, and many of the leaders of the people had married heathen wives, and he set himself with renewed vigour to correct these disorders. In the year 409 B.C., 128 after the return from captivity, was the last act of reformation by Nehemias, forty-nine years after the work had been begun by Esdras. Nehemias governed the Jews thirty-six years.

General Condition of the Jews under the Persians.—In general, the Jews were never before so faithful to God; and after they returned from captivity, we never hear idolatry once mentioned amongst them; so much were they struck with that severe punishment, and the accomplishment of the prophecies that threatened them with it. Apostates were entirely at liberty to stay among the infidels, so that there appeared none but such as were really Jews. By degrees the Jews were established again, and during the empire of the Persians they lived under their own laws, in the form of a commonwealth, governed by the high-priest and the council of seventy-two elders. They paid a light tribute to the sovereigns, who were their protectors more than their masters. The country was re-peopled, the towns newly built, and the lands better cultivated than ever. Plenty was seen again, and there was such a profound peace, that for nearly three hundred years there happened no troubles nor anything that makes the common subject of histories; and hence comes the great void that we find between the time of Nehemias and the Maccabees. The temple was honoured even by strangers, who visited it, and brought offerings thither. In short, the prosperity of the Jews was so great after their return, that the prophets in foretelling it, have left us, in the description of those times, the most magnificent types of the Messiah's reign.

The Persian empire had five other kings after Artaxerxes, who treated the Jews mildly. This empire then came to an end (B.C. 336), after it had existed, from the taking of Babylon, two hundred and nine years. It was the second of the great empires seen in vision by Daniel.

CHAPTER XVI.

STATE OF THE JEWS UNDER ALEXANDER THE GREAT AND HIS SUCCESSORS.

The Jewish republic went on in peace for many years under the protection of the kings of Persia. Alexander the Great (B.C. 332), the conqueror of Darius, founded the empire of Greece on the ruins of the Persian empire. The Jews, always faithful to the Persians, refused to Alexander what he demanded, and he marched to Jerusalem to take vengeance on the city. But on his arrival there, he seems to have been overruled by a divine power, and turned from his first intention. They showed him the prophecies which announced his victories, especially those of Daniel. He granted the Jews all they asked for, and they showed to him the same fidelity they had always shown to the kings of Persia. At the death of Alexander, his vast empire was divided into four kingdoms. But although these four kingdoms were thus formed out of Alexander's empire, there was no cessation of hostilities. On the contrary, there were almost perpetual wars among them, till they were all, one after the other, swallowed up by the Roman empire. Judæa lay between two of those kingdoms — namely, Syria and Egypt. They accordingly sometimes obeyed the king of one of those nations, and sometimes the king of the other, as one or other happened to be the stronger.

Egypt.—Ptolemy Lagus, the first and best of the race of Ptolemies, had obtained Egypt and the neighbouring countries as his share of Alexander's empire. The *second* of the name founded the great Alexandrian libraries, and caused the Septuagint version of the Scriptures to be made. It was called the Septuagint version, because it is said to have been made by seventy learned elders whom the high-priest Eleazar sent to the king for that purpose. It was for the use of the Jews, who were very much scattered over Greece and Egypt, and who had forgotten not only their ancient language, which was the Hebrew, but also the Chaldean which they had learned in captivity. They had a mixed language of Greek and Hebrew; the Septuagint and the books of the New Testament are written in this sort of language. The Jews in this reign and the following, being kindly treated, flocked in great numbers to Alexandria; but in the reign after, were persecuted for not worshipping idols. The celebrated Cleopatra ended the race of the Ptolemies, who, eleven in number, from the death of Alexander the Great, had reigned over Egypt for the space of two hundred and ninety-four years, when Egypt became a province of the Roman empire.

Syria.—The arrival of Seleucis at Babylon to take possession of the eastern provinces, his share of Alexander's empire (B.C. 312), is called the era of the Seleucidæ, which word means, the descendants of Seleucis. The eighth in succession from him was Antiochus Epiphanes, or the Illustrious (B.C. 175); he is not the same as Antiochus the Great. An increasing degeneracy among the Jews, who began to be a good deal corrupted by their intercourse with the Greeks and the neighbouring nations, and the ambition of some wicked men to get possession of the high priesthood by the help and influence of heathen kings, brought great troubles on the nation. Antiochus conceived the idea of ruining this divided nation. He began the greatest persecution they had ever suffered, and which was not inferior to any that the Christians have since endured. Antiochus thought that by destroying their religion he should strengthen his own kingdom. He took Jerusalem, plundered and profaned the temple, and abolished the sacrifices. But he found more resistance than he had expected. Eleazar, one of the chief of the Scribes, refused to submit to the edicts of this prince, and was cruelly put to death because he would not eat of things forbidden by the law of Moses. Seven brothers and their mother were also most cruelly tortured and put to death by the tyrant because they would not break the law of the only true God.

These are the first that are known in the history of the world who gave up their lives for the sake of God and the law of their fathers. Others, as Daniel and his three companions, were willing to have done it, but were saved by miracle.

The Maccabees. — Mathathias, a priest, with his five sons, of whom the third, named Judas Maccabeus, was remarkable for his courage, were determined to resist the impious commands of the king. They left the city, and gathered around them an army of men, zealous as themselves for the law. From the mountains amongst which they had taken refuge, they made inroads into the city of Jerusalem, drove the Syrian army beyond the borders of the kingdom, overthrew the Gentile altars, and roused the Jews against the tyrant who had refused them the liberty to follow their religion, which had been before allowed them by treaty.

On the death of Mathathias, his son Judas Maccabeus put to flight all the generals sent against him by Antiochus, defeated them in five pitched battles, and baffled all their attempts to recover Palestine. He at length entered Jerusalem, recovered the temple, and restored the daily sacrifice. Antiochus died a miserable death (B.C. 164), devoured by worms. The contentions amongst the Jews induced Judas Maccabeus to seek an alliance with the Roman people; he sent ambassadors to Rome, and they brought back from the Romans a friendly letter to the Jews, accepting them as allies. Judas was slain in battle, his brothers succeeded him, and the sovereignty of Judea remained in the family of the Maccabees for a hundred years.

After Antiochus Epiphanes, the Syrian throne fell a prey to a succession of usurpers who rapidly followed each other, and whose names need not be recorded, until Pompey, the Roman general (B.C. 65) overran the country, and reduced Syria to a Roman province, after a duration of two hundred and forty-seven years.

The history of the people of God under Judas Maccabeus and his brethren is contained in the two books of Maccabees. It is not known who was the author of these books. Though they are not received as Scripture by the Jews, says S. Augustine, they are received as such by the Church. The Church, in settling her canon of the Scriptures, chose rather to be directed by the tradition she had received from the apostles of Christ, than by that of the Scribes and Pharisees. The first book contains the history of thirty-seven years, from 170 B.C. to 133 B.C.. The second book is not a continuation of the first, nor does it come down to so late a period. It relates many of the same facts more at large, and adds other remarkable particulars which had been omitted in the first book, about the state of the Jews both before, as well as under the persecution of Antiochus. The author is not the same as the author of the first book.

The dissensions between the Jews became more and more violent and bloody, and the Romans at length interfered. Pompey, the Roman general, besieged Jerusalem (B.C. 63). But the people continued to be governed by one of themselves; they found, however, that their freedom was very limited. Twenty years after this date, Herod, the Idumean, was acknowledged king of Judea by the Romans. Herod not being of Jewish blood, the sceptre had now passed away from Juda, which forthwith became a tributary kingdom of the Roman empire. This was the time marked out by prophecy for the speedy coming of the Messiah. Herod became one of the most furious and bloodthirsty of tyrants. He raised some noble buildings; but his most celebrated work was the rebuilding of the temple of Jerusalem on a scale of great magnificence. Towards the close of his reign, Christ was born in Bethlehem.

CHAPTER XVII.

S. JOHN THE BAPTIST—EARLY LIFE OF CHRIST.

Promised Birth of St. John the Baptist.—WHEN the sceptre had departed from the tribe of Juda, in the reign of Herod, there lived a priest, by name Zachary, and his wife was named Elizabeth. One day, as this priest was officiating in his turn, and was offering incense, an angel appeared to him, and told him that Elizabeth, now advanced in years, should have a son, that his name should be called John, that he should be great before God, and that he should be filled with the Holy Ghost, even from his mother's womb. Zachary was struck dumb, because he did not believe the voice of the angel.

Six months after the vision of Zachary, the angel Gabriel came to Nazareth to a virgin named Mary, announcing to her that she should also be the mother of a son whose name should be called Jesus. (See the third article of the Creed.)

The Visitation.—Some time after, Mary, understanding from the angel about her cousin Elizabeth, left her home, and went to visit her.

> Jesus! whom Thy sweet Mother bore
> To Saint Elizabeth of yore,
>   On Jewry's mountain lea ;
> Oh, may Thou oft, in ways concealed,
> To heart but not to eye revealed,
>   Vouchsafe to visit me.

From Nazareth to Hebron, where Elizabeth dwelt, must have been a long journey, especially over a mountainous country. When Elizabeth had heard the voice of Mary saluting her, she was suddenly filled with the Holy Ghost, and she cried out, "Blessed art thou amongst women, and blessed is the fruit of thy womb."

Mary also, astonished at what the Lord had done for her, expressed the feelings of her heart, in that most beautiful of canticles, which begins with the words, "Magnificat anima mea Dominum," "My soul doth magnify the Lord." She remained three months at the house of Elizabeth, and then returned home. Soon after this, Elizabeth gave birth to a son. The relations would have given him the name of his father. Zachary, still dumb, signified by writing, that his name should be called John. Immediately Zachary was able to speak, and being filled with the Holy Ghost, he uttered the words of the canticle, "Benedictus." "Blessed be the Lord God of Israel, because He hath visited and wrought the redemption of His people" (St. Luke i. 68). John, in early youth, withdrew into the desert, and there led a retired and penitential life, until he was about thirty years of age, when he began to appear in public, and to prepare the people by his preaching penance, to make ready to receive the words of Christ Himself.

Six months after the birth of St. John, Christ was born in Bethlehem, and was visited on the night of His birth by Jewish shepherds from the hills round about. (See the third article of the Creed.)

The Circumcision.—Eight days after Christ was born, He was circumcised, as the Jewish law required, and He was called Jesus, as the angel had called Him before He was conceived. This day of the circumcision is kept by the Church as a day of obligation, and it falls on New Year's Day.

> Jesus! my God and Saviour, Thou,
> Sinless, didst as a sinner bow
>   To ordinance Divine.
> Oh! curb my loose and wandering eyes,
> Prune my self-will, and circumcise
>   This carnal heart of mine.

The Epiphany.—Shortly after the birth of Christ, certain persons, commonly supposed to be kings in their own country, and called Magi, or wise men, came from the East to Jerusalem, to inquire about the new-born king of the Jews. The prophet

Balaam had prophesied, fifteen hundred years before, about the appearance of a wonderful star; and the tradition of that prophecy had no doubt been kept up in those countries. God accordingly sent a wonderful star in the heavens, and gave those wise men knowledge to understand its meaning. Herod and all Jerusalem were in a state of excitement and alarm at their appearance in the city. At Jerusalem they were directed to Bethlehem, and the star still led them on their way. Arriving at Bethlehem, they found Jesus with Mary His mother, and they fell down and adored Him, and offered Him gifts, of gold, frankincense, and myrrh, the most valuable productions of their country. Warned in a dream of the wicked intentions of Herod, they did not go back to Jerusalem, but went another way into their own country. This wonderful event in the infancy of Christ was to show, that He was born not only for Jews but for Gentiles—that is, for all the world; that the Jews were no longer to be especially the favoured people of God; but that all men were to be called to the knowledge of truth and the ways of salvation; in other words, that the kingdom of Christ was not to be national, or the kingdom of one nation or place, but was to be Catholic or universal — that is, a kingdom or empire including all nations in its dominion. This had been often announced by the prophets. This Epiphany, or manifestation which Christ made of Himself to the wise men, is kept by the Church as a day of obligation, on the sixth of January, twelve days after Christmas Day, and hence is often called "Twelfth Day."

> Jesus! before Thy manger, kings
> Lay prostrate with their offerings,
>   A most unworldly throne.
> Thou to my cradle camest, Lord,
> With gifts invisibly outpoured
>   From waters of Thine own.

Presentation of our Lord in the Temple and the Purification of the Blessed Virgin. — Forty days after the birth of a first-born son, the Jewish mother had to appear before God in His temple to redeem her son from the hands of the priest, as every first-born son belonged to the Lord, and had to be ransomed by certain prescribed offerings. God claimed every first-born son as His own, in memory of His having saved the first-born of the Israelites in Egypt, from the sword of the destroying angel, while the first-born of the Egyptians perished. The Jewish mother had also to make certain offerings for her own legal purification. Accordingly, the Blessed Virgin went up to the temple to do as the law required. There was at that very time in the temple, when Joseph and Mary brought in Jesus, Anna, a prophetess, and a holy and aged man named Simeon, who was anxiously looking (as many other devout Jews were) for the coming of Christ. He was filled with the Holy Ghost, and at once knew Him whom he had so often prayed to behold. He took the Divine infant in his arms, blessed God, and uttered the words of the canticle, "Nunc dimittis." "Now Thou dost dismiss Thy servant in peace according to Thy word." It had been promised to Him, that He should not die till he had seen Christ, and now he was willing to quit this world having seen his Saviour. This event is kept as a day of devotion on the second of February, and from the procession which is often made on that day with lighted candles (in reference to Christ being the light for the enlightening of all nations) is called now, as it was by our Catholic forefathers, "Candlemas Day."

Joy! joy! the Mother comes,
  And in her arms she brings
The Light of all the world,
The Christ, the King of Kings;
And in her heart the while,
  All silently she sings.

There in the temple court,
Old Simeon's heart beats high,
  And Anna feeds her soul
  With food of prophecy;
But, see! the shadows pass,
  The world's true Light draws nigh.

> O Infant God! O Christ!
> O Light most beautiful!
> Thou comest, Joy of Joys!
> All darkness to annul,
> And brightest lights of earth
> Beside Thy Light are dull.

Flight into Egypt.—After the departure of the Magi to their own country, and the presentation of Christ in the temple, the Angel of the Lord warned Saint Joseph to take the child and His mother, and to flee into Egypt, for that Herod was about to seek the life of the Child. Accordingly, they went down into Egypt, where it is said, that the idols fell down at His approach.

> Jesus! sweet fugitive, who fled
> From Herod's bloody net outspread
> For Thy dear Infancy,
> Give me, O Lord, like modest care
> To fly the world when it speaks fair,
> To steal Thy grace away.

Herod then, in his fury and jealousy of the new-born king whom the Magi had come to inquire about, ordered all the children who were two years old and under, in Bethlehem and the country round about, to be killed. These are called the Holy Innocents, and their memory is honoured by the Church, as being the first flowers of martyrdom, who confessed Christ not by their words but by their blood (*non loquendo sed moriendo*). The Holy Family remained in Egypt perhaps for seven years, and on the death of Herod being warned by an angel, they returned to the land of Israel, not to Bethlehem but to Nazareth. There Jesus grew and was strengthened. Saint Joseph and the Blessed Virgin went every year to Jerusalem, there to keep the feast of the Pasch or Passover. At the age of twelve, Jesus also went with them. On this occasion, on their return home, He could not be found in the company of those who were travelling together, and they had to return to Jerusalem to seek for Him. There, after three days' search, they found Him in the temple, in the midst of the doctors or teachers of religion, listening to them, and asking them questions. This strange circumstance of His being thus lost, and thus found, was intended especially to teach the young the great duty of listening to their elders, and of learning the sacred duties of religion from those who are divinely appointed to teach. If Wisdom itself became a scholar, how can man, who is but Ignorance and Sin, be too proud or too idle to learn in the school of Christ!

> Jesus! whom Thy sad Mother sought,
> And in the temple found, who taught
>   The aged in Thy youth;
> How blest are they who keep aright,
> Or find, when lost, the living light
>   Of Thine eternal truth!

On His return from Jerusalem to Nazareth at the age of twelve, the Gospel tells us that He was subject to Joseph and Mary, that He laboured with Saint Joseph as a carpenter, that He spent the next eighteen years in retirement, until He reached the age of thirty, at which time those who were called to the prophetical office used to begin to preach.

CHAPTER XVIII.

CHRIST'S PUBLIC MINISTRY.

St. John the Baptist, being now thirty years old, began his public ministry. His dress was plain and mean, like that of the ancient prophets; his manner of life was severe, and though holy from his birth he was in his life a model of the virtue of repentance, which he continually preached. Those who became his disciples, were baptized by him, to show by that ceremony their desire to be cleansed from sin, and to walk in the ways of a new life. His preaching was full of spirit and power, though he confirmed it by no miracle. He was severe in his rebukes, he gave to all instructions suitable to their condition and wants. He especially laboured to prepare men's minds to believe in Him who was to come after him, whose forerunner he was. Crowds came to him from all parts to be baptized, and, amongst the rest, Jesus Himself left His retirement at Nazareth, and came to him for the same end. St. John had, perhaps, at this time, begun his ministry six months, as he was six months older than our Lord.

Hitherto St. John had not known Him or seen Him; but God made Him known on His entering into the water; on this St. John for a time refused to baptize Him. Then also His Godhead was revealed, for the heavens opened, and the Holy Spirit, in the form of a dove, visibly descended on Him, and a voice was heard from heaven, saying,—"This is My beloved Son, in whom I am well pleased." Our Lord was baptized, as tradition says, on the sixth of January, hence the reference made to that event in the Divine office of that day.

> Jesus! the Father's words approve,
> His Son in Jordan, while the Dove,
>   Bright Witness, hovers down;
> So wash me, Lord, that I may be,
> At the great day, approved of Thee,
>   Before Thy Father's throne.

Christ, after His baptism, was led by the Spirit into the desert, where He remained forty days and forty nights without eating and drinking, and afterwards was tempted by the devil. In memory of this fast, the Church keeps the forty days' fast of Lent.

> Jesus! who in the strength of fast,
> Through Adam's three temptations passed,
>   On Adam's trial-ground,
> In me let hallowed abstinence
> The issues seal of carnal sense,
>   And Satan's wiles confound.

Jesus, on coming out of the desert, chose some of His disciples, whom He took with Him to a marriage feast, to which He had been invited, to Cana in Galilee. Mary His mother was also there; and on that occasion He worked His first miracle at her request, by changing water into wine.

> Jesus! who deign'st to be a guest,
> Where Mary's gently-urged behest
>   With Thy kind power made free,
> May I mine earthly kinsfolk love,
> In such pure ways, that I may prove
>   My greater love for Thee.

From Cana, Jesus went to Capharnum, which he made the centre of His missions. As the doctrine taught by Christ was in many articles above human comprehension, and in many points contrary to flesh and blood, that is, contrary to our natural inclinations; it was necessary that He should confirm the truth of it by miracles. This He did publicly in the sight of the Jews, for the space of three years and a half, throughout Galilee and Judea. He showed His power over all parts of the creation, the heavens, the earth, the winds, and the seas. He showed His power not only over all kinds of diseases, but over death itself. He cured the sick that were brought into His presence, as well as those that were absent, by His word. The lame walked, the blind saw, the deaf heard, the dumb spoke, and the dead arose.

But His own person was the greatest miracle of all; and His life the most astonishing example of the virtues of humility, meekness, and patience. He was gracious to repentant sinners, but severe in His rebukes upon the hypocrisy of the Scribes and Pharisees. He taught the way of God in truth, without respect to the person of men, or the fear of any one. At the same time, He lived in a perfect submission, paying tribute to the civil government, and observing the laws and ceremonies of the Jewish religion, from His infancy. He went about everywhere, through towns and villages, over the mountains and desert places, and on the sea-shore, preaching the Gospel and doing good. He was so much engaged in the duties of His ministry, that He often had not time even to eat. He was often houseless and homeless, and had not where to rest His head.

> Jesus ! how toiled Thy blessed feet
> O'er hill and dale, and stony street,
>   Through weary want and pain !
> Oh, may I rather, for Thy sake,
> The hardships Thou hast hallowed, take
>   Than joys Thou didst disdain.

Christ Feeds the Multitude.—On one occasion He miraculously fed four thousand people with seven loaves and a few fishes, and they gathered up seven baskets full of the fragments which remained. On another occasion, when the multitude had followed Him into a desert place, and there was nothing to supply such a number with food, He fed five thousand men, without counting women and children, with five loaves and two fishes. It was then (John chap. vi.) that he took the opportunity to make that remarkable promise, that He would give them another bread more wonderful than that which their fathers had eaten in the desert. " I am the living bread," He said, " which came down from heaven. If a man eat of this bread, he shall live for ever; and the bread which I will give, is My flesh, which I will give for the life of the world." The Jews evidently understood our Lord as intending to make some remarkable promise, and one which appeared to them impossible to be realized. Accordingly the Jews murmured, and said amongst themselves, " How can He give us His flesh to eat ?" But Jesus quickly replied in a way, that confirmed them in the idea that He was speaking literally, and was not using any figure of speech, and that He meant exactly what He said. " Verily, verily, I say unto you, that unless you eat the flesh of the Son of Man and drink His blood, you shall not have life in you. He that eateth My flesh and drinketh My blood, hath life everlasting, and I will raise him up on the last day ; for My flesh is meat indeed, and My blood is drink indeed !" The Jews therefore, even they who had begun to believe in Him, went away, and walked no more with Him. Peter submitted his judgment, though he could not understand how it could be; but he knew that Christ had the words of eternal life.

> Jesus! who didst the multitude
> Twice nourish with miraculous food
>   Of soul and body both,
> Give me my daily bread, O Lord,
> Thy flesh, Thyself, Incarnate Word!
>   Which feeds our heavenly growth.

The Transfiguration.—One of the most remarkable circumstances in the life of Christ was His Transfiguration, when His body was changed from its natural and ordinary appearance, and became all bright and glorious. Fearing lest the faith of His disciples might be weakened at the sight of the sufferings He was to undergo, Jesus, for their encouragement, resolved to show Himself to them in His glory. He therefore took with Him Peter, James, and John; He led them apart to a high mountain, to Mount Thabor, where He withdrew to pray; and whilst He prayed, His face shone as the sun, and His garments became white as snow. Elias and Moses appeared and discoursed with Him on His sufferings which were to happen in Jerusalem. A voice from the clouds was heard saying, "This is My beloved Son, in whom I am well pleased; hear ye Him." The disciples fell upon their faces with fear, but Jesus raised them up, and as they came down from the mountain, He forbade them to tell any one what they had seen before His resurrection.

> Jesus! transfigured on the height
> Of Thabor in mysterious light
>   From Heaven's eternal fountain;
> If such the earthly type, oh, lead,
> Lead me where Thou Thy flock dost feed
>   Upon the holy mountain.

Christ came to Jerusalem in the fourth year of His public life, on the feast of the Dedication. Having declared that He was the Messiah, and of one and the same essence with the Father, the Jews would have stoned Him, but He left Jerusalem, and went beyond the Jordan to where

John had first begun to baptize. In the meanwhile Lazarus died. He was brother of Martha and Mary, in whose house at Bethania, near Jerusalem, Christ had often taken up His abode; Christ determined to return in order to raise him from the dead. When He arrived, Lazarus had been dead four days. He went to the grave, ordered the stone to be removed; He prayed to His Heavenly Father (a multitude of people standing round); He then cried out, "Lazarus, come forth." And immediately the dead man arose. On this a great number of Jews believed in Him; but the chief Priests and the Pharisees assembled to bring about His death. On this He retreated towards the desert; yet, the feast of the Passover approaching, He takes His way to Jerusalem, foretelling His apostles what would happen to Him. The nearer He draws to Jerusalem, the more He undeceives His apostles on their false notions about the nature of His kingdom. Six days before the Passover He came to Bethania. When at the foot of Mount Olivet, He sent two of His disciples, and said to them, "Go to the village which is before you; as you enter, you will find an ass tied, and a colt with her. Loose them and bring them." The disciples did as they had been commanded.

Accordingly, Christ entered into Jerusalem riding on an ass. He was received with loud Hosannas and acclamations of the people. They cut down boughs of trees, and spread their garments in the way that He might walk upon them. This happened on the first day of the week, and this triumphal procession of the Hebrew people is commemorated by the Church in the office of Palm Sunday, the Sunday before Easter. In the midst of his triumph, foreseeing the destruction of the holy city, He wept over it. His enemies could not bear to see His triumph, and the favour He was gaining with the people. They assembled the great council of the Jews, wherein it was determined that He should die, and they made an agreement with Judas (one of the twelve) that he should contrive to betray Him into their hands for thirty pieces of silver.

> Jesus ! and do I now behold
> My God, my Saviour, bought and sold,
> 	A traitor's merchandize ?
> Oh, grant that I may never be
> A Judas, dearest Lord, to Thee,
> 	For all that earth can prize.

Institution of B. Eucharist.—On the sixth day of the same week of the entry into Jerusalem was the great feast of the Pasch or Passover. The disciples had prepared a room where they might celebrate this Pasch with their Master, by eating a lamb, in the manner and with all the ceremonies required by the law. The Jewish feasts and Sabbath days were kept, not like ours, from midnight to midnight, but from sun-set to sun-set, and thus the keeping of the Passover, which fell on Friday the sixth day of the week, began on the evening of the day before. After that Paschal supper (which was His last supper) was finished, He instituted the most blessed Eucharist, but first arose from table and washed the feet of His apostles to signify with what purity, they and we, ought to receive Him in the holy sacrament.

> Jesus, who deem'dst it not unmeet
> To wash Thine Own disciples' feet,
> 	Though Thou wert Lord of all ;
> Teach me thereby this wisdom meek,
> That they who self-abasement seek
> 	Alone shall fear no fall.

Then seated again at table, He took bread and giving thanks He blessed it, broke it, and gave it to His apostles saying, "Take ye and eat; this is My body which shall be delivered for you; do ye this in remembrance of Me." In like manner, He took the chalice or cup of wine, and when He had given thanks He gave it to them saying, "Drink ye all of this, for this is My blood of the New Testament which shall be shed for you, and for many, for the remission of sin." And He said, "Do ye this in commemoration of Me." By these latter words He ordained His apostles priests, and gave them power to do what He had just done, that is, to change the bread and wine into His body and blood. This change of one substance into another is called Transubstantiation. This command only regarded the apostles and those who succeed them in the office of priests, there being none but the apostles present when the command was given. If God could create something out of nothing (as when He made the world) He could as easily change one thing into another. If we believe Him to be true God under the form of man, why need we think it hard, to believe Him to be true God and man, under the form of bread and wine, since He who is eternal truth, hath said, "This is My body; this is My blood?"

> Jesus! who Thy true flesh didst take
> Upon the Paschal night, and break
> For our most precious food,
> O Living Bread, be Thou my strength
> Through which the world and flesh at length
> In me may be subdued.

After the institution of the Holy Eucharist (which the Church commemorates on the Thursday before Easter, called Holy Thursday or Maundy Thursday) He foretold the apostles many things that afterwards happened; namely, that one of them would betray Him, others abandon Him, another deny Him; He recommended humility, love, and charity, and promised to send them the Holy Ghost, the Comforter, to abide with them for ever.

Note.—The sufferings and death of our Blessed Saviour; His descent into Limbo, together with His resurrection from the dead on the third day; His glorious ascension into heaven on the fortieth day after He rose again; and His sending down the Holy Ghost upon the apostles, ten days after His ascension, are treated of under the 4th, 5th, 6th, and 8th Articles of the Creed.

CHAPTER XIX.

FOUNDATION OF THE CHURCH.

No sooner had the apostles received the Holy Ghost than they went forth and preached the Gospel with great success in Jerusalem. In the first fervour of the faith, all the faithful had one heart and one soul. The rich with one accord sold their property, and laid the price of it at the feet of the apostles, to be distributed from a common fund to those who were in need. Ananias and Saphira having sold a field, mutually determined to keep back a part of what they had received for it. They brought a part of the money to Peter and pretended it was the total price of the property, and in punishment of this falsehood, were both struck with sudden death. A great fear was spread through the whole Church amongst those who heard of this severe chastisement. The people every day pressed round the apostles, and numbers were daily added to the Church, at the sight of their miracles. The sick and infirm were brought out upon beds and couches into the streets of Jerusalem, that the very shadow of St. Peter, as he was passing, might restore them to health.

On the first preaching of the Gospel, persecution broke out against the apostles, who were first threatened by the Jewish authorities, then imprisoned and scourged. The apostles, taking no notice of the prohibition to speak in the name of Jesus, the persecution became more furious. St. Stephen was accused of blasphemy before the great council, and stoned to death. He was the first martyr, that is, the first who shed his blood for the name of Christ. St. Stephen was one of the seven deacons. A dispute having arisen about certain widows having been neglected in the distribution of the public alms, the apostles, by prayer and the imposition of hands, ordained seven men distinguished for their holiness and wisdom, called deacons (that is, servants or ministers), to attend to the public distribution, while *they* kept themselves to the ministry of the word of God. St. Stephen, one of these deacons, was remarkable for his zeal and the conversions he made among the people.

Conversion of the Samaritans.—The same persecution at Jerusalem which brought about the martyrdom of St. Stephen caused many to fly from Jerusalem, and to spread themselves through the countries of Judea and Samaria. Saul at this time made especial havoc in Jerusalem, going from house to house, dragging away men and women, and putting them in prison. They that were dispersed, went about preaching the word of God. Amongst these, St. Philip the deacon went to the city of Samaria, where the people believed him, preaching of the kingdom of God in the name of Jesus Christ, and they were baptized, both men and women. The conversion of the Samaritans (Acts chap. viii.) is worthy of special notice, as we have here mentioned, the first clear administration of the sacrament of Confirmation, or the giving of the Holy Ghost, to men and women, by the imposition of the hands of the apostles. "Now when the apostles" (says the text) "who were in Jerusalem had heard that Samaria had received the word of God, they sent unto them Peter and John. Who when they were come, prayed for them, that they might receive the Holy Ghost. For He was not as yet come upon any of them; but they were only *baptized* in the name of the Lord Jesus. Then they laid their hands upon them, and they received the Holy Ghost." It is clear from this passage that some sacred rite or ordinance had to be administered to the converted and baptized Samaritans, which Philip the deacon had not power to do, and which required the presence of an apostle, who accordingly came a considerable journey for that purpose, from Jerusalem, the capital city of Judea, to Samaria, the chief city of another province. St. Peter (Acts ii. 38, 39) tells us, what would have been clear of itself, that the receiving the Holy Ghost, besides baptism, was intended for all times, and all persons whom the Lord shall call. We find that St. Paul, when in one of his journeys (Acts xix. 1—6), he had come to Ephesus, and had found certain disciples whom he thought had been baptized, asked them whether they had received the Holy Ghost. On finding, however, that they had not been even properly baptized, he first baptized them, and then imposed his hands on them, and gave them the Holy Ghost. The imposition of hands, by which Christians are made partakers of the Holy Ghost, is spoken of by St. Paul (Heb. vi. 1—5) as belonging, together with two other ordinances (evidently baptism and the Holy Eucharist) to the foundation and essence of religion.

The Conversion and Labours of St. Paul.—Amongst those who had demanded the death of St. Stephen was a Pharisee named Saul, one of the most furious enemies of the Christian name. Not satisfied with persecuting in Jerusalem, he obtained a commission, to go to Damascus to bring bound to Jerusalem, any men or women who believed in Christ. For on occasion of the dispersion of the chief members of the Church of Jerusalem (through the persecution which drove Philip to Samaria), many went to Damascus, others to Phenicia, Cyprus, Antioch, and some even as far as Rome. Saul, on his way to Damascus, to seize the Christians who might be there, was miraculously converted by a voice and a light from heaven (Acts ix.). He began to the astonishment of every one to preach the Gospel in Damascus itself. His principal mission was to convert the Gentiles, to whom Peter, instructed by a heavenly vision, had just opened the gates of the Church by receiving Cornelius the centurion.

Before beginning his great apostolic labours, Paul repaired to Jerusalem to see Peter, and to be acknowledged by him as an apostle. He afterwards travelled throughout Syria and Cilicia, propagated Christianity in the great city of Antioch, and went with Barnabas to preach in the isle of Cyprus, and the south of Asia Minor.

After this great mission he returned to Antioch, went to give an account of his first labours to Peter, who was still at Jerusalem, and returned a second time into Asia Minor to finish the conversion of all that country. He preached with the greatest success in Phrygia, Mysia, Lydia, and Troas; attached himself closely to his dear Timothy and the evangelist St. Luke, and passed into Macedonia, where he founded the great churches of Philippi, Thessalonica, and Berea. Thence he embarked for Athens, where he announced before the Areopagus the "Unknown God," and terminated this glorious mission by the establishment of the Church at Corinth.

These labours kept him away from Antioch for a year and a half. He returned there after this long absence, passing through Ephesus, Cæsarea, and Jerusalem. He made afterwards a third mission into Asia Minor. Having heard of the troubles raised among the Corinthians and the Galatians, he wrote to them, to put an end to the controversies which agitated them. He visited the churches of Macedonia, sent a second letter to Corinth, and went himself to that city, in order to smother the seeds of division which the spirit of darkness had sown amongst them. From Corinth he wrote to the Romans.

He collected at Corinth abundant alms for the faithful of Jerusalem. He knew that persecution awaited him in this last city; but nothing could stop his zeal. When he appeared before the governor of Judea, he used the rights which his title of Roman citizen gave him, and appealed from him to Cæsar. He was accordingly sent to Rome, where he remained a prisoner for two years. When set at liberty, he began his apostolic labours anew, and preached the Gospel in the East. Unfortunately, the Acts of the Apostles stop here, and we possess only, concerning the last missions of the Apostle of the Gentiles, some traditions, very respectable no doubt, but which, however, do not suffice to give us complete certainty. He was beheaded at Rome, under Nero, the same day that St. Peter was crucified.

The Apostolic Labours of St. Peter.—The Holy Scriptures have not preserved as many details regarding the missions of the chief of the apostles as regarding those of St. Paul. But it seems that the Holy Spirit, which has dictated them, has taken care by facts to show his priority of honour and jurisdiction. Thus we see him at the head of all important affairs. He presided at the election of the apostle Matthias. He spoke the first to the people, after the descent of the Holy Spirit. It was in the name of all the apostles that he spoke to the Sanhedrim. He worked the first miracle, and first pronounced a terrible judgment against Ananias. He first opened the gates of the Christian Church to the Gentiles. It was Peter, whom Paul sought for at Jerusalem after his conversion to converse with him. It was Peter who presided at the first council of Jerusalem, and it is always Peter whom the evangelists style the *first*, although he was not the first to follow Jesus Christ; a clear proof that his primacy was acknowledged by all the apostles.

About his apostolic labours, we know that he founded the first Christian Church at Jerusalem, and that he was the head of all the new communities of the first Christians throughout Judea and Samaria. When the faith was spread in the East, he resided for some time at Antioch, the capital of all that part of the world. He then preached the Gospel successively in Pontus, Cappadocia, Galatia, Asia, and Bithynia. The kingdom of Christ having spread into the West as well as into the East, Peter left Antioch, to fix his seat at Rome, the queen and mistress of all nations. There he sealed his faith with his blood, and was crucified like his Divine Master. St. Peter suffered death about the year 65, the thirty-seventh after the death of Christ. On this calculation he had lived about five years at Jerusalem, and had presided over the Church of Antioch (where the faithful were first called Christians) for seven years. He had been Bishop of Rome nearly twenty-five years, though often absent on his apostolic journeys. No one of St. Peter's two hundred and fifty-five successors has occupied the See of Rome so long as St. Peter.

The sacred books have not recorded the miracles, virtues, and sufferings of the other apostles, as they were similar to those related in the lives of St. Peter and

St. Paul. The other apostles preached in the various countries of the inhabited world, and through the different provinces of the Roman empire. St. John dwelt principally at Ephesus, from which city he watched over the Churches of Asia Minor.

From this it appears that the apostles really visited all nations, and hence we may understand how some years after the Ascension of Jesus Christ, St. Paul could write to the Romans that the Gospel had been preached to every country.

The Books of the New Testament.—The New Testament contains an account of the life of our Lord, the principal events of the first thirty years after His Ascension, the Epistles of some of the apostles, and the Revelations of St. John, called the Apocalypse.

The four Gospels, written by the four evangelists, Sts. Matthew, Mark, Luke, and John, contain an account of our Lord's life until His Ascension.

The Acts of the Apostles, written by St. Luke, contain an account of the first thirty years of Christianity after our Lord's Ascension. The Epistles of the New Testament are twenty-one in number, fourteen of which were written by St. Paul. They were written some to a particular Church, as some occasion called for them, as for example, to Rome, Corinth, Ephesus, etc. Some are called Catholic Epistles, because written not to a particular Church, but to the faithful in general of a certain district. Some were written to individuals.

The Gospel of St. Matthew was the first book of the New Testament which was written, about six or eight years after our Lord's Ascension. St. John's Gospel was written sixty-three years after the Ascension. The book of the Apocalypse was written a little later, as also his three short Epistles. The Apocalypse contains an account of heavenly visions with which he was favoured, and in it, he prophetically and in mysterious language, speaks of what will happen to the Church till the end of time.

CHAPTER XX.

HISTORY OF THE CHURCH (*continued*).

ABOUT the same year that St. Peter and St. Paul were martyred (A.D. 65), the civil wars began in Judea, and the seditions of the Jews against the Romans. The Christians residing in Jerusalem, were divinely admonished of the destruction that was at hand, and ordered to withdraw from that city. Accordingly, they retired beyond the river Jordan with their bishop St. Simeon, successor of St. James, and remained in a city called Pella, until after the taking and burning of Jerusalem, when they returned to settle themselves in the midst of its ruins. It is said, that for forty years before the destruction of the city, there were all manner of wonders seen in the temple; a terrible noise was heard by the priests in the sanctuary on the day of Pentecost, and a voice issued from the sacred place, saying, "Let us go hence, let us go hence."

Jerusalem Destroyed (A.D. 71).—It was expedient that the city of Jerusalem and the temporal republic of the Jews should last until the spiritual kingdom of Christ, and the new Church of the Gentiles, should be formed and grafted on the ancient stock and root of the synagogue of true Israelites. The time was at length arrived, when Jerusalem and its beautiful temple were to be demolished. The Divine vengeance which they had incurred, came upon them about forty years after the death of Christ. Vespasian (A.D. 70) had been ordered by Nero, to chastise the Jews who had revolted. When Vespasian aimed at being proclaimed emperor, he left the command of the army to his son Titus, who laid siege to Jerusalem. Titus did not wish to deal harshly with the Jews; but they would listen to no terms. He sent to them Josephus, the celebrated Jewish historian, their fellow-citizen, one of their captains and priests, who had been taken prisoner; but they would not listen to his advice. Titus, moved by their misfortunes, called his gods to witness, that he was not the author of their destruction. During these evils, they still believed in the false predictions which promised them the empire of the world. Soon after the city was taken, fire raged on every side, and the madmen still believed the false prophets, who assured them the day of salvation was come, in order that they might continue their resistance, and that there might be no mercy for them. In fact, all were massacred, the city was utterly overthrown, the temple was burnt, and except some remains of towers, which Titus left to serve as a monument to posterity, there remained not a stone upon a stone.

So great was the spoil, that the price of gold sunk to half its value in Syria. Eleven hundred thousand Jews died during the siege, ninety-seven thousand were sold as slaves (buyers could hardly be found for the worthless outcasts), several thousand Jews perished by fire and wild beasts, or by the hands of each other as gladiators. At Rome, Titus and his father triumphed over Judea. John and Simon, the Jewish rulers of Jerusalem, marched in chains behind their chariot. Medals were struck in memory of this event, representing a woman covered with a mantle, seated at the foot of a palm-tree, her head resting upon her hand, with this inscription, *"Judea captive."* The destruction of Jerusalem took place in the pontificate of St. Linus, the successor of St. Peter, who had been ordained by that apostle, to supply in his absence during his apostolic journeys.

St. Cletus.—St. Cletus, a disciple of St. Peter, succeeded St. Linus as Bishop of Rome (A.D. 78). Fleury remarks that when the apostles established the seven deacons at Jerusalem, it does not appear that they had ordained any priests; on the contrary, they reserved to themselves the functions since communicated to priests. St. Paul, giving his orders to Titus and Timothy for the government of new churches, only speaks of bishops and deacons, nevertheless, we are assured that St. Cletus ordained twenty-five priests for the different portions of the city of Rome. St. Cletus is said to have lost his life (A.D. 91) in the second persecution of the Church raised by the Emperor Domitian. About this time, St. John the Evangelist, who had generally lived at Ephesus, was banished to the isle of Patmos, in the Ægean Sea, where he wrote the book of the Revelations. He had long outlived all the other apostles; he had seen executed on Jerusalem and the Jewish nation, God's just judgments and our Saviour's predictions. After four or five years' exile in Patmos, on the death of Domitian, the edict of Nerva, his successor, restored him to liberty; so that he returned to Ephesus, where he died in peace, at a great age, under the next emperor, Trajan, about the one hundredth year of our Lord.

St. Clement.—St. Clement, the fourth from St. Peter, had been for some time the companion of St. Paul, and was with him at Philippi. He afterwards received episcopal ordination from the hands of St. Peter (as his two predecessors had), and probably assisted the apostle in his labours. The persecution of Domitian had caused St. Clement to appoint seven notaries for different parts of the city of Rome, to take down in writing what passed at the trial of the martyrs before the pagan tribunals, the questions of the magistrates, and the answers of the Christians. These records are called the Acts of the Martyrs, and are, next to the Scriptures, the most ancient and venerable monuments of Christian antiquity. A division happening in the Church of Corinth, on occasion of two priests who were unjustly deposed, this Pope wrote to that Church an admirable letter, which, with the fragment of another, are the only writings which remain of him. St. Clement saw the close of the first century of Christianity. He was banished to the Tauric Chersonesus, and afterwards, by order of the Emperor Trajan, was drowned.

Trajan issued no new decree against the faithful; but allowed the former cruel laws against the Christians to be put into execution. This is called the third persecution. Pliny the Younger (A.D. 105), governor of Pontus and Bithynia, wrote to the emperor that the Christians were very numerous in the provinces of his jurisdiction, that the temples of the gods were abandoned, their feasts interrupted, and scarcely any victims purchased for sacrifices, and therefore wished to know what should be done. Trajan's answer was, "Let the Christians not be sought for; but if they be accused and convicted as such, let them be punished." Tertullian confutes this absurd and unjust answer, and asks, "If they are criminal, why are they not sought for? If innocent, why are they punished?" St. Simeon, Bishop of Jerusalem, and brother and successor to St. James the Lesser, suffered martyrdom under Trajan at the age of one hundred and twenty years. St. Ignatius, Bishop of Antioch, was sent by him to Rome to be torn to pieces by wild beasts in the amphitheatre. St. Ignatius wrote seven epistles, still extant, which breathe the spirit of every Christian virtue. The acts of his martyrdom, written by the Christians who had come with him to Rome, record the great respect shown to his relics, and that they were carried to Antioch, and deposited in the church as an inestimable treasure.

End of the Jewish Nation.—Adrian, the successor of Trajan (A.D. 124), put a stop to the persecution; moved probably by the apologies of Quadratus and Aristides, and by a letter which the pro-consul of Asia had written to him in favour of the Christians. It was Adrian who built the wall (called Adrian's wall) between England and Scotland. Adrian visited Judea, rebuilt Jerusalem, but forbade the Jews to enter it except they bought permission to go and weep over the ruins of their country. At length, under the leadership of a man named Barcochebas (son of the star), who gave himself out as the Messiah, and assumed the title of King of the Jews, the Jews (A.D. 134), about fifty years after the destruction of Jerusalem by Titus, rose in a body in different countries where they were settled against their rulers; they massacred with all manner of cruelties about a million of human beings. The sword of the Romans, with an enormous slaughter of the Hebrews, destroyed their foolish illusion. Fifty strongholds and nine hundred and eighty-five country towns were demolished. Then the total destruction of the country, took away from that unhappy nation, not only the hope, but also the possibility of its ever being restored.

In order to annihilate their religion, a temple for idols was built upon the foundations of the temple of Solomon. The name of Jerusalem was changed into that of Ælia Capitolina, and its ancient name was so completely forgotten, that about one hundred years after, in the time of Diocletian, a martyr having said that he was born at Jerusalem, the governor of Palestine and the inhabitants of that province, did not know even where it was situated.

Julian's attempt to rebuild the Temple.—The last event connected with the history of Jerusalem worthy of notice is the attempt which the Emperor Julian, an apostate from Christianity, made to rebuild the temple (A.D. 362). He did this through a desire to make false the words of Christ, who had declared that not one stone of it should be left on another. Jews in multitudes, from all parts of the world, answered to the invitation of the emperor to join in the work; gold and costly ornaments were abundantly contributed to the expense. When they had dug up the old foundations, and removed the old ruins, and were preparing to lay the foundation of the new building; then the finger of God visibly defeated all their attempts. Earthquakes cast back what had been dug up into the trenches, dreadful whirlwinds scattered the lime and loose materials, balls and flames of fire repeatedly bursting forth near the foundation, melted the iron instruments, burnt and scorched the workmen, drove them to a distance, not once, but as often as they made a fresh attempt, until at last they were obliged to desist. A flaming cross appeared in the sky over Jerusalem, surrounded with a circle of light, as if to celebrate the triumph of Christ, and to confound the impiety of Julian. These wonders were recorded by both Pagan and Christian writers, were witnessed by multitudes of spectators, and induced many Jews and heathens to confess the divinity of Christ.

Part the Second.

LESSONS ON DOCTRINAL SUBJECTS.

Lessons on Doctrinal Subjects,

FOLLOWING THE ORDER AND ARRANGEMENT OF THE ELEMENTARY CATECHISM APPROVED FOR THE USE OF THE FAITHFUL IN ALL THE DIOCESES OF ENGLAND AND WALES.

CHAPTER I.

INTRODUCTION.

God is our first beginning and last end. He made us, and not we ourselves. He is our Creator; we are His creatures. The sun, moon, and stars, and all the beautiful and magnificent works of nature, tell us of God's existence, and silently praise Him. There is also something within us, that is, our conscience, which continually tells us of that Great Being, who will reward our good works, and will punish our evil doings, and who knows all things, even our most secret thoughts. A man who disbelieves in a God is called an atheist; but it is hard to believe that such a person ever existed, though many have professed atheism.

God who made us, could alone appoint and fix the end and object for which He made us. He made us to know Him, to love Him, and serve Him in this world, and to be happy with Him for ever in the next. We must *know* God—that is, not merely believe and know that there *is* a God, but we must know His will, His works, His perfections, as far as it is given to beings like ourselves to know such things. We are not said to know a person if we only know that there is such a person, but have perhaps never seen or spoken to him, and know nothing of him; but to *know* a person means much more than this, and so it is when we speak of knowing God. If we knew God as we ought, we should soon also begin to love Him, and that love would continue to increase, unless we began to turn from Him to created things. If we loved God as we ought, we should soon show that love by serving Him faithfully—that is, by keeping His commandments. "If you love Me, keep My commandments" (John xiv. 15).

This knowing, loving, and serving God, is the way by which we are to arrive at the great end for which we were created,—the enjoyment of God in a happy eternity; for God made us to be happy with Him for ever in the life to come. God might have made us for some happiness inferior to this, and still have shown His great goodness in creating us; but He made us for a supernatural end. Existence would have been a blessing in any state, in which it would be better to be, than not to be; how great a blessing then it must have been, when it was to be an eternal existence with God Himself!

God made man to His own image and likeness. Other creatures may have existed on earth before man was made. But God said, "Let us make man to our own image and likeness" (Genesis i. 26). He might have made a being much inferior to man, and not one who is little less than angel. The likeness of man to God is in the spiritual and immortal soul, which God breathed into the lifeless body of Adam which had been fashioned from the clay. The soul is immortal—that is, it never dies, it does not perish and cease to be when the mortal body is dissolved. It is plain, therefore, that it is of far greater consequence, to take more care of the soul than of the body. The sins of men, are for the most part, committed through their desire to take more care of the body than of the soul, through their seeking more eagerly after what they should eat, and wherewith they shall be clothed, than after the food and the life of the soul; through their seeking this world, and its riches and pleasures, before the kingdom of God and His justice. God will not give Himself to us in the next life to be our happiness unless we, as His creatures, give ourselves to Him in this life. Therefore, by faith we must know Him, in hope we must serve Him, and by charity we must love Him all the days of our life. We should often pray that those virtues of faith, hope, and charity may be more and more increased and strengthened in us. For this end we should often say from our hearts, "O my God, I believe in Thee, do Thou strengthen my faith; all my hopes are in Thee, do Thou secure them; I love Thee with my whole heart, teach me to love Thee daily more and more."

By faith we believe without doubting whatever God has revealed, and this, because God is the very truth, and cannot deceive nor be deceived. It is true that God has not revealed His truths to each of us individually. The Almighty, in former times, made His will known to men by Moses and the prophets and the divinely appointed authorities of the Jewish Church. Afterwards, He sent His only Son Jesus Christ upon the earth, to bring to men a more perfect knowledge of His will. Christ especially taught the twelve apostles His doctrines, and when He was about to leave the earth, ordered them to preach those doctrines to all the world, and that men were to believe, or else to be condemned. Those apostles who thus bore witness — that is, gave testimony as to what the doctrines of Christ were, and who had authority from Christ to teach those doctrines to others, constituted in themselves what we call the Church of Christ. Those who succeeded age after age to the authority and office of the apostles, are called the Church of Christ, and it is from that Church which speaks to us now, with the authority which Christ in the beginning gave to the apostles, that we have to learn the things which God has revealed. Some of those things are points which we have to believe, and others are duties which we must practise, in order to please God, and thus save our souls unto life eternal.

CHAPTER II.

FAITH — APOSTLES' CREED.

THE chief things which God has revealed to man are contained and named in the Apostles' Creed. There are other points besides those mentioned in the Creed; but we sufficiently profess our belief in them, when we profess our belief in the Holy Catholic Church as having authority from Christ to teach us all things necessary for our salvation. It is called the Apostles' Creed because it is commonly believed that the apostles, before they separated to preach the Gospel, as Christ had commanded them, composed a form of words which all Christians might know and make use of; and this Creed, which is of most ancient use in the Church, is perhaps the very one which the apostles themselves composed. It is divided into twelve parts, or articles.

1ST ARTICLE.

In the first article we profess our belief in God the Father Almighty, Creator of heaven and earth.

God is a spirit; but as we are beings made up of a body and spirit, we cannot understand what a mere spiritual being is. God alone is self-existent — that is, exists of Himself. He depends upon no other for His being; but all other beings that exist depend on Him for their being, and therefore they belong entirely to Him, and are bound by the law of their nature to give themselves to Him in whatever way He wishes them to serve Him. God alone is goodness or perfection in Himself; and that infinite perfection of God in His own essence and nature, is necessarily the object of the love, admiration, homage, and adoration of His creatures, who have reason and are able to become acquainted with it. This love of God for His own essential goodness and perfection is the highest act of worship which the creature can offer to its Creator. That we may be able to love God for His own infinite perfection and goodness, we must study and learn, as far as we can, in what His perfections consist. These attributes and perfections are often spoken of, in the Sacred Scriptures, and are treated of by spiritual writers.

God is called "Father," because being the first Person of the Blessed Trinity, and proceeding from no other, He is by nature the Father of the second Person. The Son, whom in His human nature we call Jesus Christ, is the second Person of the Trinity, because He proceeds from the Father by eternal generation. The Holy Ghost is the third Person, because He proceeds from the Father and the Son. Yet we must not imagine that there is any inequality among them. They have and are the same Godhead, and are in every respect equal.

To remember the doctrine of the Church upon the Holy Trinity, it would be well to read occasionally the first part of the Athanasian Creed, which may be found in most Prayer Books.

The unity of nature and Trinity of persons in the Godhead is the greatest mystery of religion. There must be mysteries in religion—that is, things beyond our comprehension. What wonder that we cannot understand God's nature, when we cannot understand our own!

God is especially called "Almighty," because He can do all things. Nothing to Him is impossible or difficult. It is this attribute of God, above any other, with which men at all times have been most deeply impressed. We see everywhere around us the power of God made manifest, and we know that He is Almighty both in punishing the wicked and in rewarding the good.

God is called the "Creator of heaven and earth," because He made them out of nothing by His only word. He said, "Let there be light, and there was light," and so of all the other works of creation, "He commanded, and they were created." The belief of one God, the Creator of the world, is the foundation of all religion; hence, the Creed and the Scripture begin with the and forgiveness for actual sin which He has left for us in His Church. Christ is therefore called our Redeemer, our Saviour; and the blessing He procured for us by His coming is called redemption and salvation. To redeem, means to purchase by money from his master the freedom of a slave. So long as we were shut out of heaven by the effects of the first sin of Adam, which was brought about by the malice of the devil, we were called the slaves of the devil. But Christ has made us free from that slavery, having purchased our freedom, not with gold or silver, but with His own blood.

From the name Christ we are called "Christians," which means believers in Christ's doctrine and imitators of His life. The believers in Christ very soon received that name, and first of all in the city of Antioch, where they were very numerous. Before that time they were called "disciples"— that is, scholars of Christ; and "brethren," because they were remarkable for the love they bore to one another, being all of one heart and one mind. The apostle exhorts all Christians to walk in a manner worthy of their profession, which is not merely to believe in the heart, but to show holiness in their lives. Christians in Scripture are also called "saints," because by baptism they are made holy, and ought ever after to remain holy. The words "Christian" and "saint" remind us what we ought to be; that we should be holy in all things; that we should put on the Lord Jesus Christ (Rom. xiii. 14).

3rd Article.

"Who was conceived by the Holy Ghost."

He who was the Son of God from all eternity, when the appointed time was come, took to Himself a body and soul like ours. He did not take a body made from the dust, as was the body of Adam, but He was conceived in the womb of the Blessed Virgin Mary. This conception took place by the power of the Holy Ghost—that is, by a miracle contrary to the ordinary course of nature. The prophet Isaias had long before foretold that Christ should be born of a virgin. St. Luke tells us (chap. i. 26—38) that the angel Gabriel was sent from God into a city of Galilee called Nazareth, to a holy virgin whose name was Mary. The angel being come in, said to her, "Hail, full of grace; the Lord is with thee: blessed art thou amongst women." The holy virgin being troubled and disturbed at this strange salutation, the angel bade her not fear; he announced to her the designs of God, that she should be the mother of a son, whose name should be called Jesus, that He should be the Son of the Most High, the Son of God, and that of His kingdom there should be no end. On understanding the will of God, she bowed in submission, and exclaimed, "Behold the handmaid of the Lord; be it done to me according to Thy word." At that wonderful moment the mystery of the Incarnation was accomplished — that is, a human body and soul were united to the Divine nature of the Eternal Son of God in the womb of the Blessed Virgin Mary. This great event is commemorated by the Church on the 25th of March; it is called the Annunciation of the Blessed Virgin Mary, and more commonly Lady Day. It used to be a day of obligation; but though now kept in England only as a day of devotion, it may in reality be considered, as to the fact which is commemorated, as great as Christmas Day itself. To commemorate this mystery, the devotion prevails almost everywhere of reciting every day, morning, noon, and night, the "Angelus," at the public ringing of the bell. Though it may seem frequent to commemorate three times every day, in such a public manner, the mystery of the Incarnation, and Christ's miraculous conception in the womb of the Holy Virgin, we should ever remember, that it is by this mystery, that the salvation of the world was brought about, and from it all our good must come. Moreover, in the Mass, at the words, "Et incarnatus est," "He was made flesh," in the Creed; and again at the words, "Et verbum caro factum est," "And the Word was made flesh," in the last Gospel; we each time kneel down to commemorate and to reverence the mystery of the Incarnation.

"Born of the Virgin Mary."

Nine months after His conception in the womb of the Blessed Virgin Mary, Christ was born at Bethlehem. He was born in a stable. The birthday of Christ is kept on the 25th of December; it is called Christmas Day. It is a day of obligation in the Catholic Church; it is a day well remembered and thought of by all Christians; but often more on account of the worldly feasts and festivities of Christmas time than on account of any spiritual joy. Bethlehem, a little town about six miles from Jerusalem, was, according to prophecy, to be the birth-place of Christ. The Blessed Virgin Mary lived at Nazareth, a distance of about ninety miles from Bethlehem; but in consequence of the decree of Augustus, the Roman emperor, requiring a general registration of the people in all the provinces of the empire, she and her espoused husband, St. Joseph, had to make a long journey from Nazareth to Bethlehem. She went to Bethlehem; for, humble and poor as she was, she was a descendant of King David, and Bethlehem was the city of David and his family. Through the throng of those who on that occasion claimed to belong to the royal house of David, every house and inn was filled, so that the only place, where that unknown, humble-looking pair could find any shelter was in a hovel or stable. Here Christ was born. Though the people in Bethlehem knew nothing of what had just taken place, angels came down, and on that same night gave notice to certain poor shepherds who were watching their flocks in the country close by, of what had just happened. The shepherds were greatly afraid at the brightness that shone round them; but the angel said to them, "Fear not, for behold I bring you good tidings of great joy, that shall be to all the people; for this day is born to you a Saviour in the city of David; and this shall be a sign unto you, you shall find the infant wrapped in swaddling clothes, and laid in a manger. And suddenly there was with the angel a multitude of the heavenly army, praising God, and saying, Glory to God in the highest, and on earth peace to men of good will." And the shepherds left their flocks, and came in haste to Bethlehem, and found Mary and Joseph and the infant lying in the manger. The shepherds spread the news of what had happened, and returned glorifying and praising God.

Christ was born at a time when the world was in peace everywhere, which was a thing seldom before ever known to have happened. This was to signify, that He came to make peace between heaven and earth, to reconcile man with God. He was born of a *virgin* to show His great love for purity, and how pure our souls ought to be, especially when we receive Him in the Holy Communion. He was born in the midst of *poverty*, and suffered great hardships, intending thereby to teach His real followers, that they are not to think too much of riches, nor of enjoyments, but that they are to be willing and satisfied to live in poverty, with very few pleasures; and never, by seeking riches and pleasures, to neglect religion and the care of their souls. He began very early to teach the same lessons which He taught during the rest of His poor and self-denying life, and especially in the time of His painful sufferings and death.

> Jesus! the spacious world was Thine,
> Yet, when Thou would'st Thy head recline,
>   It scarce found room for Thee;
> And, oh! shall sinful man be bent
> On self-sought greatness, not content
>   With Christ-like poverty?

> Jesus! for whom the shepherds sought
> An infant, by the angels taught
>   From out the midnight sky,
> Oh, may I love Thy praise on earth,
> That I may one day share the mirth
>   Of angel hosts on high.

4TH ARTICLE.

"Suffered under Pontius Pilate, was crucified, dead, and buried."

Christ having spent His life in retirement beneath the roof of Joseph and Mary, at the age of thirty made Himself known to the people by beginning His public preaching. He spent three years and a half in teaching the multitudes, and especially His own disciples. He went through towns and villages, everywhere doing good and working miracles to confirm His mission. But His enemies were continually watching to ensnare Him in His speech, and were becoming more and more bitter against Him, and at last they determined to take away His life.

After the last supper, a hymn having been sung, Christ went out of Jerusalem with the eleven, Judas having gone out a little before. He crossed the brook Cedron, and went to the foot of the Mount of Olives to a garden called Gethsemane, where He warned them to watch and pray. Going a little further, He took with Him, Peter, James, and John. Then He fell into an agony of mind at the prospect of His sufferings, which so affected His body, that falling on His face, He sweated drops of blood, which ran upon the ground. "My soul," He said, " is sorrowful even unto death." Thrice He prayed that the bitter cup of suffering might pass away, if such was His Father's will.

O soul of Jesus, sick to death,
Thy blood and prayer together plead ;
My sins have bowed Thee to the ground,
As the storm bows the feeble reed.

Oh, by the pains of Thy pure love,
Grant me the gift of holy fear,
And give me of Thy bloody sweat
To wash my guilty conscience clear.

Ever, when tempted, make me see,
Beneath the olive's moon-pierced shade,
My God alone, outstretched and bruised
And bleeding on the earth He made.

And make me feel it was my sin,
As though no other sins there were,
That was to Him who bears the world
A load that He could scarcely bear !

At the end of this agony an angel came from heaven to comfort Him. He thrice went to His disciples, who slept instead of praying. Shortly after this, Judas Iscariot, who had just been seated with Him at His last supper, and who well knew the usual place of His retirement for prayer, appeared with a company of soldiers to apprehend Him. The words of Christ to the soldiers caused them to recoil before Him, and to fall to the ground; but after this He freely gave Himself up to them. Peter with a sword cut off the ear of one of them. Christ healed the wound; yet, notwithstanding these wonders, they carried Him away, and the disciples fled.

> Jesus! who saw'st on that sad night
> Thine own, Thy chosen, take to flight,
>   And leave their Lord by stealth;
> Oh! may we learn in grief and care
> Those harder trials still to bear,
>   Prosperity and wealth.

Then He was carried prisoner, about midnight, to Annas, who caused Him to be led to his son-in-law Caiphas, who was the high-priest for that year. Here, in the judgment-hall of Caiphas, several false witnesses were brought against Him.

On His declaration that He was Christ, the Son of God, He was judged worthy of death, beaten, blindfolded, buffeted, spit upon, and left till morning in the hands of the soldiers. Peter had followed from a distance, and had entered with others into the court of Caiphas. He stood warming himself at a fire with other attendants of the court, when he was recognised as being one of Christ's disciples; and being asked upon the subject by three different persons, he three times most vehemently denied it. Then the cock crowed the third time; Christ looked upon Peter, who knew His meaning, felt his guilt, and went forth and wept bitterly.

> Jesus! whom Peter then denied,
> Thou with one gentle look didst chide

> The weak disciple's fears;
> If ever I deny Thy name,
> Thy cross, oh, send me speedy shame,
>   Oh, give me Peter's tears.

Morning being come, the senate of the nation was assembled by Caiphas, when our Saviour, persisting in His first confession of being the Son of God, His condemnation was confirmed. Then they led Him to Pilate, the governor of Judea under Tiberius, to obtain from the civil authorities His condemnation and execution, as the Jewish ecclesiastical court had not the power of life and death. Pilate tried in all ways to excuse himself, and to escape the cruel task that was being forced upon him. Pilate declared Him innocent, and, hearing that He was a Galilean, sent Him to Herod, the Tetrarch of that province, who was in Jerusalem on account of the Passover. Herod, not having his curiosity satisfied by Him, for he expected to see some miracle, treated Him with contempt, clothed Him with a white garment in derision, and sent Him back again to Pilate.

Pilate, knowing His innocence, proposed to scourge Him, and then to acquit Him; but, as this did not satisfy His enemies, Pilate hoped to release Him another way. It was the custom to release a prisoner on the festival-day of the Passover, and, as if to make sure of the deliverance of Christ, he proposed to them either to release Christ, or a man named Barabbas, a notorious robber and murderer. But the people would have Barabbas set free, and cried out that Christ should be crucified.

> Jesus! for whom the wicked Jews
> A vile and blood-stained robber choose,
>   Have mercy, Lord, on me,
> And keep me from a choice so base
> As taking wealth, or ease, or place,
>   Barabbas, Lord! for Thee.

Pilate still endeavoured to obtain His release; and, to move their compassion, he then ordered Him to be scourged. Then He was left in the hands of the soldiers, who platted a crown of thorns, and put it upon His head. Then they clothed Him with a purple garment, put a reed in His hand for a sceptre, and, kneeling before Him, saluting Him as King of the Jews, they struck His head with the reed, and spit in His face.

> Jesus! when scourged, and buffeted,
> And spit upon, Thy sacred head
>   Was bow'd to earth for me;
> Oh, may I pardon find, and bliss,
> And expiating love in this
>   My Lord's indignity!

> Jesus! with crown of reedy thorn
> The Jews Thy tortured brow adorn,
>   And, jeering, hail Thee king;
> May I, O Lord, with heart sincere,
> My humble zeal, my love and fear,
>   And real homage bring!

Pilate brought Him forth in this condition, and in compassion said, "Behold the man!" They cried out, "Crucify Him." Pilate at last, fearing that if He dismissed Him, he should be accused to the emperor, at length condemned Jesus to be crucified; but, washing his hands, declared himself innocent of His blood. Judas, seeing Him condemned, was filled with remorse for having betrayed Him, brought back the money he had received, and went away and hanged himself. The money was laid out in buying a piece of ground, which was used as a burial-place for strangers.

THE WAY OF THE CROSS, AND THE SEVEN LAST WORDS.

For the rest of the sufferings of Christ we may follow the order observed in the devotion called "The Stations," or "The Way of the Cross." This devotion was established and encouraged in the Church to promote meditation on the Passion of Christ, and as an imitation or representation of the real way of the cross from the court of Herod to the top of Calvary, which in past ages used to be trodden by thousands of devout pilgrims from every Christian nation.

> From pain to pain, from woe to woe,
> With loving hearts and footsteps slow,
> To Calvary with Christ we go.
> See how His precious blood
> At every station pours !
> Was ever grief like His !
> Was ever sin like ours ?

The stations are fourteen in number, in the following order :—
1st. Pilate, after trying in vain to effect His release, condemns Jesus to death. 2nd. A heavy cross is laid upon the bruised shoulders of Jesus Christ. 3rd. Jesus, bearing His cross, advances on His way to Calvary in the midst of a furious rabble; but at last, exhausted with the loss of blood, sinks upon the ground.

> Jesus ! along Thy proper road
> Of sorrows, with Thy weary load,
>   How didst Thou toil and strain !
> Oh, may I bear the cross like Thee,
> Or rather, Lord, do Thou in me
>   The blessed weight sustain.

4th. Jesus is met by His Blessed Mother. 5th. A countryman, named Simon of Cyrene, is made to assist Christ, for a time, in carrying the cross. 6th. A pious woman in compassion wipes the face of Jesus with a veil, and in reward of her piety the impression of His divine countenance is left upon it. 7th. Jesus bearing His cross, falls a second time beneath its weight. 8th. Jesus, seeing some holy women following Him and weeping over Him, said to them, "Weep not for Me, but for yourselves and your children." 9th. Jesus falls a third time. 10th. Having arrived at Calvary, Jesus is violently stripped of His clothes before He is nailed to the cross.

Jesus! on that most doleful day,
How were Thy garments stripped away,
  Thy holy limbs laid bare!
Oh, may no works or ways unclean
Despoil me of that modest mien
  Thy servants, Lord, should wear.

11th. Jesus is nailed hands and feet to the cross about noon.

Jesus! what direst agony
Was Thine upon the bitter tree,
  With healing virtues rife!
Oh, may I count all things but loss,
All for the glory of the cross,
  The sinner's tree of life!

Pilate placed at the top of His cross this inscription in Greek, Latin, and Hebrew, " Jesus of Nazareth, King of the Jews."

Jesus! around Thy sacred head
There is an ominous brightness shed,
  The name which Pilate wrote;
Save us, Thou royal Nazarene!
For in that threefold name are seen
  The gifts Thy Passion brought.

12th Station. After three hours' agony, He dies on the cross. During the three hours He was on the cross the sun was darkened. The seven last words which fell from those sacred lips were:—

First.—" Father, forgive them, for they know not what they do."

Jesus! who to the Father prayed
For those who all Thy love repaid
  With this dread cup of woes,
Teach me to conquer, Lord, like Thee,
By patience and benignity,
  The thwarting of my foes.

Second.—" Amen, I say to Thee " (to the good thief) " this day thou shalt be with Me in Paradise."

> Jesus! who came to seek and save,
> Absolved the thief, and promise gave
>   Of peace among the blest;
> Oh, do Thou give me penitence
> Like this, that I, when summoned hence,
>   In Paradise may rest.

Third.—" Woman " (He said to His Blessed Mother), " behold thy son;" (and to St. John) " Behold thy Mother."

> Jesus! who bade the virgin John
> Thy mother take when Thou wert gone,
>   And in Thy stead to be;
> Oh, when I yield my parting breath,
> Be Thou beside me, and in death,
>   Good Lord, remember me.

Fourth.—"My God, My God, why hast Thou forsaken Me?"

> Jesus! true Man, who cried aloud,
> Toward the ninth hour, "My God, my God,
>   Oh, why am I forsaken?"
> Lord! may I never fall from Thee,
> Nor e'en in life's extremity
>   My humble trust be shaken!

Fifth.—" I thirst." And the soldiers gave Him wine to drink made bitter with gall, reaching to His lips by means of a sponge at the end of a reed.

> Jesus! athirst, the soldiers think
> To mock Thee, giving Thee to drink
>   What might inflame Thy pain;
> Ah! mindful of the loathsome draught
> Which for my sins my Saviour quaffed,
>   May I my flesh restrain!

Sixth.—" It is consummated." The work of man's redemption is finished.

Seventh. — " Father, into Thy hands I commend My spirit." And saying this, He gave up the ghost.

Jesus! Thy Passion at an end,
Thou didst Thy blameless soul commend
　Unto the Father's care;
When my last hour is come, may I
Hasten with meek alacrity
　To do Thy will elsewhere!

Jesus! all hail, who for my sin
Didst die, and by that death didst win
　Eternal life for me;
Send me Thy grace, good Lord! that I
Unto the world and flesh may die,
　And hide my life with Thee.

When He yielded up the ghost, all nature proclaimed His divinity. The veil of the Temple was rent in two, from the top even to the bottom, the earth quaked, the rocks were rent, the graves were opened, and many bodies of the saints that had slept, arose, and, coming out of the tombs after His resurrection, came into the holy city, and appeared to many. And some of those that witnessed the crucifixion, having seen the earth quake, and the things that were done, said, "Indeed, this was the Son of God." And all the multitude of them that were come together to that sight, and saw the things that were done, returned, striking their breasts.

Come, take thy stand beneath the cross,
And let the blood from out that side
Fall gently on thee drop by drop;
Jesus, our Love, is crucified!

A broken heart, a fount of tears,
Ask, and they will not be denied.
A broken heart love's cradle is;
Jesus, our Love, is crucified.

The Jews, desirous that condemned persons might not remain on the cross on the Sabbath-day, requested of Pilate that their legs might be broken to hasten their death. The soldiers accordingly broke the legs of the two others that were crucified with Him; but Christ was already dead, to the surprise of Pilate, as such sufferers often lingered for some days. One of the soldiers, probably out of mere brutality, thrust his spear into the side of our Saviour's body, whence issued forth blood and water.

> Jesus! from out Thine opened side
> Thou hast the thirsty world supplied
>   With endless streams of love;
> Come ye, who would your sickness quell,
> Draw freely from that sacred well,
>   Its heavenly virtues prove.

13th Station. Jesus is taken down from the cross, and is laid in the arms of His Blessed Mother. 14th. He is laid by Joseph of Arimathea and Nicodemus in a new sepulchre.

> Jesus! in spices wrapped, and laid
> Within the garden's rocky shade,
>   By jealous seals made sure,
> Embalm me with Thy grace, and hide
> Thy servant in Thy wounded side,
>   A heavenly sepulture!

Every Friday of the year is observed as a day of penance, by abstaining from flesh meat in memory of Christ's death on that day; but on the Fridays in Lent, there are more especial commemorations of some of the circumstances of Christ's sufferings.

Sign of the Cross.—We also sign ourselves with the sign of the cross, to put us in mind that Christ died on the cross, and by the words which we say at the same time, we profess our belief in the Blessed Trinity. The sign of the cross is a short creed, by which we profess our belief in the two principal mysteries of the Christian faith — namely, the unity and trinity of God, and the incarnation and death of Christ. We begin and end our prayers with the sign of the cross, to signify that we can obtain nothing of God but through the mediation and merits of Christ. The Church also makes frequent use of the sign of the cross in the administration of the sacraments, to signify that their virtue comes from the death and passion of Christ. Many miracles have been wrought by the sign of the cross. The Christians from the earliest times made continual use of it on all occasions, and not merely before and after praying. The cross, whether we carry it about us, or have it in our houses, or see it in our churches, reminds us of Christ on the cross, of whom we cannot think too often.

5th Article.

"He descended into hell; the third day He rose again from the dead."

When Christ died upon the cross, His soul was separated from His body, but still the Divinity remained united with the body, and also with the soul. Joseph of Arimathea took the body of Jesus, and laid it in a new sepulchre, to the entrance of which a large stone was rolled, and the Jews sealed the stone, and set a guard of soldiers to watch, lest the disciples should steal away the body, and say He had risen from the dead as He said He would.

His soul descended into hell—not the hell where the wicked are tormented, but to that part of hell called Limbo; for every state in the other life which is not heaven is called hell. Limbo was a place of rest, not a place of punishment, and in it were detained the souls of all those who from the beginning of the world had died in the state of perfect holiness, or who had expiated the remains of lesser sins which they had taken with them out of this into the other life. For such as died in lesser sins, the Jewish Church used to offer prayers and sacrifices. To all those who with Lazarus were at rest in Abraham's bosom, Christ came to bring them the good tidings of salvation, and to set them free, that they might soon go up with Him to heaven. For, though Enoch and Elias had been taken away somewhere from among men to appear again on earth in the latter times, no one as yet had ever entered into heaven, the gates of which had been shut against us by Adam's sin. No one could enter heaven till Christ Himself had opened the way thither.

> Thousands of years had come and gone,
> And slow the ages seemed to move
> To those expectant souls, that filled
> That prison-house of patient love.

But see! how hushed the crowd of souls!
   Whence comes the light of upper day?
What glorious Form is this that finds
   Through central earth its ready way?

'Tis God! 'tis Man! the living soul
   Of Jesus, beautiful and bright,
The first-born of created things,
   Flushed with a pure, resplendent light.

So, after four long thousand years,
   Faith reached her end and Hope her aim,
And from them as they passed away,
   Love lit her everlasting flame!

"The third day He rose again from the dead."

The soul of Christ remained in the abodes of the ancient saints, changing their prison into a Paradise, from the hour of His death, at three o'clock on Friday afternoon, till early on Sunday morning.

Then His soul and body were united together, and by the power of His Divinity He rose up from the dead. At that moment there was a great earthquake, the soldiers on guard fell in terror upon the earth like dead men. When they had recovered, they ran into the city, and told everywhere that Christ had risen, till by money they were bribed to conceal the truth. An angel had come down, and had rolled back the great stone that closed the mouth of the sepulchre, and sat upon it, and told some holy women who had come to the sepulchre, that Christ had risen, and was no longer there.

All hail! dear Conqueror! all hail!
   Oh, what a victory is Thine!
How beautiful Thy strength appears,
   Thy crimson wounds, how bright they shine!

Thou camest at the dawn of day;
   Armies of souls around Thee were—
Blest spirits, thronging to adore
   Thy flesh, so marvellous, so fair.

Ye heavens, how sang they in your courts,
   How sang th' angelic choirs that day,
When from His tomb th' imprisoned God,
   Like the strong sunrise, broke away!

Christ appeared as often as five times on the day of His resurrection. After that He appeared many times during the next forty days that He remained on earth, between His resurrection and His ascension. He ate and drank with His disciples. He gave them the power of forgiving sins, and to Peter the charge to feed His lambs and His sheep, and full commission to all the apostles to preach the Gospel to all nations, baptizing them in the name of the Father, and of the Son, and of the Holy Ghost.

> Jesus! who from the dead arose,
> And straightway sought to comfort those
>   Whose weak faith mourned for Thee;
> Oh, may I rise from sin and earth,
> And so make good that second birth
>   Which Thou hast wrought in me!

6TH ARTICLE.

"He ascended into heaven."

After Christ had remained on earth forty days with His disciples, and had confirmed them in the faith of His resurrection, He led them out of the city to the top of Mount Olivet, and, having lifted up His hands, and given them His blessing, He raised Himself up from the earth, and ascended into heaven.

> Thou through the starry orbs this day
>   Didst to Thy throne ascend;
> Thenceforth to reign in sovereign power
>   And glory without end.
>
> There seated in Thy majesty,
>   To Thee submissive bow
> The heaven of heavens, the spacious earth,
>   The depths of hell below.
>
> With trembling there the angels see
>   The chang'd estate of men;
> The flesh which sinn'd by Flesh redeemed,
>   Man in the Godhead reign.

When the disciples, in wonder, still continued to look up to heaven after He had gone, two angels said to them, "Ye men of Galilee, why stand you looking up into heaven? This Jesus who is taken from you into heaven shall come again as you have seen Him going into heaven" (Acts i. 11), which was spoken of His coming again at the day of judgment. Heaven had not been opened again since the fall of Adam to the human race, till the day of Christ's ascension. It was on that day that "ascending on high He led captivity captive" — that is, Christ made those who had been captives and prisoners in Limbo His own captives, and placed them in eternal mansions in heaven. With reason, then, does the Church celebrate Ascension Day as a great festival. That day closed the course of Christ on earth, and put the saints of old in possession of eternal happiness. Ascension Day is kept as a day of obligation.

> Jesus! amid yon olives hoar,
> Thy forty days of sojourn o'er,
>   Thou didst ascend on high.
> Oh, thither may my heart and mind
> Ascend, their home and harbour find
>   With Jesus in the sky.

"Sitteth at the right hand of God, the Father Almighty."

Christ as God is not next but equal to His Father in all things. It is only speaking of Him as man that we say He is next to God in heaven; in other words, that "He sitteth at His right hand." Our human nature, therefore, which Christ had joined to His divine nature, was on the day of His ascension raised above the very highest of angelic natures, next to God Himself. The body of Christ is in heaven, and no Catholic doubts that the sacred body of His Immaculate Mother is there also; but *our* bodies will not enter heaven until after the general resurrection, when, if we live having our heart in heaven, we shall in the flesh see the glorious humanity of our Saviour.

> Jesus! who at this very hour
> At God's right hand, in pomp and power,
>   Our nature still dost wear,
> Oh, let Thy wounds still intercede,
> And, by their simple silence, plead
>   Thy countless merits there.

7TH ARTICLE.

"From thence He shall come to judge the living and the dead."

Christ, having come upon earth to be our Redeemer, ascended up into heaven to be also our Mediator. He who is now our Mediator with God will one day come to be the Judge of all mankind. He will come to judge "the living"—that is, those who shall be living at the time of His coming, who nevertheless shall all "once die," when the world will be destroyed. And He shall come to judge "the dead"—that is, all who had died from Adam to that day.

Particular Judgment: Purgatory.—We shall each of us immediately after death appear at the tribunal of God, and each of us will be judged for the thoughts, words, and deeds done in the years, few or many, of that life which has just ended. This is called the *particular* judgment. Sentence of punishment or reward will be pronounced upon each one according to the good or evil done. Those who have died in the guilt of grievous sins, or even of one really grievous sin, are condemned to hell, and their torments then begin, and never come to an end. Those who die in such a state of holiness that there is no spot or stain of sin upon their souls, are admitted at once into heaven, where nothing defiled can ever enter. Those souls which leave this world in a state of not such grievous guilt as to condemn them to hell, and yet not so holy as to make them fit for immediate entrance into heaven, are detained in some middle state, for a longer or shorter time, in proportion (we must suppose) to the number and greatness of those lesser sins and imperfections which they took with them out of this world. They are there detained until they are cleansed and purified by some sort of punishment, and are made fit to enter into the kingdom of God. This place of departed souls we call purgatory, which word means a place for cleansing and purifying. The mere privation of the sight of God would be punishment enough to a soul separated from the body, if there were no other punishment besides. The ancient fathers believed, and it is the general belief, that this purgatory will end at the destruction of this world by fire. That *after* the final judgment there will be but two places, heaven and hell, is sufficiently implied in Scripture; but that there are only these two places between death and that final judgment, is not only not the doctrine of Scripture, but cannot be reconciled with Scripture, and is contrary to reason and tradition. Some have vainly pretended that the souls of the departed remain in the sleep of death, in a state of utter insensibility, till the day of the general resurrection.

General Judgment.—Besides the particular judgment immediately after death of each individual by himself, there will also be a *general* judgment of all mankind assembled together. As the terrors of Mount Sinai, at the giving of the commandments, were intended to fill every human heart with the dread of breaking them, so the terrors of the last day and of the general judgment, so fully set forth in Scripture, are intended to make an impression on the hearts of men, that they may always live in the remembrance of what is to come, and in such a manner as to have no reason to fear when that day arrives. There are other reasons for a second and general judgment: — 1st. Because the *first* judgment concerns the *soul* only; the second regards the whole man, both soul and body. 2nd. Because the first judgment can unfold and justify no more than the dealings of Providence with *each individual* during life; but the second will unfold and justify the ways of Providence with the whole human race, especially in prospering the bad and afflicting the good. 3rd. That Christ, who was denied on earth by many, may at the last day be glorified before all.

Signs of the Last Day.—Before the last day, some especial and great enemy of religion called Antichrist will appear on earth, and will prevail for three years and a half. False Christs and false prophets will appear, working such wonders as to seduce many, and almost to prevail against the elect. To oppose this spiritual desolation, Enoch and Elias, who are yet living in some unknown paradise, having been taken away from this world without dying, will again return to the earth to defend the Church. They will oppose those false teachers, support the good in their faith, convert great numbers, and then both will suffer martyrdom. Afterwards there will appear terrible signs of God's anger in the sun, moon, and stars; the sun and moon shall be darkened, the stars will not give their light, all nature shall be thrown into confusion, and the whole world will be destroyed by a fire universal as the waters of the deluge. Then there will appear in the heavens the cross (the sign of the Son of Man), to the confusion of the wicked and of unbelievers, but to the comfort and triumph of the good.

Coming of the Judge.— After this, our Saviour, who has been appointed by His Father to be the Judge of the living and the dead, will be seen in the clouds, coming with great power and majesty, attended by millions of angels. Then He will send forth an angel, who with a loud voice and the sound of trumpet, which will be heard from the highest heaven to the lowest hell, will summon all generations to appear before the judgment-seat. Then shall the books be opened, and all the sins of men, even the most secret and hidden, be brought to light. The devils who tempted and seduced men to sin will then become witnesses and accusers against them. God, who is unchangeable in His decrees, and whose words shall never pass away, will pronounce the final sentence of eternal punishment, or of happiness without end. Then time shall be no more, and eternity begins.

> Jesus! who shalt in glory come
> With angels to the final doom,
>   Men's works and wills to weigh,
> Since from that pomp I cannot flee,
> Be pitiful, great Lord! to me
>   In that tremendous day.

8th Article.

"I believe in the Holy Ghost."

In this article we believe and put our trust in the third Person of the Blessed Trinity, who proceeds from the Father and the Son, being the same God with them, and who came down upon the apostles on Whit-Sunday in the form of fiery tongues—that is, of flames of fire.

In the first article of the Creed we are taught what we are to believe of God the Father, and His work of the creation. In the six following articles we learn what we are to believe of God the Son, made man, and His work of man's redemption. In the present article is declared what we are to believe of God the Holy Ghost.

"Ghost" is an old English word for Spirit; but this word *Spirit* has not the meaning which is commonly given to it, but it is in reality a Latin word, which means a breath of air, the motion of the wind, and suchlike. As the second Person of the Blessed Trinity, who "in the beginning was the Word," spoke in human words God's truths to men, so the third Person of the Blessed Trinity, who from all eternity was the Spirit of God, or the Holy Ghost, breathes into us a new spiritual and supernatural life by His heavenly grace. With this explanation of the word Spirit, we may see the meaning of Christ breathing upon the face of the apostles when He said to them, "Receive ye the Holy Ghost." He signified by the outward action of breathing, the grace inwardly given. Thus, too, the Holy Ghost Himself signified His presence by the strong wind, which shook the house in which the apostles were.

Again, we see the meaning of the Holy Ghost being called "the life-giving Spirit," because He is by His graces to our souls, what the natural breath of life is to our bodies. In allusion to the word "Spirit" meaning the same as "breath," the Holy Ghost is said to *inspire* us with, that is, to breathe into us, good thoughts and desires. He is said to have spoken by the prophets of old, because He inspired them and directed them what to say, and the books of the Old and of the New Testament were written under *inspiration*—that is, under the teaching of the Holy Ghost. All the divine wisdom of the prophets, of the apostles, and of the Church, is spoken of as the gift of the Holy Ghost. The Holy Ghost is called the "Spirit of Wisdom" and the "Spirit of Truth," and many of His gifts — for example, wisdom, understanding, counsel, knowledge—evidently show that a great and chief grace of the Holy Spirit is to enlighten the mind, and to teach us what is right and just to do. He is the "Comforter" whom Christ promised to send the apostles, to abide with them for ever—that is, with their successors in the apostolic office. The word "Paraclete" is a Greek word, which means consoler and comforter.

The Holy Ghost descended on our Saviour in the visible form of a dove, a fit emblem of that peace and reconciliation between God and man which He was to bring about by His death. He appeared thus at our Saviour's baptism, to signify also that baptism makes us pure and innocent as doves. The same Holy Spirit descended on the apostles in the form of fire, an emblem of the change which He was about to make in their hearts by purifying them from all sensual notions and affections, as metals are purified from their dross in the fire. "He," says the Baptist, "shall baptize you with the Holy Ghost and with fire" (Luke iii. 16). As the Holy Spirit descended upon Christ before *He* began to preach, so He descended upon the apostles before they entered on their mission. This happened on the tenth day after our Lord's ascension into heaven, and on the first day of the week. It was on the feast of Pentecost (the word means fiftieth), when the Jews were celebrating the memory of the first giving of the law on the fiftieth day after they left Egypt, that the Holy Ghost came down, and on the same day the Christian law was, for the first time, published to the world. By the wonderful change which He made in the apostles, filling their minds with wisdom and their hearts with strength, they were at once fitted for their office of apostles—that is, of messengers of Christ. The apostles, as long as our Saviour remained on earth, seem to have been incapable of understanding His doctrine; but on the coming of the Spirit, they were able at once to act as authorized and infallible teachers. The Jews, who for three years had been obstinate and unbelieving, were converted in great numbers, three thousand by one sermon, and as many as five thousand by another. Thus by the Holy Ghost, through the ministry of the apostles, was laid the foundation of the Christian Church, first in Jerusalem, and afterwards in the different countries which they visited. The Holy Ghost is not only the founder but the preserver of the Church; for if the Spirit of Truth, according to the promise of Christ, is to be with the Church for ever; the consequence of His presence must be, to preserve it from falling into error.

> Ten days and nights in acts divine
>   Of awful love were spent,
> While Mary and her children prayed
>   The Spirit might be sent.

> The hour was come; the wings of Love
>   By His own will were freed:
> The hour was come, th' Eternal Three
>   His mission had decreed.

> He comes! He comes! That mighty Breath
>   From Heaven's eternal shores;
> His uncreated freshness fills
>   His bride, as she adores.

Earth quakes before that rushing blast,
  Heaven echoes back the sound,
And mightily the tempest wheels
  That upper room around.

What gifts He gave those chosen men,
  Past ages can display;
Nay more, their vigour still inspires
  The weakness of to-day.

Those tongues still speak within the Church,
  That fire is undecayed;
Its well-spring was that upper room,
  Where Mary sat and prayed.

The Spirit came into the Church
  With His unfailing power;
He is the Living Heart that beats
  Within her at this hour.

Oh, let us fall and worship Him,
  The love of Sire and Son,
The Consubstantial Breath of God,
  The Coeternal One!

9TH ARTICLE.

"The holy Catholic Church, the communion of saints."

The word in the Scriptures, by us translated "Church," originally signified a society of men *called out*, or chosen from amongst others—that is, men who in obedience to the call of God had separated themselves from the wicked world, and had joined together in the profession of the Christian faith. The Church, therefore, now means the union of all the faithful—that is, of all true believers under one head. Every one knows that Christ is the Head of the Church; but since He went up into heaven He is invisible to us. Before He went into heaven, He appointed a vicar, or deputy, to be the visible head in His place. From the history of St. Peter in the Scriptures, it is quite clear that he was the person on whom Christ bestowed that dignity. The office was not personal to Peter, but was of course to descend to his successors; for if Christ gave to His Church a visible head, who could have power to change that form of government afterwards? If the apostles required a head, much more would the successors of the apostles, having become numerous and scattered over the whole world, require a head. The Bishop of Rome, who is the successor of St. Peter in the see or bishopric of Rome, has always from the beginning been acknowledged as the head of the Church and as the vicar of Christ.

All Christians believe that the true Church of Christ must be one, holy, Catholic, and apostolic.

One.—Christ's Church must be *one*, for Christ did not establish a number of Churches, each having its own doctrine and separate government. "There is but one Lord, one faith, one baptism." The members of that one Church may differ from each other in mere *opinions* upon certain religious questions, but they must agree upon those questions which the Church positively teaches and has decided. They must also submit to the appointed government of the Church; to refuse this obedience would be *schism*, and obstinately to maintain or teach a doctrine contrary to the teaching of the Church would be *heresy*. Many who are ignorantly, and without any fault of theirs, in outward heresy or schism, may by the virtue of Christian baptism which they have received belong to the "soul" of the Church, and may produce fruits of holiness in their lives.

Holy.—The Church is *holy* in her founder, in her doctrines and worship; and she invites all to the practice of holiness. Still it depends on the free will of each individual, whether he profit or not by the call to holiness. Hence it is no wonder, if at all times, many professors of Christianity disgrace their profession by their evil lives. Such was the incestuous man at Corinth (1 Cor. v. 1), and even Judas, among the personal companions of our Blessed Lord. There are reasons why the tares are allowed to grow with the good grain till the time of harvest.

Catholic.—The Church of Christ is *Catholic*. This is a Greek word, and means universal. "The Catholic Church," says St. Cyril of Jerusalem (A.D. 350), "is so called because she is spread over the whole habitable globe, from one end to the other." The Church of God before Christ, the Jewish Church, was a *national* church, confined to one place and people; the other nations of the earth were left to follow that light of reason and conscience which God had given to man in the beginning. But the kingdom of God which is His Church, the kingdom of the Messiah, had been often spoken of by the prophets, as intended to be the kingdom of *all* nations and places. In the New Testament we see that the name of Christ was to be preached to *all* nations, beginning from Jerusalem; Christ commissioned the apostles to preach to *all* nations; the saints in heaven (Apoc. v. 9) are spoken of as redeemed by the blood of the Lamb, out of every kingdom, and tongue, and people and nation. As the redemption brought by Christ and the truths which He preached were necessary for all men, Christ necessarily intended that all men should be made partakers of them; in other words, that His Church should be everywhere, that it should be the Church of all places, and for the same reason of all ages. Not only did Christ, its founder, intend His Church to be everywhere, that is, to be Catholic, but it has *actually* been so from the beginning, we may say, from the day of Pentecost, when there were believers out of every nation in Jerusalem. There is only one Church which can claim Catholicity: that Church, therefore, alone must be the Church of Christ. A "Catholic," therefore, means a believer, who is a member of that Church, which is everywhere more or less diffused throughout the world. No single sect of Christians can, in its numbers, bear the least comparison with those of the Catholic Church, which with its two hundred millions even doubles all other so-called Christians put together.

Many sects have from the days of St. Cyril and St. Augustine wished to call themselves Catholic, but as these two saints in the fourth century remark, a stranger on entering a town and on inquiring for the Catholic Church is never directed to a conventicle of heretical worship. Others not Catholics derive their name generally from the founder of some new doctrine. The word Protesters, or Protestants, was assumed by, or given to those who, in the sixteenth century, made a formal protest against the doctrines of the Catholic Church. This is a title common to a number of sects, but they have also, each of them *specific* titles, and are called Anglicans, Lutherans, Zuinglians, Calvinists, Wesleyans, &c.

Papist and Roman Catholic. — Catholics are often called "Papists" (from the Latin word "Papa," which means Pope), because they reverence and obey the Pope as the Vicar of Christ. There would be nothing objectionable in the name as conveying any erroneous idea, but it is objectionable because it is used as a nickname and a term of contempt. The term "Roman Catholics" by which we are described, chiefly in legal and official documents, is free from objection *in itself*, but is often used by non-Catholics in an objectionable manner, as if there were any Catholics who are not Roman. An "English Catholic," a "French Catholic," a "German Catholic," &c., merely points to the nation of the individual spoken of, but a Roman Catholic does not point to the nation of the individual, but it signifies a Catholic in communion with the Church of Rome, which is the Mother and Mistress of all Churches.

Apostolic.—The Church must be *apostolic;* that is, its doctrine, orders, and mission, the three essentials to a Church, must have come from the apostles of Christ. Its *orders* must be apostolical; that is, its pastors must have been ordained by those who were in like manner ordained before them, by the real successors of the apostles. Now, who can show such a succession of pastors down from the apostles, but the Catholic Church ? As to other sects, they own that for many ages, there were neither pastors nor people of their communion to be found anywhere in the whole earth. To keep up the apostolic succession unbroken, ordination is not of itself sufficient, it is moreover necessary that the ordainer be duly authorized, that is, there must be apostolic *mission*. Those who commission others, must first be commissioned themselves. To make this plain, let us suppose a person to have been ordained and commissioned by the apostles, and afterwards to have been deprived of his commission for misconduct by the same apostles. No one could pretend that he, or any person whom he might ordain after the withdrawal of his commission, could be the successor of the apostles. He was disowned by the apostles, and consequently no one could inherit from the apostles through him. Such a one would be unlawfully ordained, and would be totally deprived of apostolic *mission*.

Infallible.—The Church of Christ is also *infallible;* that is, she cannot fall into error, and teach error to her members. If Christ came on earth not only to die for us, but to found a Church which was, at all times, to teach His saving doctrine to mankind, it must follow that He intended to save His Church from falling into errors, either in matters of faith or morals. If this were not the case, it would follow that having a particular end in view, Divine Wisdom adopted for the accomplishment of that end, means which might not at all answer the purpose. It would follow that Christ founded a Church to teach truth and holiness, and yet permitted her, while she was under His own guidance, to become the teacher of error and the corrupter of morality. But what was *naturally* to be expected from the Divine Founder of the Church, we have besides His own word for. He *promised* His apostles that the Spirit of truth should abide with them, not for their natural lives, but "for *ever,*" and, therefore, not with them only, but with their successors. He promised to remain with them Himself, not while *they* preached the Gospel, but "all days even to the consummation of the world;" a promise which most plainly extends to their successors. He declared that the "gates of Hell," that is, the whole power of Hell, "should never prevail against His Church." The infallibility of the Church is clear from this text, for if the Church ever fell into error, if she had ever taught any one of those horrible doctrines which her enemies have so often imputed to her; then the gates of Hell would have prevailed against the Church, and the positive promise of Christ would have proved false. Men have in all ages been baptized, but no one was ever baptized without declaring his belief in the holy Catholic Church; but that surely could not be in a Church that *had* fallen, or was *liable* to fall into error! Though the Church is composed of men who are by *nature* fallible, yet we may be sure from the promise of Christ, without inquiring where or among what particular men that promised infallibility is lodged, that God by His superintending providence will so watch over the Church in her decisions, as never to suffer her to become the teacher of error. It is from the *Church* then, and not from the *Scriptures*, that we are to learn the articles of our faith. The Creed refers us to the Church, the Scripture refers us to the Church and to living teachers, and gives us no instruction about any course of reading to bring us to faith. Christ sent His apostles to *preach*, and not to *write*, and what they did write was for the comfort of those who were already Christians, and are addressed as "saints." Besides, we observe that those who profess to follow Scripture alone, cannot agree upon very important points; for instance, the Divinity of Christ. The New Testament was written by the first pastors of the Church, not to furnish texts for foolish men to use against the authority of themselves or of their own successors; and the same Holy Spirit which directed the writers of those books, directs and guides the body of teachers who have succeeded them.

"THE COMMUNION OF SAINTS."

The Holy Catholic Church is described in the Creed as "*the communion of saints.*" The original word (κοινωνια) *communion,* means a union or association of men joined together for some common purpose, and for their joint participation in some common benefits. The word "saints" signifies Christians, for all Christians in Scripture are called saints, because they are called to the profession and practice of a saintly life. That the Church was the association of all the faithful, in the above sense, was more clear in the early Christian times than at present. For they were then all "of one mind and one heart," and they had all things in *common.* This was the case also in other places, though not to such a degree as in the model Church at Jerusalem. Moreover, in the more early ages, Christians, when they travelled from home, were careful (as appears from the letters of St. Cyprian) to take with them *letters of communion,* in virtue of which, on the principle that all things were *in common* to the saints, they were in every place received by the Christians as brothers, were admitted into their religious assemblies, and to the participation of the sacraments, and if they were in want were relieved in the same manner as the poor Christians of the place. We may see from this, how, especially in primitive times, the Church was the mutual fellowship of the saints (that is, of Christians) in order to a joint participation in spiritual and in *temporal* goods.

But though that fellowship of primitive times is not to be seen in such perfection now, still the members of the Church always assist each other by their prayers and share in each other's prayers and good works. The prayers of the sacred Liturgy, the sacrifice of the Mass offered everywhere, the divine office said by the ministers of the Church, and the prayers of private individuals, are offered up, for the general good of the members of the Church throughout the world, for the conversion of sinners, and the perseverance and perfection of the good. Only those cut off from that communion of saints, who are said to be *excommunicated*, are deprived of the benefit of those prayers and sacrifices.

If we can ask each other's prayers and can benefit by them now on earth, much more are we likely to be helped by the prayers of those who are in heaven. Certainly the saints in glory can do as much for us, as we poor sinners can do for one another.

Besides this, the saints in heaven and we on earth can pray for those that are dead, but who did not die in such a state of holiness as to make them fit to enter at once into heaven. Two causes will render any one unfit for *immediate* entrance into heaven. In the *first* place, to have died in venial sin unrepented of; *secondly*, to have died after having repented of mortal sin so that its guilt has been forgiven, yet not to have fully paid that debt of *temporal* punishment which God in His justice often awards to the sinner after the eternal punishment has been remitted. It is easy to see and reasonable to believe that while one man may repent of grievous sin so perfectly as to merit, even on the very day of his death, to see God without delay; another may, by his less earnest sorrow, deserve to undergo yet in this world or the next, some further penalties of a temporal nature for his past sins.

The belief in this intermediate state between heaven and hell has always been held in the Church from the earliest times, and certain passages of Scripture were always considered as alluding to such a state. The Scripture certainly proves nothing *against* a purgatory, but on the contrary clearly *implies* the existence of such a place or state. To suppose that God, who renders to every one according to his works, has no way of dealing with men but to award at once eternal happiness or eternal damnation, is against reason. That a human being should fall short by a little of that virtue which would have procured his immediate admittance into heaven, and in consequence be sent to hell; or that any one being stained with sin so as only just to escape hell, should therefore, as the only alternative, be sent at once into heaven, is evidently absurd. This would be making the entrance of heaven and hell to be very near to each other, though they must be as wide apart as light and darkness, as sin and holiness can make them, and as the belief of all ages has always supposed them.

It seems quite natural to suppose that the saints in heaven can help us by their prayers, as also that they can help the souls detained in purgatory; perhaps we might not have so readily supposed that we on earth could help the souls in purgatory by our prayers. But we find that prayers and sacrifices for the dead were offered by the Jewish Church, which was God's Church, and the same has since been practised in every Christian age. It is therefore a want of charity in us if we neglect to pray for the dead, especially for those who were our relations, friends, and benefactors, or for those to whom we may have been the occasion of sin. The public offices of the Church and private forms of devotion continually end with a prayer for the faithful departed in these words: "May the souls of the faithful through the mercy of God rest in peace."

By this *communion of saints* therefore, not only do the faithful on earth assist each other, but we keep up a communication with those who have gone before us and whom we are soon to follow. We keep up a communion with the saints in heaven, whose trial is over and who can help us in the midst of ours; and also with the holy souls in purgatory not yet admitted into heaven whom our prayers may help thither, and who one day may be able to repay us a hundredfold by their prayers when we are in the greatest need of them.

10th Article.

"The forgiveness of sins."

There was a forgiveness of sins before Christ, through faith in Him, to such as sincerely repented; when, therefore, the " forgiveness of sins " becomes a distinct article of Christian faith, it must be a forgiveness, in some way or other very different from that forgiveness which could always be obtained from the beginning. The peculiarity of Christian forgiveness of sins consists, amongst other things, in this, that Christ left in His Church a ministry of reconciliation and positive ordinances, the sacraments of baptism and penance, by which that forgiveness was to be conveyed to our souls. He distinctly gave this power of forgiving sins to His apostles after His resurrection, when, appearing to them, He said, "Peace be to you; as the Father hath sent Me, I also send you." When He had said this, He breathed on them, and He said to them, "Receive ye the Holy Ghost; whose sins you shall forgive, they are forgiven them; and whose sins you shall retain, they are retained." God alone can forgive sins in His own name and by His own power; but He can commission others to do it, as His ministers, in His name and by His power; and it is plain that He has given this commission to the apostles and their successors. But this forgiveness of sins is only given to us in consideration of the merits and death of Christ, and on condition of sincere repentance on the part of the sinner.

Sin is anything which we think, say, or do, against what we know to be the law and the will of God. We sin also by *omitting* to do what we know we ought to do. By the *law* of God is meant, all that God has commanded or forbidden, whether by Himself, or by His Church, or by our lawful superiors, or by our own conscience, which is the voice of God within us. Sin naturally offends God, for he who breaks a law, shows a contempt of Him that made the law, and makes himself liable, in proportion to his offence, to more or less punishment; which can only be done away with at the good will of the Lawgiver. The sins which we commit ourselves are called *actual*, because they are our own doing. But there is a sin which we did not commit ourselves, but in which we are all conceived (with the exception of the Blessed Virgin) through the sin of our first parents, "in whom all have sinned." This is called *original* sin, &c. (See chapter on the Fall of our First Parents, page 20). This sin is removed from the soul by the waters of baptism, together with any actual sins which may have been committed, as is the case when baptism is administered to those who have attained the use of reason.

Actual sins are more or less sinful and displeasing to God, according to the nature and circumstances of them; but they are divided only into two classes, in reference to their greatness, namely, *mortal* and *venial*.

"*Mortal*" means deadly, because a mortal sin is so great an offence against God, that in punishment of it, He strikes the soul with death; not by destroying the soul and depriving it of its *natural* life, but by taking away from it His favour and grace, which is its *supernatural* life. The consequence of this loss of grace would, without repentance, be eternal death in hell, and separation from God for ever. To make a sin mortal, the offence to God must not only be in a *serious* matter, but there must be a *knowledge or belief* that it is a serious offence; and it must also be done *wilfully and deliberately*. No one can commit a sin sufficient to ruin him for all eternity without knowing what he is doing.

Venial Sin. — All sins which are less grievous than mortal sins are called "*venial*" sins. Though every sin which we commit, even the least, is against God's law, and therefore to be feared, yet reason tells us that there must be a great difference between sin and sin. To steal a farthing is not so great a sin as to steal a hundred pounds. To speak an idle or an angry word is not so bad as blasphemy, &c. "The just man falls" into sin, and "in many things we all offend" (James iii. 2); but these are not such sins and offences as to exclude us from heaven. These sins may vary in guilt, from a little idle word up to a sin which comes near to what is absolutely grievous, but they all are still called venial. The word *venial* means *pardonable*, so called, because venial sins, though often great, are of course more easily pardoned than mortal sin. But in the use of the word venial we must guard against the common meanings attached to it. The word venial, in ordinary use, means pardonable, excusable, permitted, allowed, trivial, &c. We must never attach such ideas as these to the commission of what we call venial sins. Venial sins are often committed through frailty and inadvertence; but when committed, as they often are, deliberately and habitually, they are an evil next to mortal sin, to which they commonly lead. Deliberate venial sins lessen our love of God, of prayer, and of everything good. They cause us to lose nearly all the graces of the sacraments, to grow weary of religion, and by degrees to abandon its duties. Venial sins may keep us a long time in purgatory, away from Heaven and the sight of God. Venial sins often become mortal; for example, when they are committed with so much wilfulness and such affection, that a person is determined to commit them though they were mortal. They may also become mortal, when a person commits a sin which in itself is only venial, yet he thinks in his conscience it is a mortal one.

The sacrament of penance, in reality or desire, is absolutely necessary for the remission of *mortal* sin, and therefore mortal sin must of necessity be confessed, if we intend to obtain forgiveness. The sacrament of penance is not absolutely necessary to obtain forgiveness of venial sin, because it may be removed from the soul by prayer and other good works; therefore, it is not of obligation to confess venial sin. Still, the sacrament of penance is the best remedy for venial sins also, though not absolutely necessary. He that does not make use of it shows an indifference about venial sin, a desire to commit it, or no desire to get rid of it. In practice, therefore, every one in the confession of sin with a view to obtain forgiveness should not aim too much at making distinctions, but would do well to confess all his sins alike to the extent that he feels himself to be guilty.

11th Article.

"The resurrection of the body."

At the moment of death, the soul is separated from the body. The soul appears before God, and is judged according to its works. The body is buried in the grave; but though reduced to dust and scattered abroad by the winds, it will rise again on the day of the general resurrection. This shall take place by the power of that same God, who made the body from dust, and in the beginning made all things out of nothing. This general resurrection will come to pass after the whole world shall have been destroyed by fire, and when there will not be a single person *living* on the face of the earth. Then God will send His angel to call the dead to life. On that day the body shall be united to the soul to which it had before been joined; and all the children of Adam, from first to last, shall come again to life. The sentence of eternal happiness or misery already passed upon each *soul* after death, and which immediately began to take effect, shall be confirmed and passed upon all mankind assembled together; and all shall, immediately after that sentence, begin to be punished or rewarded, both *in soul and body*, according to their deeds. As the body was partner with the soul in good or evil during this mortal life, so it will be afterwards partaker of its punishment or reward in that life which never ends.

Our Saviour proved the resurrection of the dead to the Sadducees who denied it. The bodies of those who rise to the resurrection of life and happiness will be bright and glorious like the body of Christ on the day of His transfiguration; they will be spiritual like the body of Christ after His resurrection. The prospect of the glory that awaits the human body ought to encourage us to bear bodily hardships, pain, and want; to deny the flesh with its lusts, and to keep our bodies from the corruption of sin now, that they may rise hereafter in incorruption.

12th Article.

"Life everlasting. Amen."

In the seventh article of the Creed, we have considered the general judgment which takes place after the general resurrection. After the last sentence has been passed, inviting the good, who are on the right hand, to the kingdom of heaven, and condemning the wicked, who are on the left, to everlasting fire; then "life everlasting" begins. The blessed will be placed in the enjoyment of happiness which will never end, and which will be so great and wonderful that no thought of man can conceive it, nor any human words describe it. It is the sight and the enjoyment of God which makes the happiness of heaven, and we have to begin now that love of God which we hope to be our employment for all eternity. But those who lived without God here, or died out of His grace by grievous sin, will have to live without His presence for ever. In hell the wicked will be tormented by a fire that shall never be extinguished, by a worm that never dies; there shall be weeping and gnashing of teeth, eternal darkness without one ray of light or the least hope of deliverance.

"Amen" is a word which the Jews were in the habit of using, and which means, "even so," "truly so." It is expressive of agreement, and of assent to what has just been said before, whether it be a prayer that has been uttered, or some truth that has been stated.

CHAPTER III.

HOPE — THE LORD'S PRAYER.

IN the Creed we are instructed in what relates to faith. The next great virtue is hope. Hope is a gift of God by which we expect with confidence that God will give us all things necessary for salvation. Salvation in heaven is promised to such as do good works. Faith is necessary to save us, for "without faith it is impossible to please God" (Heb. xi. 6); yet it is not sufficient by itself, for good works are also necessary. "Faith without works is dead." Christ came to teach us what to *believe*, and also what to *do*, in order to be saved. To believe and to do, that is, faith and works, are therefore both necessary for salvation, and neither can be neglected.

But of ourselves we cannot do any good work that will be of any use towards *our salvation*. We can do actions of mere *natural* goodness of ourselves, without the grace of God, such as the heathens did, and which may receive from God a temporal reward. But to do anything that will be of any use towards salvation is not within the power of nature, but requires a grace or help given to us from above, and which is supernatural—that is, beyond nature. Grace acts upon the soul, enlightening the understanding to see what is good, inclining the will to choose the good, and strengthening it to do what is right.

Prayer.—Grace is given to us through the merits of Christ, and ordinarily on the condition of our asking for it. "God who made us without our concurrence," says St. Augustin, "will not save us without our concurrence." Man lost heaven by the sin of Adam; he will not be restored to it but by his own striving for it, and knocking at the gate to gain admission. God knows our wants, but He wishes that we should know them, and come to Him for a remedy. If all that men needed was given to them without asking, they would be more unmindful than they are now of their Creator and Preserver. Christ commanded us to pray. He said, "Ask and you shall receive," which implies that asking is a necessary condition of receiving, and that if we ask not, we shall not receive. Prayer then is a great duty of every Christian, and is necessary for salvation.

Prayer is the lifting up of our minds and hearts to God, that is, it consists in thinking of God with our minds; and with our hearts, loving, admiring, fearing, honouring, worshipping Him, on account of His greatness and goodness. Prayer does not require that we make use of any words whatever. The best prayers are speechless and silent. It is in the thoughts and feelings of the mind and heart that prayer essentially consists. Religious feelings habitually entertained are a continual prayer. This notion of prayer removes many difficulties, and makes the practice of it very easy, for in this sense of prayer we can pray always and everywhere. It is true that *forms* of prayer have been made to be learnt by heart, or to be read from books; these are often convenient, and help to prevent distraction; but we must always remember that a mere repetition of words is not prayer. Prayer with the use of words is called *vocal* prayer, or "saying prayers;" the prayer of the mind and heart without words is called *mental* prayer. If the essence of prayer consists in the mind and heart being employed about God and holy things, it is clear that when this is wanting there can be no prayer, but rather a mocking of God. The best Christians in the midst of their prayers often find their minds wandering away from God to other things, but these distractions if not wilful, are not sinful. The distractions of most Christians too often proceed from want of care and preparation of the mind for prayer.

The object of prayer is fourfold,—to worship God as our Creator and sovereign Lord; to thank Him for past blessings; to ask for new blessings; and, fourthly, to beg pardon for sin. We must pray in the name of Jesus Christ. "If you ask the Father anything in My name,

He will give it you" (St. John xvi. 23). Therefore all our prayers end with these, or such-like words: "Through Jesus Christ our Lord." We must pray with *reverence*, remembering that we are in the presence of God; we must pray with a feeling of our own unworthiness. We must not grow weary with asking, that is, we must persevere in prayer, for God does not always give at once what we ask for; and as our wants during this life always continue, our prayer must never cease but with life itself. We must pray not only for ourselves, but for all mankind, for the living and the dead. The "communion of saints" mainly consists in the share which we all have in the general prayers of all the members of the Church throughout the world. We should pray especially for our relations, friends, and benefactors; for those who are in trouble and temptation; and for those to whom we have been the cause or occasion of sin. We should pray also for our enemies, who perhaps hate and persecute us, that they may repent and be saved. We should pray in the *evening* before we go to rest, to return thanks for the blessings of the past day, to beg pardon for the sins of that day, and protection for the night that is closing over us. We should pray in the *morning* for grace for the day that is beginning, and offer all the thoughts, words, and actions of that day to God. We should not rise up and lie down, day after day, like dumb beasts, without thinking of God, and opening our mouths to bless Him. We are still more strictly obliged to pray when we are in temptation and danger of falling into any sin, and to repent speedily when we have sinned. We should pray every day (the oftener in the day the better), but especially on days consecrated to God, when we have more time and opportunity.

Seven Petitions of the Lord's Prayer.

The best of all prayers is the Lord's Prayer, so called because Christ our Lord taught it to His disciples. It was made short and easy, that all men, even the most unlearned, might be able to learn it. Though short, it is full of meaning, and contains the chief things we can ask or hope from God. It contains seven petitions.

"Our Father who art in heaven." God in the Creed is called "Father," because He is the Father of our Lord Jesus Christ; but here in the Lord's Prayer, we call God our Father, because we, as Christians, are the adopted sons of God by His grace; and Christ has taught us to address Him by that title. Moreover, God is the Father of all creatures, because He created them, and continually provides for their wants. In saying "our," we speak as a member of a family of which God is the head, and we pray for the wants of the whole family, and therefore not for ourselves only, but for all mankind. Though God is everywhere, we chiefly fix our thoughts on Him as being especially "in heaven," because in heaven He especially shows His glory and greatness, for the happiness of the blessed.

1st Petition. "Hallowed be Thy name." "Hallowed" means made holy, treated as holy. "All Hallows" is an old English expression for "All Saints." We here pray, that not only the name of God may be always spoken of and used with reverence, but that God Himself may be more and more known, loved, and worshipped by all mankind.

2nd. "Thy kingdom come." God's "kingdom" means His Church on earth; also His kingdom in our hearts by His grace, in opposition to the power of sin and Satan, which rules in too many hearts. It means also His kingdom in heaven, to which we are all invited. We may utter this petition in any one or all of these meanings.

3rd. "Thy will be done on earth as it is in heaven." The saints in heaven do the will of God in loving and praising Him so perfectly that they have but one will with God; they cannot commit the least sin. Here on earth our will is continually in opposition to the will of God; God wills us to think and do one way; we are always wishing to think and do the contrary. Following our own will against God's, is *sin*. We here pray that the will of God may be the only rule of our whole being, as it is to the blessed in heaven.

4th. "Give us this day our daily bread." The plainest and most natural meaning of these words is, that we ask God to grant us our food for each day, and to bless our daily labours and endeavours. We pray for "bread," that is, for the necessaries, not the luxuries, of life; for "this day," that we may be reminded that we have to ask God again on the morrow, and that we are not to be too anxious about the morrow. We may also in this petition pray not only for what is necessary for the body in the way of food, raiment, and habitation, but also for all that is necessary for the soul, especially for the "bread" of life in the Holy Eucharist.

5th. "Forgive us our trespasses as we forgive them that trespass against us." To trespass is to leave the public beaten road, on which we have a right to walk, and to pass beyond the fence or boundary into a private field or property on which we have no right to enter. It plainly means here to break through God's commandments, and so to sin against Him. We pray therefore that God will forgive us all such sins and trespasses, in as much as we are willing to forgive our fellow-men who trespass against us. To forgive others is the condition on which we are to be forgiven. "If you will not forgive men, neither will your Father forgive you your offences" (Matt. vi. 15).

6th. "Lead us not into temptation." In scriptural language God is often said to *do*, what He only *permits* to be done; as in this expression, "Lead us not into temptation." It means therefore the same as "Let us not be led into temptation." God is not the tempter of evil: "He tempteth no man" (James i. 13). We are tempted by the devil, the world, and our own flesh. We must always expect to be tempted as long as we are in this world. It is no sin to be tempted. Temptation becomes sin when we give some consent, or take some delight in it. As a remedy against temptation, we must avoid the occasions of it, and pray for strength to resist it. Temptation firmly resisted increases our merit and adds to our future glory.

7th. "But deliver us from evil." We pray to be delivered from evil, whether of soul or body. The only real evil is sin, because this is absolutely contrary to the will of God, and comes not from God, but from the devil's malice, our own corrupt nature and perverse will. Against this evil of sin therefore we chiefly pray. As to the evils of this life, pain, poverty, sickness, and such like, we pray to be delivered also from these, so far as they may hinder our progress in virtue, or tempt us to murmuring or impatience.

Prayer to the Saints. — We not only in the Lord's Prayer pray for ourselves, but we pray for others, as they also pray for us. We not only ask our fellow-men on earth to pray for us to the Almighty, but we ask the saints in heaven also to pray for us and with us, to our common God and Lord. To God we say, "Have mercy on us," and such like expressions, but to the saints we say, "Pray for us." We do not make the saints in heaven mediators in any other sense, than as we on earth are mediators for one another, by praying for each other. Certainly in the sense of St. Paul (1 Tim. ii. 6), "there is but *one* mediator of God and man, who gave Himself a ransom for all," namely, Jesus Christ. Without attributing to the saints and angels *omnipresence*, we know that by their rejoicing at the conversion of a sinner (Luke xx. 7—10) they must be made to know what passes on earth, and therefore are able to hear our prayers. Amongst the *saints* we especially pray to the saint of our name, the one whom we have chosen as our patron, or whose virtues we particularly desire to study and imitate. Amongst the *angels* we pray chiefly to the one whom God has appointed to be our Guardian Angel, and who is deputed especially to take care of us. There was always a belief amongst the true people of God, in ancient times, in the ministry and guardianship of angels; and the Church teaches us to believe, that we each of us have a guardian angel, and she has appointed a day in their honour (October 2nd).

Dear angel! ever at my side,
  How loving must thou be,
To leave thy home in heaven to guard
  A guilty wretch like me!

And when, dear spirit! I kneel down,
  Morning and night to prayer,
Something there is within my heart
  Which tells me thou art there.

Then love me still, O angel dear!
  And I will love thee more;
And help me when my soul is cast
  Upon th' eternal shore.

THE HAIL MARY.

Since God has honoured the Blessed Virgin above all the children of Adam, and exalted her above all creatures, we believe it to be a duty to honour her, and to ask her prayers above all the other saints, and therefore we say so frequently the Hail Mary, the prayer to the Blessed Virgin which the Church teaches. It is a prayer in which we beg the intercession of the Blessed Virgin, and especially turn our thoughts to the Incarnation of Christ, and the part which she had in that great mystery of man's redemption. Next to the Lord's Prayer, it is the most frequently used, and therefore should be well understood. This prayer must of necessity be odious to the devil, because it shows how his wicked designs were ruined, and his head was crushed by the seed of the woman. No wonder that he tries to raise up men to oppose such a prayer, on the pretence that the honour we show to the Mother for the sake of her Divine Son, takes away the honour due to the Son Himself. No doubt also the evil spirits, while busy in tempting us to sin, desire that we should not pray to saints and angels to help us, that so we may be left alone in our encounters with the powers of darkness.

"Hail, Mary! full of grace," were the words of salutation addressed to her by the angel Gabriel. "Ave," or "Hail!" is a word of salutation or address to a person when you begin to speak to him; as "Vale," "Farewell," is a word at parting. Though saints have been said to be "full of grace," yet no one of them was so full of grace as she was, who was chosen to be the mother of our Lord. No wonder then that in her conception, in her birth, and her whole life, she was Immaculate—that is, never subject to the stain of sin; that she who was to be the mother of Him, who came to destroy sin, should by His grace be preserved from all sin. "The Lord is with thee," not only by love and grace, but He descends upon thee, to take flesh of thee, to be conceived of thee, and in due time to be born of thee.

"Blessed art thou amongst women, and blessed is the fruit of thy womb." These were the words of St. Elizabeth, when the Blessed Virgin entered her house, soon after the conception of the Son of God. On that occasion, the Blessed Virgin herself, filled with the deepest sense of what God had done in her regard, and of the blessings that would come to the world through her, exclaimed, "From henceforth all generations shall call me blessed."

"Holy Mary, mother of God, pray for us sinners, now and at the hour of our death." These words were added by the Church. She was called "Mother of God," in opposition to the heresy of Nestorius and his followers, who would have her called only the "Mother of Christ," as if the person of Christ was different from the person of God the Son. She is called Mother of God, because her son Jesus, who was born of her, is truly God. We invoke the aid of the Blessed Virgin, knowing that while she is without sin, we are sinners, and stand in need of help. We have need of her help every day, but we shall chiefly require it at our last moments, when her enemy and ours will gather his strength against us. We say the Hail Mary after the Lord's Prayer, that by the Blessed Virgin joining her intercession to our petitions, we may more easily obtain what we ask for in the Lord's Prayer.

We say the Hail Mary very often, not only to invoke and honour the Blessed Virgin Mary, but also to put us in mind of the Incarnation. This may easily be seen in the use of the Hail Mary in the "Angelus." In like manner, in the devotion of the Rosary, we often repeat the Hail Mary, while we contemplate one or other of the fifteen mysteries, joyful, sorrowful, or glorious, of the life and death of her divine Son.

Next to the Our Father and Hail Mary, there is no form of prayer more commonly used than the Litany of the Blessed Virgin. It contains in all forty-five addresses to her, each one referring to some honour or privilege which she possesses; and at each of those addresses we beg of her to pray for us. Some of these titles refer to her dignity as Mother of God, some refer to her as a virgin adorned with every grace and virtue. Some which are less easily understood, such as Mystical Rose, Tower of David, &c., contain some scriptural allusion, or have been found in the writings of the Holy Fathers of the first five centuries. Some refer to her as a "queen," because she is above all saints, before or since Christ, in consequence of her dignity of Mother of God. One title, "Help of Christians," dates from the great naval victory of the Christians over the Turks at Lepanto (1571), won, as was believed, by her intercession. "Queen conceived without original sin" has been added, especially since the decision of the Church on her Immaculate Conception, and the decree of Pius IX. on that subject, on the 8th of December, 1854.

CHAPTER IV.

CHARITY—THE COMMANDMENTS.

CHARITY is that virtue by which we love God above all things, and our neighbour as ourselves. As the belief of the articles of the Creed is an exercise of faith, and prayer is the exercise of hope, so also to keep the commandments is the greatest and surest proof of our charity. The ten commandments and all our obligations are by our Lord included in two; the first of which is the love of God, and the second is, "Thou shalt love thy neighbour as thyself." The first three of the ten commandments regard our chief duties to God; the remaining seven point out our principal duties to our neighbour—that is, to all mankind.

The first portion of the law was published by the Almighty Himself in the midst of thunder and lightning; the rest of the covenant, containing a great variety of laws upon religious and social questions, was delivered to the people by the mouth of Moses, because they were so terrified at hearing the voice of God. The first portion, spoken by the Almighty Himself, is generally known as the *ten* commandments, because Moses, in speaking of it, tells us that the words of the covenant were *ten*. They were inscribed on two tables — that is, on two smooth slabs of stone. This was the ancient mode of preserving on record important events, and some of these ancient inscriptions exist to this day. Though there were *ten* words, we are not told in what way the division into ten was made. It matters little how they are divided, provided that none of them are left out. They were differently divided in the ancient Christian Church. Origen and St. Jerome had one division, St. Augustine used another, which latter is followed now by the Catholic Church. The ten commandments were not new to the people, but were for the most part a portion of that natural law which God in the beginning had written upon the heart of man in plain characters, but which had now become almost worn away and defaced by time and the wickedness of the world. God now repeated those laws in a solemn manner, that the people might tremble and obey. So far as they formed a part of the eternal moral law they remain to us, and were confirmed by Christ in the new law; whatever portions of them were merely ceremonial belonged to the Jews only, and are no longer binding on us.

No one can doubt that we are able and are bound to keep the commandments, for God would not give us laws that we might break them, neither would He command impossibilities. While the commandments seem chiefly to warn us from doing evil, they imply also, that we are to keep as far as possible from the evil, and in order to do this, we must practise the opposite of what we are forbidden—that is, we must not only avoid evil, but do good. We must avoid any act of sin, and practise acts of those virtues which are most opposed to the sins that are forbidden. The commandments forbid by name the *greater* sin of each kind; but of course include all lesser sins of the same sort, and all those acts and occasions which may lead to that *greater* sin.

1st Commandment.

" Thou shalt not have strange gods before Me. Thou shalt not make to thyself any graven thing, nor the likeness of anything that is in heaven above, or in the earth beneath, nor of those things that are in the waters under the earth; thou shalt not adore them, nor serve them."

In those days when the law was given on Mount Sinai (A.C. 1500), idolatry prevailed everywhere. Every nation, tribe, and place had its own God. There were gods of the mountains, of the valleys, and of the streams. All these false gods were the gods of other nations, and therefore, with respect to the Israelites, were "strange" gods — that is, the gods worshipped by foreigners and strangers, and not by Israelites. The Israelites, during their long stay in Egypt of four hundred and thirty years, appear to have forgotten the God of their fathers, and to have adopted the idolatrous worship of Egypt. They carried the idols of Egypt with them in their long journey through the wilderness, and must have been very prone to idolatry, for Joshua said to the next generation, "Put away the gods which your fathers served in Egypt, and serve ye the Lord" (Josh. xxiv. 14).

The first commandment therefore contained—

1st. A prohibition of the *worship* of strange gods, commonly done under the form of some image or likeness, called an idol. The Israelites fell into this idolatry at the foot of Mount Sinai, before Moses had returned from its fiery summit, when they set up a golden calf, intended for an Egyptian deity, and worshipped it, saying, "This is thy God, O Israel, who brought thee out of the land of Egypt."

2nd. The first commandment probably forbade the very *making* of all images and likenesses. There was nothing immoral or sinful in the making of such things, for God ordered Moses to make the figure of a cherub in gold at each end of the Mercy-seat. This prohibition then, if it existed, as is supposed, was a national regulation, binding only that people to whom it was addressed, and imposed on them on account of their proneness to idolatry. For, such were the habits and notions which they brought with them from Egypt, and handed down to their posterity, that notwithstanding the most positive commands of God, and His severe judgments upon the nation, nearly a thousand years passed before they were cured of this folly.

This prohibition of *making* images was called for by circumstances peculiar to the children of Israel, but does not prohibit Christians from making images. They are bound not to worship images—a folly which no one but an idiot could be supposed to be capable of committing. So far from its being evil to have the images and pictures of Christ and of His saints, the practice is good, and tends to promote religion, because such objects in a church, or in a house, often help to remind us of those whom they represent. As bad pictures and immodest statues and images are calculated, as all the world knows, to excite unholy and wicked thoughts, so a crucifix, a picture, or an image of the Blessed Virgin or of the saints, is very likely to put good thoughts into the mind. We do not pray to such things, because no one prays to wood, clay, marble, or canvass; but we have them in churches because such things are the most fitting ornaments of places of worship. Though we do not pray *to* them, we often pray *before* them, and perhaps bow down before them, but our prayers and our marks of reverence, whatever they may be, are directed to those whom these objects represent, and of whom they remind us. If I bow my head or my knee at the name of Jesus, I bow not to the sound which I hear, but to Him whom that sound brings to my recollection.

True Religion.—The first commandment binds Christians not as it bound the Israelites, but only inasmuch as it includes the moral precept of not giving to any created being, the worship due to God. As it required the Jews to worship Him alone, and in the manner which He prescribed to them; so it requires us to worship Him, by that system of religion, both as to matters of faith, government, and sacraments, which Christ came on earth to teach. To encourage in any way false religions, or to doubt or disbelieve any article of true religion, is contrary to this commandment. Faith is a virtue which may be lost like any other virtue (like chastity for example), by going into dangerous occasions. Nothing therefore can be so dangerous to faith, and so likely to weaken it, as to read books against religion, to be continually in the company of those who do not believe, and above all to be joined *for life*, by marriage, to one who has no faith, but perhaps a dislike, or even a hatred of the truth.

Superstitious Practices.—God has reserved to Himself alone the knowledge of future events; it is therefore sinful and contrary to the true worship of God, to endeavour to know the future, by dealing with the devil (as some have been said to do), or by seriously consulting those who make profession of knowing the future. Superstition is also sinful, because it is a silly and wicked attempt to pry into the future known to God alone. Superstition, as commonly understood, consists in making conjectures, and expecting that certain things will happen from certain circumstances of chance or accident which could by no law of nature produce the effect or event which is looked for. Thus some have made conjectures from the stars which were supposed to have a certain influence on human affairs. This once favourite superstition is called *astrology*. Some believe in *omens*—for example, the spilling of the salt on the table, certain days being unlucky; some use *charms* and spells—that is, they keep about them certain words or things which are supposed to prevent or cure certain evils. Some again pay too much attention to their *dreams,* commonly the mere effects of a diseased state of body, and quite unable to tell them anything that is to happen. As to mesmerism and animal magnetism, which are so much spoken of now, they often give grounds to suspect that they are not natural but diabolical; "and to seek truth from the dead," was one of the things forbidden in Deuteronomy (chap. xviii.), and by doing which Saul sinned so grievously.

2ND COMMANDMENT.

"Thou shalt not take the name of the Lord thy God in vain."

"To take the name of God," "to take an oath," or "to swear," mean the same thing, that is, call upon God to witness the truth of our words, and invoke a curse upon our own heads, if they are not true. "So help me God," words often used in taking an oath, are the same as to say, "May God send me blessings or punishments, according as my words are true or false." No particular ceremony or form of words is necessary to make an oath. The taking of God to witness in *any manner,* or form of words, is sufficient; and, therefore, we should be careful how we make use of many common expressions in affirming or denying, which if strictly explained, can have no other meaning, but calling upon God as a witness. "In vain" means falsely, or irreverently. To do this, that is, to call upon God to witness the truth of what you know to be false or doubtful, is called *perjury.* This is a grievous crime of irreverence to God, and as it is likely to be most injurious to the good of society, it is severely punished by the civil tribunals of all nations. In all ages men have had the custom, on important occasions, of appealing to God to witness the truth of their words, and an oath has everywhere been looked on as something very solemn and sacred. In the Scripture there are some texts which seem to forbid us to swear *at all*, and therefore some persons, chiefly of the Society of Friends, have a religious objection to take an oath on any occasion whatever. These Scripture texts were directed against the common and too frequent use of oaths in *common* conversation. The practice of the Christian Church has never interpreted these texts as forbidding the proper use of an oath, on suitable occasions. An oath when employed must be taken with due consideration as to the truth of what we are saying—that is, not rashly. It must be on a serious and important occasion—that is, not without necessity. It must be just—that is, not in any matter that would be a sin against God, or an injustice to man.

A *vow* is a deliberate promise made to God of doing something that will be good and pleasing to Him, with the intention of binding one's-self under pain of sin, to do it. This is a much more serious thing than those good *resolutions* which Christians make and very often break, without any sin. It is not always easy to distinguish one from the other. A vow should never be made without the advice of a spiritual director, even when it is in a matter where we are our own masters, and so have a right, and are able, to make it.

Cursing is forbidden by the second commandment. To curse is to utter a wish, or to pray that God would bring some evil or mischief upon some person or thing. Though the name of God be not used in the words of the curse, yet it is implied, because the evil wished or prayed for cannot happen without God's permission and knowledge. Persons often use the language of cursing without meaning or desiring what they say; but even this is very scandalous and unchristian. The curses which men utter are often known to fall back in a wonderful manner on their own heads.

To *blaspheme* is to speak irreverently of God, or of that which is holy, or consecrated to His service. By the law of Moses this sin was punished with death.

Persons, again, in this matter often use expressions which are blasphemous, but which they do not mean as such. If Christians always were accustomed to think with reverence of God, and of things of His appointment, they would not easily be betrayed by passion or thoughtlessness into the use of words or speeches, which sound impious or irreligious.

Besides blasphemy and cursing, *profane words* and discourses are also forbidden by the second commandment. To speak of holy things, in a trifling, frivolous manner,—to make them and the sacred Scriptures furnish the subject of jokes, or of witty remarks in common conversation, shows a great want of reverence to what is holy; an unbecoming familiarity, instead of respect; which is likely to be injurious to those who use such speeches, and to produce a bad effect on all, especially on young persons who hear them.

3RD COMMANDMENT.

"Remember that thou keep holy the Sabbath-day."

The Jewish Sabbath.—There is no clear mention in Scripture of the observance of a Sabbath, or day of rest, till after the flight of the Israelites out of Egypt. In the second month, their provisions being all consumed, Moses announced to them that a certain food, afterwards called manna, would be sent to them from heaven, which they might gather on the six following mornings; but that on the seventh day, God would observe a day of rest, and there would be no manna to be gathered. So it happened, and the people kept the rest on the seventh day (Exodus xvi. 30). This was the *first* Sabbath.' In the same manner it happened during their forty years in the desert.

It must be observed that God fixed a seventh day, the seventh from the first fall of manna, and not any one day out of the seven days. A day of rest was appointed in memory of the rest and peace in the land of Canaan, to which the Israelites were brought after being delivered from the slavery of Egypt; and the *seventh* day was appointed in memory of God resting on the seventh day from the work of Creation. It was appointed also in compassion to the great mass of the people, who have to live by their labours, that they might have one day of rest out of the seven, from the oppression of hard masters.

Christian Sabbath.—The Jewish Sabbath does not bind Christians. We do not keep any Sabbath as the Israelites did, either as to the time or manner. Not as to *the time*, for they kept their Sabbath from sunset on Friday to sunset on Saturday; we keep ours from midnight on Saturday to midnight on Sunday. The ancient Christians (their teachers being Jews) kept it from sunset on Saturday to sunset on Sunday; but afterwards it was found more convenient to adopt the Latin and Greek way of counting time from midnight to midnight. But even now, the first vespers, or evening service, of greater feasts, is celebrated on the preceding evening. This *change* of the Saturday, or seventh day, to Sunday, the first day of the week, was made by the authority of the Catholic Church, in memory of Christ's resurrection. The Scripture is silent as to the *obligation* of keeping Sunday as a day of rest. It is one of those traditions coming down from the time of the Apostles, which those are compelled to adopt in practice, who profess to reject it in theory. Again, as to the *manner* of keeping it, the Sunday differs from the Jewish Sabbath. In the first place, our rest from work is not so strict as was that of the Jews. The Mosaic law forbade labour and traffic of every kind; it did not allow so much as a fire to be lighted on the Sabbath-day, and a poor man who had gathered a few sticks on that day, was punished with death.

The first teachers of Christianity, when they began to observe the first day of the week as a day of rest, probably had no other intention than to procure for everybody time and opportunity for joining in the public service, and for celebrating with joy the memory of our

Lord's resurrection. Sunday, from that event, was called the "Lord's day." The observance of the Sunday as a day of rest, from being simply the *custom* of Christians, in course of time, by various laws of the Church, was made a matter of obligation. *Servile* work was therefore in time forbidden on that day—that is, all that kind of work which in those ages was generally done by slaves, and this in order to give to them time to attend better to the duties of religion. But this prohibition of servile work was made with due consideration to the wants and habits of men, and therefore with the allowance of that amount of work which custom had rendered necessary, and which could not be omitted without very considerable loss or inconvenience. Hence the preparation of food, attention to personal cleanliness and domestic comfort, the necessary care of cattle, the occasional sale or purchase of small articles, which cannot be conveniently procured on any other day, and other such like things, have always been tolerated, as *necessary* work, and not inconsistent with the rest enjoined on Sunday.

Moreover, the Sunday, from its first institution, was especially a *day of worship*, but the Sabbath was not, but was simply a day of rest from labour, both for man and beast.

It is plain, therefore, from what we have just seen, that the Sunday is a very different institution from the Sabbath. The Sabbath was a *Jewish* ordinance, and belonged to the ceremonial code of another form of worship which has now passed away. It therefore seems desirable not to call Sunday "the Sabbath-day." It is nowhere so called in Scripture, and to call it so, leads men to confound the Jewish Sabbath and the Christian Sunday together; and causes many to think that the severity of the Jewish Sabbath belongs to the Christian Sunday. In consequence of this idea, Sunday is often made a day of gloom and sadness, on which every innocent recreation is forbidden; but with the ancient Christians it was a day of joy, on which it was almost a sin to fast or mourn.

Obligations of the Sunday.—The first of these is to abstain from all works which are commonly called *servile*—that is, all such kinds of bodily works as are commonly done by servants, mechanics, tradesmen, &c., for gaining a livelihood. We have seen above that necessity justifies some of these on Sundays, such as cooking meals, &c. But when real serious necessity occurs, as it sometimes does, persons may, especially with a dispensation, work the *whole* or the *greater part* of a Sunday. There may arise questions as to whether certain things would be servile work or not, but on such occasions as these, as also on occasion of apparent or real necessity for working on a Sunday, we should ask the advice of prudent persons, and especially of our spiritual director. This rest from servile work is ordered by the first commandment of the Church.

The *second* obligation of the Sunday is to hear Mass. It is sinful to be absent through carelessness or neglect from any even a small part of the Mass; but to be absent during a considerable part of the Mass, is not to comply with the obligation of hearing Mass at all. In like manner, to be wilfully distracted during a part of the Mass is more or less sinful, in proportion to the time of such wilful distraction. Again, the reasons for which persons absent themselves from Mass will excuse that absence more or less according to the weight of those reasons, but he who is absent without any reason at all, but through idleness, is guilty of a grievous sin. To be absent from Mass for a weighty reason, is not a sin, and need not be mentioned in confession. The laws of the Church are intended for the spiritual good of the faithful, and not to be a burden to them. No one, therefore, is bound to hear Mass, when there would be very great difficulty or inconvenience in doing so. Catholics will reason very differently, according to their earnestness or sluggishness, as to what may be called a *great* difficulty or inconvenience, but those who sincerely wish to know their duty and to do it, will always form a sufficiently correct opinion of what they ought to do. The obligation of hearing Mass is fixed by the second commandment of the Church.

Sunday well spent.—But besides hearing Mass, which is binding under grievous sin, every one who would do what even a moderately good Catholic ought to do, will make it his rule and his ordinary practice to attend some other public service, either in the afternoon or evening. This is especially important for the generality of persons who have so little time to give to God's service on other days of the week. But to attend instructions on the Sunday is of absolute *obligation* for those who have no other opportunity, and have not yet received the Sacraments, or who are very ill-instructed in their holy religion. Most persons who generally on other days are so much occupied in worldly things, should by prayer, and reading, and self-examination, make the Sunday a day of real spiritual improvement, and not merely a day of vanity, dress, and worldly pleasure. On that day we should repent of the sins of the past week, and prepare to do better for the week that has just begun. We should on that day rest from worldly labours in such a manner that we shall find ourselves more fitted to enter into the eternal rest of heaven. Many complain of want of time during the week, to pray and think of God; only let them make good use of the Sunday, and they will not have anything to fear about their salvation. But what hope can *they* have, who spend the six days without thinking of God, and pass even the Sunday itself, in sleep, idleness, and pleasure, without feeling any desire for improvement or holiness?

THE SECOND TABLE OF THE LAW.

4th Commandment.

"Honour thy father and thy mother."

This honour which we owe to parents, implies love, reverence, and obedience.

We must *love* all persons; how much more, then, our parents! If we love them as we ought, we shall show that love in our words and actions, in our whole manner and behaviour to them. It will make us willing on all occasions to do what we can to relieve them in their necessities, whether corporal or spiritual. We shall not forget them when they are dead, but do what we can to help them even then by our prayers. We shall never show any dislike by look, manner, or by any unkind and harsh words. In general, anything which would be sinful to any ordinary person is more sinful when done to parents.

We must *reverence or respect* our parents. We sin against this duty if we reproach or mock them, or give them any kind of evil language. We sin against this duty if we speak to them in a hasty, harsh, or passionate manner; or if we give them sharp or short answers, or rudely contradict, or vex and distress them by undutiful behaviour, especially in the presence of others. We sin against parental respect if we make known their weaknesses and defects, instead of concealing them, or if in any way we expose them to contempt or ridicule. We sin if we refuse to consult them or to study their feelings, especially in matters of great importance.

Children must also show *obedience* to their parents. "Children, obey your parents in all things, for this is well pleasing to the Lord" (Coloss. iii. 20). They should do what is commanded them, and avoid what is forbidden. This should be done with willingness and cheerfulness—that is, without making needless excuses or delays, without murmuring or disputing the point, without showing opposition or stubbornness. Children should receive correction and chastisement with patience; they should own their faults, and promise amendment. When sent to school, or placed under the care of others, they should respect and obey those who have to teach them or take care of them; they should strive to learn, and not give unnecessary trouble to any one. They should never, by word or example, encourage others in disobedience, or in resisting the commands of parents or teachers.

Disobedience is more or less sinful, according to the nature of the case. A great many acts of disobedience of which children are guilty, are in matters of less importance. But when a command is made in such a way that the child knows and understands it to be a matter of consequence, then disobedience would be a great sin. Such are the commands given to children, not to go to particular places or to remain in certain company. When children are grown up and come to man's estate, they are not bound to obey their parents as they were when they were in childhood; yet even then the advice of parents should be received with deference and treated with respect. Children must never obey their parents in what is clearly sinful, and they would do well in doubtful cases to seek proper advice. If parents, or other members of the family (as too often happens), are drunken, irreligious, profane, or immoral, children should, from their earliest childhood, begin to guard against such example; they should remember the good instructions given them in school and church, and always bear in mind that no bad example will excuse them in the sight of God. They are bound, notwithstanding, to respect their parents, and should often pray for their conversion.

Duties of Parents to Children.—This commandment treats of the duties of children to their parents, but parents also have duties towards their children, and those of the highest consequence. As long as the child is unable to provide for himself, or to govern himself, it is the duty of parents to supply his wants, to watch over his health and safety, to fashion and fit him for his future station in life, and to provide for him instruction in the doctrines and practices of religion. Above all, they must be careful that there be nothing to corrupt the child's mind in his home—that is, in their own example, or in that of their family, or of his companions. Parents should strive to regulate their feelings, their words, and their whole conduct to their children, by the dictates of religion; so as not, on the one hand, to injure them by too much fondness, nor to harass them by too much severity; nor to say or do or encourage anything that may be calculated to lessen their reverence of religion, their fear of God, or their esteem for salvation.

Duties to other Superiors.—Christians owe obedience also to the authorities in Church and State. In the Church they owe obedience and reverence to the Chief Bishop, the *Pope*, the Vicar of Christ, for whom they should often pray, knowing that he is always the object of contradiction, through the fear or hatred which all unbelievers and heretics throughout the world always have of him. He is also continually resisted and thwarted in the government of the Church, even by Catholic governments and individuals, who prefer their own political notions, or national traditions, or private opinions, to the principles of Catholicity and the general good of the Church. Christians also owe obedience to their own bishop, in the government of his own diocese, and they should pray that through him, religion may be extended and all abuses corrected. They owe obedience and respect to their own pastor and priest in all those things which belong to his office, in the spiritual management of his parish, and the direction of the souls intrusted to his care. They should be willing to help him in the various arrangements which are made, with a view to the general good. They should not allow any difference to arise, or cherish any feeling towards him, which might be a hindrance to them in attending to their sacramental duties. All idle gossip on the conduct of priests should be avoided. Besides this, the faithful are bound to contribute according to their means to the *support* of their pastors. Priests have received a longer course of education, to fit them for their office, than lawyers or medical men, and have as much right as these have, to live by the exercise of their profession. Besides the personal maintenance of the priest, the faithful should contribute to the education of new priests, and to the various expenses necessary for carrying on religious worship; whether it be towards building, repairing, or decorating, furnishing the requisites for the altar, or for assisting in what may add to the dignity and beauty of the service of the Church. Many look too much to a few rich people to do all these things; but it is the duty of *all* to give in proportion to their means; and the constant supply of the "widow's mite" and of the pennies of the poor is in many places the chief means by which the work of the Church can be begun or carried on.

Servants and Masters.—Servants also owe a becoming obedience and respect to their masters. They should not expose their faults, nor betray family secrets. The injustices in various ways by waste, carelessness, dishonesty, loss of time, &c., belong to the seventh commandment. Masters also have duties to their servants, such as to treat them in the first place with *justice*, and in no way to defraud them of what is due to them. They should also treat them with gentleness and kindness, and not with harshness and contempt. Masters should look to the *spiritual* well-being of those dependent on them, allowing them time to attend to instructions, to Mass, and to the Sacraments. Masters would be better served, if by word and example they encouraged their servants to be more faithful to Him who is the common Master, both of rich and poor, in heaven.

5TH COMMANDMENT.

" Thou shalt not kill."

This commandment forbids the taking away without lawful authority the life of another. Notwithstanding this commandment, it is lawful to fight in a just war, and to kill another when necessary for the defence of our own life. Capital punishment, that is, punishment by death for certain crimes against society, is also lawful. The general design of this commandment is to forbid all actions that may have any tendency, however remote, to destroy life unjustly, and all feelings that could have any such tendency. It forbids, therefore, everything from murder, even to a little angry word. Therefore, uncharitable disputes, injurious and provoking language, contentions, strifes, quarrelling, fighting, and the like, are forbidden by this commandment. These are mentioned in Scripture with other crimes, as "the works of the flesh," which exclude from the kingdom of heaven.

Anger is a feeling of displeasure on account of some real or supposed evil done. It is just, when the cause is just, when the feeling is moderate, kept within bounds, and subject to reason. Parents and superiors may be angry without sin, on account of the faults of children and others. Anger is sinful when it is without just cause, when it is unreasonable, immoderate, and violent. Such anger as this may soon become settled hatred and revenge. It is easy to see how anger differs from hatred and revenge. Anger is a passing feeling for an injury we have received; *hatred* is a settled dislike of another, which is often shown by refusing the customary signs of civility and goodwill, by not speaking to him, by grieving at his prosperity, or rejoicing at his misfortunes.

Revenge often springs from hatred. It consists in returning evil for evil, and inflicting injuries on those from whom we have received injuries. Anger, hatred, and revenge are more or less grievous, according to the amount of evil which we desire, or inflict on another; according to the length of time we cherish those passions; and the number of times we indulge in those desires and feelings.

Scandal and Bad Example.—The fifth commandment forbids everything that can be injurious to the body of our neighbour. But all injuries that may be caused to the *soul* of another are included also under the fifth commandment. The two principal and common causes of such injury named here, are scandal and bad example, though bad example is only one of the various ways of giving scandal.

The word "scandal" in common conversation means

the same as slander or detraction; but it is in reality a Greek word, and means a stumbling-block, or anything put in a person's way to trip him up, and make him stumble, and perhaps fall down. Such a stumbling-block may be put either on *purpose*, or by *thoughtlessness*, or it may be something that was left in its place which would be no hindrance except to a careless and thoughtless person. This will explain what is meant by the three different kinds of scandal, which consist in the *first* place in doing something evil on purpose to lead another into sin, or when the person knows, or ought to know, that it will cause sin, or is calculated to cause it. Thus, bad example to inferiors, enticing others to sin, ridiculing virtue, advising or encouraging what is sinful, flattering others for doing evil, uttering immodest words, &c., would be examples of this sort of scandal. *Another* sort of scandal consists in doing or saying things which, especially to weak or ignorant persons, may have the appearance of evil, and might lead them to do what was *really* evil. Thus, to eat meat, even when lawfully dispensed with, in the presence of strangers, on a forbidden day, without any explanation or excuse, would be an example of this sort. To do this, and many such like things, which are not evil, but from peculiar circumstances may have the appearance of evil, is not a sin, except when we foresee, or ought to foresee, that scandal will be taken from it. Many are very careless upon this point, and often make a boast of not caring what others may think, or say, or do, if what they do is right in itself, but yet is calculated to produce a bad effect on others who see or know it. *Again*, the Pharisees took scandal at our Saviour doing a good work, even working a miracle on the Sabbath-day; but we are not bound to omit good actions, if people without reason, but through their own malicious and bitter dispositions, make evil out of what is good. This *third* kind of scandal would be a case of scandal maliciously *taken*, but not really *given*.

6th Commandment.

"Thou shalt not commit adultery."
Though this commandment mentions only the greatest sin of this class as being forbidden, yet all other lesser sins, in word or deed, which spring from the same source, are also here included. Though these other sins may be less grievous than the one here mentioned, yet every deliberate violation of chastity is always a mortal sin, on account of the evil and danger attending such sins. The sixth commandment, then, forbids all impurity of every kind. The various sins forbidden by this commandment are called by different names, according to their nature and circumstances and the person who commits them; but it would not be suitable to explain or mention them here. These sins are so contrary to purity and holiness, that no one ever commits any of them, or even comes near to them by any imprudence, but he feels, especially in the beginning, a trouble and an unhappiness of conscience. That trouble and uneasiness should be explained with the cause of it to a spiritual director, who will advise, as the case may require. But if the uneasiness is concealed, and the sin or the imprudent conduct is repeated, the conscience becomes more and more hardened; very commonly a course of sacrilegious confession follows; religion is at length forsaken, and the soul is lost in sin for years, perhaps for ever. Why are so many young persons lost to the duties of religion, except for the cause just mentioned? Parents, priests, and all who have the care of youth, find it a very anxious, difficult, and delicate task, to give proper warnings and cautions upon this subject to the young of both sexes, at that dangerous time when they are growing up to manhood and womanhood; but God has given to all, especially to young women, instincts of modesty and chastity so keen and acute, that if these were followed, and never slighted, these alone, with God's grace, would be enough to protect their virtue, by giving them timely notice of coming danger.

Preventives.—It is often more easy to prevent than to cure. This is especially the case with the sin of impurity. A person, then, who wishes to be saved from a sin which causes more bad confessions than all the others put together, which sends more souls to hell than all other sins, which is the ruin of so many young persons, must use all possible precautions and preventives. This is an enemy that we must keep at a distance by avoiding every occasion of temptation. Some things may be a more dangerous occasion to one person than to another; but whatever we have reason to believe, either from past experience or in any other way, to be dangerous to us, we must shun. Immodest plays, dances, or books, are clearly sinful; but it is dangerous to become fond of plays, dances, and light reading, which are not positively and plainly immodest, but which are all calculated to favour sensuality, which breathe luxury and self-indulgence, are full of vanities, and totally opposed to a true Christian tone and frame of mind. Avoid dangerous intimacies and familiarities with the other sex. Do not look upon things or persons which excite improper feelings or thoughts. Always check a certain dangerous curiosity to know, to speak, to inquire, or hear about things with which the corrupt and depraved, even in early youth, soon become familiar; but of which the innocent and virtuous long remain in happy ignorance. But all human efforts to correct the violent propensities of nature will fail without God's grace, which must be obtained by daily prayer, by a regular system of sincere and humble confession, and by often receiving Him who is the great lover of holy purity.

7th Commandment.

"Thou shalt not steal."

This commandment forbids every kind of injury that can be done in any way to another in regard to his property and worldly goods. It forbids taking or keeping what belongs to another, without the actual or implied consent of the owner. This sin of injustice is committed in a great variety of ways. It is done by theft when property is secretly taken, or by robbery when it is taken by open violence; these require no explanation. Injustice is committed by *fraud in the dealings* of one man with another. There may be customs in trade which are so well understood, that however suspicious they appear, they cannot always be condemned as absolutely unjust. A man may also seek to obtain the best price for his goods, knowing well at the same time that he would soon injure himself if his prices were exorbitant or too high. But when people use false weights and measures, or impose upon others by falsehoods, and thus obtain an unreasonable price, or sell an article as being of a superior material, when it is of an inferior and different material altogether; these and such like things are positive acts of injustice which require restitution. It is plain, that whoever obtains possession of another man's money or property by such deceit, does not possess it with the consent, either actual or implied, of the owner. Untruths which are told in selling goods, but by which goods are not sold beyond their real value, do not involve the obligation of restitution, as no injustice is committed, though such untruths are of course sinful.

Injustice is often committed by *breach of contract*. This often happens between master and man, the employer and the employed. If the workman takes his stipulated wages, though he has spent part of his time in idleness; if he receive the price which was agreed on, though he has not performed his work in a workmanlike manner, or, in place of sound, has employed unsound materials; he becomes possessed of that to which, by the terms of the contract, he has no right. In like manner, the employer, if he refuse without just cause to pay according to agreement, becomes possessed unjustly of the property of the employed; for the property of the poor man is his labour.

Injustice is committed by *getting into debt* without the means or the intention of paying. This is often the case; for how can there be such an intention when there was no probability, when the debt was contracted, that it ever could be paid?

All sins of injury and injustice vary in guilt, according to the amount of the injury and injustice done. Small thefts from the same person, at different times, which amount in the total to a considerable injury, is a grievous violation of the commandment; for the owner has the same right to his goods when stolen at different times as when taken all at once.

Restitution.—All injustice committed on the property of our neighbour requires, in conscience, restitution and reparation. Injuries from accidents, unless the result of gross neglect or carelessness, are not injustices, and do not require, in conscience, restitution. The obligation of restitution concerns not only the person who did the wrong, but also those who were concerned in it, by counsel, assistance, or partaking of the ill-gotten goods. Many perplexing difficulties often arise as to the extent of the duty of restitution in certain cases, and the manner in which the restitution should be made. In these and all other difficulties of conscience, a spiritual director should be consulted, to whom the case must be truthfully exposed, with a determination to abide by the decision, and speedily to put the matter right. The longer the property of another is kept from the owner, and the restitution is delayed, if we are able to make it, the longer does the sin hang upon us, and the greater it becomes. A person who cannot from poverty, or from the circumstances of the case, make complete restitution or reparation, must make it, as far as he is able, and must make it, at some future time, if he should have the means of doing so.

8TH COMMANDMENT.

" Thou shalt not bear false witness against thy neighbour."

The words of this commandment forbid us to bear false witness against another. But it is always understood to include many other sins besides this. Its object is to forbid everything contrary to *truth*, and every injury that can be done to our neighbour's *character* and good name.

Calumny.—It forbids, then, in the first place, that worst kind of lie by which a *false charge* is made to the injury of another, whether in a court of justice or elsewhere. This is called *calumny, or slander*. This is so absolutely unjust, that any one who has committed this sin is bound before God to recall the slander, and repair the injury. He is bound, if necessary, to avow himself guilty of falsehood, and often of falsehood of the most disgraceful nature, if he hope to obtain the pardon of his sin. But who can tell the extent to which the slander has spread, or the real amount of pain, loss, and disappointment which it may have caused? Yet for all this, reparation is to be made as far as possible. If calumny has caused injury to property, reparation is necessary for this also, as well as for injured reputation. The law often punishes slanderers with severity, as they are the greatest enemies of the peace of society.

Lies of every kind.—Besides this worst sort of lies, every kind of lie is forbidden. A lie consists in saying anything with the intention of deceiving; it is having one thing in the mouth, another in the mind. Some are malicious and injurious to others, some are told to excuse ourselves or others, some to cause amusement, some for the sake of boasting, some for flattery. It is never lawful to do evil that good may come from it, therefore it is never lawful to tell a lie for some good intention, or for the benefit of another, much less to another's injury. " The devil is a liar, and the father of lies " (St. John viii. 44). " All liars shall have their portion in the pool which burneth with fire and brimstone" (Apoc. xxi. 8). Lies are more or less grievous according to their nature and the circumstances in which they are uttered, some being exceedingly grievous, some venial, but all sinful. Many have a continual habit of lying, and this evil is very common in children, and should be corrected as soon as possible, or it will grow beyond correction.

Detraction.—Every man who has committed secret faults, that is, faults known only to one or two persons, has, for all that, an absolute right to the good opinion of other persons, and of the public in general, perhaps as much as if he had never committed those sins at all. Any one, then, who makes those secret sins known to others, especially who makes them widely known, does him an injury and injustice, perhaps a most grievous one. This is called *detraction*. It is a sin against the law of justice and charity; and it shows a shameful ignorance of both, for people to pretend to justify themselves when they are making known the secret faults of others, by saying that it was all true. Most commonly, much falsehood is, sooner or later, added to the truth; and thus the detractor is in danger of being the cause of calumnies. But even if all that is said, or is likely to be said, were the exact truth, to speak such truth, which is injurious to another, is sinful, and, according to the nature of the case, might be grievously sinful. The individual right of our neighbour, the law of charity, and, besides these considerations, the general good of society require that the *secret* sins of others should be kept secret. This general rule has an exception. If the good of the offender, or the good of others should require such secret sins to be mentioned to certain individuals, so far they may be mentioned with prudence and charity, but no further. Many who have had some religious instruction, and frequent the sacraments, violate this law habitually, and without remorse, and never properly reflect till it comes to be their turn to smart from the detractor's tongue.

Backbiting.—When persons, all of whom are acquainted with the sins and weaknesses of others, make them the subject of their conversation, and indulge in ill-natured, unkind, uncharitable, or witty and jocose remarks at their expense, it is called *backbiting*. This is contrary to that law by which we should be willing to do to others as we should wish others to do unto us. No one, certainly, ever wishes himself or his faults to be the subject of conversation to others, and to furnish them with matter either for ridicule, amusement, or contempt.

Rash Judgment.—" Charity thinketh no evil;" therefore rash judgment, which is also forbidden by the eighth commandment, is contrary to charity. A judgment of our neighbour is *rash* when we suspect, or in our own minds judge another to be guilty of some evil, without having any grounds, or without sufficient grounds. To judge so far as there is reason, is not a rash but a reasonable judgment. We are in general too apt to form unfavourable judgments; some have minds peculiarly given to evil suspicion; and many judge evil of others in proportion to their own consciousness of the like guilt.

9TH AND 10TH COMMANDMENTS.

" Thou shalt not covet thy neighbour's wife."
" Thou shalt not covet thy neighbour's goods."
The other commandments forbid outward acts, these forbid inward thoughts and desires. The thought and desire are as well known to God as the act could be. A man certainly would have great reason to be offended if he knew of some one who was engaged in thinking, desiring, and planning some insult, injury, or mischief to him, though it was never effected. The Almighty, therefore, must necessarily be displeased with any one who is pleasing himself with the idea, or the desire of something which He has forbidden ever to be done. In a moral point of view, there is little difference between the guilt of him who actually sins, because he has the opportunity; and of him who desires to sin, but does not, because he has not the opportunity. The latter is restrained, not by the love or fear of God, but by human,

M

and therefore selfish considerations. God, therefore, requires us to regulate our thoughts, desires, and intentions, as well as our acts, according to His commandments. Whatever it is unlawful for us to do, it is unlawful for us to desire, or to deliberately think of with pleasure. All the commandments may be broken by sins of thought, but God has more expressly forbidden sins of thought contrary to chastity and justice, because these are especially dangerous, and lie at the root of many other sins. As the sixth commandment puts a restraint on our eyes, ears, hands, and tongue, so the ninth puts a restraint on the powers of our soul, our will, memory, heart, thoughts, and desires. The tenth commandment forbids us to think or desire anything which the seventh forbids. The design, then, of these two commandments is to teach the proper regulation of the thoughts and desires, that is, the government of the heart, because it is from the heart that all good or evil issues forth.

Evil thoughts and desires may and do come into every human mind. Such thoughts of themselves are not sins, they are only temptations; and Christ Himself was tempted. So far from their being imputed to us as sins, they may add to our future reward. We make evil thoughts our *own*, and render them sinful if we bring them into the mind wilfully; if we love the evil, and wilfully allow our thoughts to dwell upon it, and if we desire and intend to commit the evil thought of. It is not easy for any one to say precisely how far he has sinned in his thoughts. Every one should always look upon it as part of the duty of a Christian to examine his thoughts and feelings and dispositions, as well as the things that he actually says or does. We have to avoid the occasions which are apt to bring bad thoughts, for such thoughts will come fast enough of themselves without any invitation. We should avoid the beginnings of all temptations, especially of such as are contrary to chastity.

CHAPTER V.

THE COMMANDMENTS OF THE CHURCH.

BY the commandments of the Church, we mean those general laws and regulations which the pastors of the Church have made and rendered binding on the faithful, by virtue of the authority they have received from Christ. These commandments of the Church for the most part regard duties which God Himself has commanded. The Church has merely fixed *the time and manner* of fulfilling them, as there is every reason to believe that if Christians were left to themselves, and nothing definitely marked out for their observance, they would delay too long, and even fall into total neglect. The ten commandments of God enjoin duties obligatory in themselves from which there can be no release or dispensation. The laws of the Church, on the other hand, which chiefly define times and seasons when certain duties are to be performed, admit of exceptions and dispensations. These do not bind at all under circumstances of extreme hardship, and in cases of less severe difficulty, a dispensation from them can be obtained from the pastors of the Church. Some laws suitable or necessary in one part of the Church might not be suitable in another; and laws which are good at one period of time might be unnecessary or even injurious at another. It is the same in political laws and enactments. While, then, the doctrine of the Church is always one and the same, it is evident that discipline, that is, her laws, may vary according to the wants of different times and countries.

There are only six commandments which regard the Universal Church, and bind all the faithful, and are therefore called the *chief* commandments. They seem to be nothing else but holy practices and customs, received by tradition; for the most part, from apostolical times, which the Church at length reduced into laws, and enjoined all Christians to observe, as things highly conducive to the general good.

1st and 2nd Commandments of the Church.

The first is "to keep certain days holy with the obligation of resting from servile works;" and the second is "to hear Mass on Sundays and the holy days of obligation." Nearly every day of the year is dedicated to the memory of some saint, or to some religious commemoration, but certain days being remarkable for some greater event in the life of Christ, or in the history of religion, are observed as holy days—that is, though they fall on a week day, they are kept like Sunday by resting from servile work, and by the obligation of hearing Mass.

There are eight such days in the year, and they are called *holidays of obligation*. These days in England are: (1) New Year's Day, or the Circumcision of our Lord. (2) The Epiphany, or the Manifestation of our Lord to the Gentiles, in the persons of the wise men. (3) The Ascension of our Lord into heaven. (4) Corpus Christi, or the festival in honour of the real presence of Christ in the Blessed Sacrament. (5) The Feast of St. Peter and St. Paul. (6) The Assumption of our Blessed Lady into heaven. (7) The Festival of All Saints; and (8) Christmas Day, or the birth of our Lord. Formerly there were many more days of obligation, which are now kept only as *days of devotion*—that is, as days on which we are recommended, as a matter of devotion, to hear Mass, and to approach the Sacraments. The same authority which ordered the observance of the Sunday has ordered days of obligation to be kept in the same manner as Sunday, which therefore must be so kept as far as circumstances render possible. To be present at Mass is required on Sundays and days of obligation, in preference to any other religious duty, because the Mass is the greatest act of religious worship, as every one knows, who knows the Catholic doctrine upon this subject. Besides, in the other acts of religion, there is nothing which essentially requires attendance at public worship; nothing which any individual may not offer to God in his own private house. But the Mass is a *sacrifice;* it cannot be offered without the ministry of a priest, who offers, not only in his own name, but in the name of all present. Personal attendance is, therefore, necessary. Whosoever is absent joins not in the common worship. On the twofold obligation of Sundays and days of obligation, see other remarks under the third of the ten commandments.

3RD COMMANDMENT OF THE CHURCH.

"To keep the days of fasting and abstinence appointed by the Church."

Fasting a Scriptural Observance.—In the Old Testament there are numerous instances of the practice of fasting, and of its acceptance with God. In the New Testament we do not indeed meet with any express command of it given by our Saviour; for as it was universally practised, there was no necessity; yet we cannot doubt that He recommended it to His disciples both by word and example. He fasted Himself forty days in the desert; He declared that His apostles after His departure should fast (Matt. ix. 15); He gave to them instructions concerning the manner of fasting (Matt. vi. 15); and after His ascension we find the apostles themselves, fasting before the ordination of ministers (Acts xiii. 3, and xiv. 22); and the practice of fasting universally prevailed among their disciples in the earliest ages of Christianity. When we consider all these circumstances, we cannot doubt that the Christian precept of fasting originated with our Blessed Lord Himself, for it was universally practised. There were many laws of abstinence also imposed upon the Jews in the old law. Eleazar and the seven Machabees with their mother suffered death rather than eat forbidden meats. The apostles commanded the early converts to abstain from blood and things strangled, as well as from things sacrificed to idols (Acts xv. 28, 29).

Fasting in Scripture is spoken of as a good work, and ranks in merit with prayer and almsdeeds. As fasting is a work so meritorious and conducive to spiritual good, the Church has thought it necessary to make it a matter of obligation, by appointing days of fasting, from time to time, during the year; lest, if left to our own discretion, we should altogether neglect to do any works of penance.

Manner of Fasting.—On a fasting day we can take but one full meal, and are forbidden to eat flesh meat. A person who fasts may take in the *morning* one ounce or at most two, but this is not to be flesh meat nor anything produced from animals, as milk, butter, cheese, eggs, &c., but it must consist of such things as are produced by the earth, as bread, fruit, olive oil, &c. About *midday* a person may take the one full meal, but it must consist of abstinence food and not of flesh meat, unless special permission is granted for a particular day, as is commonly done at the beginning of Lent. A supper or collation is allowed in the evening, on a fast-day, which must not exceed eight ounces, and must be of the same quality of food as the small allowance permitted in the morning, unless there be some dispensation to the contrary. Liquids—such as beer, water, tea, and coffee—do not break the fast, but such liquids as soups or milk are not allowed, except at the principal meal.

Exceptions in Lent.—The following are the permissions which were granted in most of the dioceses in England, by authority of the Holy See, for the Lent (1864), and probably will be generally granted, to lessen the severity of the Lenten fast:—

"1. Flesh meat is allowed at the single meal of those who are bound to fast, and at the discretion of those who are not so bound, on all days except Mondays, Wednesdays, and Fridays, Ember Saturday, and the four last days in Holy Week. On Sundays, even those who are bound to fast, may eat flesh meat at their discretion.

"2. Eggs are allowed at the single meal of those who are bound to fast, and at the discretion of those who are not so bound, except on Ash Wednesday and the three last days of Holy Week.

"3. Cheese under the same restrictions is allowed on all days except Ash Wednesday and Good Friday.

"4. The use of dripping and lard is permitted at dinner and collation on all days except Good Friday."

"On those days, Sundays included, whereon flesh meat is allowed, fish is not permitted at the same meal."

It must be observed, that *on all fasting days* throughout the year, when flesh meat is allowed by a general or particular dispensation, fish and flesh are not allowed at the same meal. This prohibition of the joint use of fish and flesh-meat applies (see above) to the Sundays of Lent, but not to any of the other *abstinence* days throughout the year.

Who are not bound to fast.—Persons are not bound to fast till they have completed their twenty-first year, as to fast sooner might be injurious to the constitution. For the same reason those who are past sixty are considered exempt. In general those persons are not bound to fast to whom it would probably be injurious. This is determined by the nature of a person's constitution, the nature of his work, the general or particular state of his health, at a given time. Doubtful cases should be referred to a confessor. Those who in consideration of their age and strength are not bound to fast may, as a general rule, in most dioceses in England (see above the Lenten dispensations), eat at *each* meal what those who are bound to fast should eat at dinner only.

Fasting Days.—*Lent* is the greatest and most solemn fast of the year; it is kept in memory of our Saviour's fast of forty days in the desert, and as a preparation to celebrate the approaching Easter in a worthy manner. It begins on Ash Wednesday, and consists of forty fasting days, without counting the six Sundays of Lent.

Vigils or Eves were so called from the custom of watching or keeping vigils during the night on the eves of certain festivals. Only five of these vigils now remain in England as fasting days—namely, the vigils of Christmas Day, Whitsunday, SS. Peter and Paul, the Assumption, and of All Saints.

The Ember Days. — The Wednesday, Friday, and Saturday in each Ember Week, at each of the four seasons of the year, are fasting days. The object of this fast is to draw down the blessing of God upon those who enter into Holy Orders, which is generally administered at those times, and also to draw down God's blessing on the fruits of the earth. The weeks for this purpose are the first week of Lent for the spring season, Whitsunweek for the summer, the third week of September for the autumn, and the third week of Advent for the winter.

In *Advent*, the Wednesdays and Fridays are fasting days in England.

Abstinence.—This consists in not eating flesh meat on certain specified days, but on those days we are allowed the usual number of meals. All fasting days above mentioned and the Sundays of Lent are abstinence days, unless leave to the contrary be given, as is done in the Indult given, by authority of the Holy See, at the beginning of Lent by each bishop in his own diocese. Also all Fridays in the year, except the one Christmas Day may happen to come on, are abstinence days. Friday has always been considered as a very suitable day for the practice of penance, in memory of the crucifixion and death of Christ, who died on Good Friday. On abstinence days we are strictly forbidden to eat flesh meat, or anything which is made up with flesh meat; but by a rescript of our Holy Father Pius IX., in England the use of dripping and lard is permitted on all days throughout the year except Good Friday. Children from the age of seven years are bound by the law of abstinence. Those who are not bound to fast are still bound to abstain unless there is a sufficient cause to the contrary, and then a dispensation should be obtained. A dispensation always supposes a reasonable cause, and therefore no one should seek to obtain it without a proper ground of exemption.

To violate in a great degree the law of fasting or

abstinence without sufficient cause, is a grievous sin of disobedience to the Church.

4TH COMMANDMENT OF THE CHURCH.

"To go to confession at least once a year."

The general command of God to confess our sins is implied in the very institution of confession. The power which Christ gave to the apostles of forgiving or retaining sin could not be exercised unless a confession of sins were to be made. The Church commands us to comply with this general command of God at least once a year. But for this command of the Church many would not confess and repent of their sins for years together, and would run every risk of living and dying in the guilt of them. This obligation of yearly confession begins at the time when children come to the use of reason, so far as to be capable of mortal sin. When they begin to know good from evil, they begin to be accountable to God for their actions. Children who are not seven years old may have sufficient knowledge to commit *venial sin;* but it is commonly supposed that at about seven years of age they are capable even of *mortal sin.* As soon as mortal sin exists, or may exist, the necessity and the obligation of confession begins, as a preventive or cure. No precise time in the year is fixed for the yearly confession, as if to teach us that as soon as sin is committed it ought to be repented of immediately, and that there should be no delay till the coming Easter, or to any future time, which may never arrive. The yearly confession is of course, in most instances, complied with at Easter by those who go to communion only once a year.

The expression to go *at least* once a year implies that we ought to go much oftener. The frequency of confession ought to be determined by the necessity which each one feels for it, whether as a remedy against past sin, a preservative against future sin, or a means of improvement and perfection. As those who are very cleanly in their persons cannot endure the least dirt, and are frequently washing to keep the hands and face perfectly clean, while others, though covered with dirt, have no sense of uncomfortableness, and feel no necessity of making themselves clean ; so the frequency of confession will depend much on the feeling which persons have about purity of conscience, or upon their being able to bear easily a conscience soiled and stained with sin. Many, especially young persons, who by the violence of their passions and the dangerous occasions to which they are exposed, are every day in danger of mortal sin, have more necessity to go to confession *every week* than others more advanced in life have to go once every year. Whatever laws may be given as to the frequency of confession, it is quite clear that every one should go so often as to keep himself from committing mortal sin, or to get free from mortal sin at once, if he has unfortunately fallen into it. Sin not repented of is a continual provocation to God, and likely to bring other sins after it. If the Church makes a law as to once a year for every one, every Christian should make a law for himself of *several times* in the year, and have times *marked* and *fixed* for so important a duty. Some wish and resolve all their lives to go more frequently to confession, but seldom improve. The Church's law of at least once a year was intended to be a *warning* and a check to libertines, to the irreligious, and to the most careless members of the Church, and was not given as a rule of life for those who are really in earnest in the affair of salvation, and who aim at a devout life. The Church could not command less, but in commanding the least thing possible, she hoped for much more, but left the rest to the piety and the earnestness of all who seek to cultivate holiness of life.

5TH COMMANDMENT OF THE CHURCH.

"To receive the Blessed Sacrament once a year, and that at Easter or thereabouts."

We read that in the second century of Christianity, on the Sundays, the Communion was distributed to all present at the Mass, and was sent by the hands of the deacons to the absent. In the fourth and fifth century it excited surprise that any one who had been present at the Holy Sacrifice should withdraw without having received the Communion. But in course of time, as Christians grew more negligent, many persons passed even a great part of their lives without receiving the Blessed Sacrament. As a remedy it was decreed in the Fourth Council of Lateran (A.D. 1215), and confirmed by the Council of Trent, that every Christian should communicate at least once a year, and should prepare himself for that duty by the confession of his sins. The penalty of disobedience to this law was to be excluded from entrance into the Church during life, and from Christian burial after death.

The time of complying with this yearly communion is about Easter, because about that time — that is, on Maundy Thursday—the Holy Sacrament was instituted; and it has also to be received in memory of the passion and death of Christ which are then commemorated. The time for complying with this duty is in England extended over several weeks, and begins on Ash Wednesday, and ends with Low Sunday. The general command of God on the duty of receiving Holy Communion is evident from the words of Christ,—" Amen, amen, I say unto you, except you eat the flesh of the Son of Man, and drink His blood, you shall not have life in you " (John vi. 34). The Church defines the time beyond which we are not allowed to defer the receiving of the Holy Sacrament.

Those are bound by this commandment of the Church who by their age and reason are capable of being instructed sufficiently, so as to understand the sacredness of Holy Communion. Though seven is the age when children should be taught the duty and practice of confession, they are not generally capable of receiving sufficient instruction for Holy Communion till between the ages of ten and thirteen. This is left to the discretion of the pastor. Persons who are judged capable are bound to get ready, and to make the necessary preparation, and parents are bound to see that their children are prepared in time for Communion, and should do what they can themselves to get them ready.

But though the Church on this subject, as in the former commandment of yearly confession, could not command *less*, yet there is nothing on which she has expressed more continual and urgent wishes than that the faithful should receive communion *frequently*, once a month, or once a week, or oftener, even every day. How can any one believe in Christ's real presence, and yet be satisfied to receive Him only once a year? This heavenly bread is the food of our souls, and given to be our *daily* food; how then can any one feel quite satisfied in his conscience to partake of that food only a few times in a year? The body is fed every day; why should the soul be left in want for weeks together? "So live that thou mayest receive daily," says St. Augustin. *He* is not accounted a worthy member of society and a good citizen, who only just escapes the severest punishment which the law can inflict upon transgressors. Neither can any one who goes to Communion about once a year, and thereby only escapes the very heaviest punishment the Church can inflict (the excommunication threatened to those who neglect their Easter Communion), be considered a good Catholic.

6th Commandment of the Church.

"Not to marry within certain degrees of kindred, nor to solemnize marriage at the forbidden times."

The State has a general power to forbid and to declare certain contracts null and void; it has also the same power over the marriage of *infidels*, because their marriage is a mere *natural* contract. But marriage between *Christians*, being a sacrament of the new law, is not subject to the power of temporal princes, who have no authority to alter or ordain anything that relates to the substance and matter of sacraments, nor consequently to the contract of marriage, which is now the *matter* of a sacrament. The *Church* alone has the power of regulating the conditions of a marriage contract, and not the State. The State punishes with civil disabilities those who marry contrary to the laws of the land, which have been made with a view to the general good.

Forbidden Degrees. — A marriage which has been entered into within the forbidden degrees is null and void. There are four forbidden degrees of *consanguinity*, or relationship by blood. Brothers and sisters are said to be related by blood in the first degree; the children of brothers and sisters—that is, first cousins—are related in the second degree. *Their* children, again, are second cousins, and related to each other in the third degree. Third cousins, therefore, will be related in the fourth degree. Hence, when relationship exists which takes in third cousins, the contract of marriage between such persons is null and void.

The Church also annuls marriage entered into by persons who are related to each other within the fourth degree of *affinity*. Man and wife by marriage are *one* flesh. All who are related by *blood* to the husband are related in the same degree by *affinity* to the wife; and, for the same reason, all who are related by blood to the wife are related in the same degree by affinity to the husband. Hence, the meaning of the law of the Church is, that if the husband were to die, his wife could not marry any of his relatives within the fourth degree; and, on the same principle, the husband, after the death of his wife, could not marry any of his wife's relations within the fourth degree.

When special reasons exist, dispensations are given to enable persons to marry who are related either by blood or by marriage in the third and fourth degree, and, in peculiar cases, in the second, or even in the first degree, when the relationship is by affinity.

Godfathers and godmothers, in baptism or confirmation, contract a spiritual relationship or affinity with the person to whom they are sponsors, and with his parents, which would prevent marriage.

Forbidden Times.—To *solemnize* marriage is to celebrate a marriage with the festivity and ceremonial usual on such occasions, and especially with the nuptial mass, or the nuptial blessing, commonly given out of the mass. These *solemnities* of marriage are forbidden at certain times. But it is lawful to *marry* without those solemnities at any time, though no good Catholic would, by marrying within forbidden times, wish to marry *without* the blessing of the Church. The forbidden times are holy seasons, when Christians should have their thoughts engaged in works of penance, or in spiritual joy, and not distracted with worldly cares and pleasures. Hence, the law and the wish of the Church.

CHAPTER VI.

THE SACRAMENTS IN GENERAL.

THE Sacraments are certain things which Christ has appointed to be said or done, by which grace may be given to our souls. The words and actions and the things made use of by the priest when he administers a sacrament, are called the *matter* and *form* of the sacrament. Each sacrament gives a special grace of its own for a particular purpose. If they all gave the same grace, seven sacraments would not be required, but one would have been sufficient, if repeated when necessary. The seven sacraments which have been instituted seem to suit the various necessities of the soul, which bear a certain resemblance to the wants of the body. 1. As we must first be born into this world, so by *baptism* we must be regenerated—that is, spiritually born again. 2. As we must gain strength and grow before we become perfect men, so by *confirmation* we are made strong and perfect Christians. 3. As we require every day a sufficient support for our bodies, so the bread of the *Holy Eucharist* was intended for our daily and constant food, to give nourishment and strength to our souls. 4. As we require to be cured of our wounds and diseases, so by the sacrament of *penance* the diseases and wounds made in the soul by sin are healed. 5. As we stand in need of special cordials and strengthening draughts in the agonies and pangs of death, so by *extreme unction* our souls are comforted and strengthened in the last assaults of the devil. 6. As we must be governed by laws and magistrates, so *holy orders* provide us with spiritual rulers to direct and govern us. 7. As an earthly kingdom must be constantly supplied with a succession of citizens, so by the sacrament of *matrimony* the married state is blessed and sanctified, that children may be born, and be trained up as citizens of an eternal kingdom.

There are various ceremonies used and many prayers said in the administration of the sacraments which are not all essential to the validity of the sacrament, but which the Church has ordered to be done, in order both to give greater solemnity to the sacred rite, and to signify more plainly by words, and to express more clearly the grace which is given to us.

Three of the sacraments—namely, baptism, confirmation, and holy orders—are said to leave a *mark* or *character* on the soul, by which "God has sealed us" as His own. These sacraments, therefore, can only be given *once*. When a letter or a document has once been duly signed and sealed, it would be useless to sign and seal it again. So when men have once been registered as *members* of Christ's kingdom by baptism, enrolled as His *soldiers* by confirmation, and duly appointed and ordained as His *ministers* by holy orders, any repetition of these several acts could not add to the effect of what had been already done.

He who receives a sacrament must receive it with proper dispositions; and he will receive grace more or less abundantly according to the holiness of his dispositions and the preparation he has made use of. To receive a sacrament knowingly, with a want of all proper dispositions, would be to receive it *unworthily*, and would bring upon the soul the guilt of *sacrilege*. If a window be covered all over with thick black paint it will admit no light, and if it be slightly stained or covered with dust the light will come in, but less abundantly. So also the soul which is covered with the black stain of mortal sin unrepented of, cannot receive the grace of the sacraments at all; while grace will enter, but less abundantly, when the soul is stained with the dust of venial sin.

BAPTISM.

Baptism is that sacrament by which we are cleansed from original sin in which we are all born, and also from actual sin, if we be guilty of any. By this sacrament, therefore, we are made capable of being admitted into God's kingdom in heaven, at the same time that we are made members of the Church of Christ on earth.

The converts from Judaism and Paganism were put under a course of instruction, as a preparation for baptism, and were called *catechumens*, but immediately after baptism they were called *neophytes*, as being newly implanted in the Church. The catechumen had to make a solemn renunciation of the devil and of his works and pomps—that is, of the sinful practices and the false worship of the age. Those things to which he had been habituated from his childhood were inconsistent with that belief and that holiness of life which the profession of Christianity required of its followers; and, therefore, he was called upon to renounce them publicly before he was admitted to baptism. The same form of renunciation has been continued to the present day, and every Christian should constantly keep before his eyes the promises which at his baptism he made to God.

Modes of Baptizing.—Baptism is administered by the application of water to the body, accompanied with the words, "N, I baptize thee, in the name of the Father, and of the Son, and of the Holy Ghost." The water in baptism has been applied at different times, either by *dipping*, *pouring*, or *sprinkling*, and each of these ways in different parts of Scripture has been called "baptism." In warm countries, in which bathing was of almost daily use, the baptism of adults (that is, of grown-up persons) was very commonly done by immersion or dipping. From warm countries the custom passed into the colder climates of the north, and was in general use as long as the baptism of *adults* was continued. As to the baptism of *infants*, in England, in Catholic times, *sprinkling* was used in the cases of lay and conditional baptism, but when the sacrament was regularly administered in the church, a total or partial dipping was required. It was done in this way, in England, till the seventeenth century, when the missionaries, in times of persecution, having to baptize in private houses, adopted, for convenience, the practice of affusion, or *pouring*, which was prescribed in the Roman ritual, and is now in use amongst us.

Sponsors.—In ancient times, when an adult desired baptism, some person or persons were appointed to aid him with advice during his course of instruction, and to bear testimony in his favour when he came to the font. At an infant baptism no such offices were requisite. But now a godfather or a godmother, or both, assist at the baptism of a child, and are called *sponsors*, because they answer for it, as it cannot answer for itself. They also undertake to perform the part of spiritual parents if the natural parents should not live, or should neglect to instruct the child in the doctrine and practice of religion. Sponsors ought themselves to be able to do the duties they undertake, and be at least Easter communicants. They contract an affinity with the godchild and its parents, which prevents them marrying one or the other.

Baptism in Necessity.—A priest or deacon is the ordinary minister of this sacrament, but in case of necessity any man, woman, or child may, and ought to, administer it. Such baptism, whether it be given by a Catholic or heretic, Christian or infidel, is valid, provided he intended to do what the Church does, and Christ has ordained. It is probable that Ananias, who baptized St. Paul (Acts ix.), was a layman. But whether he were or not, the validity of baptism administered by lay persons was never disputed in the ancient Church. To render it lawful, two things are required—namely, the absence of the ordinary minister, and the danger of death on the part of the person to be baptized. The same person who says the words "I baptize thee," &c., must pour the water at the same time, in such a manner that the water may flow, and wet the skin. When baptism is given by a lay person, the person who best understands the ceremony should be preferred to another. The child thus baptized must be taken in due time to the church for the rest of the ceremonies, but the baptism is not repeated.

Necessity of Baptism.—Baptism is absolutely necessary for the salvation of all. Infant baptism has always been reputed valid and necessary, and has always been practised in the Church. The words of Christ, "Unless every one be born again of water and the Holy Ghost, he cannot enter into the kingdom of heaven" (St. John iii. 5), seem to imply the necessity of baptism, of a new spiritual birth, for every one, without exception, *who has been born* into the world. But though the Scripture is not at all clear upon this point, many who profess to follow Scripture alone, still retain the traditional practice of infant baptism. Faith was required in Scripture for the baptism of those who were adults, but the absence of it in infants cannot exclude them from the benefit of baptism, inasmuch as having been *born*, and born in original *sin*, they are included in the words of Christ, and also stand in need of it. Children who die without baptism can never see God—they are sometimes said to *be lost;* but it must carefully be noticed that this simply means that they have lost God, whom they can never see, but it does not signify, that they suffer any positive pain; it being probable, on the contrary, that they are in some sort of natural happiness, though not in heaven. God, in excluding them from heaven, does them no wrong, for they never had a right to go there; heaven is a place of happiness in no sense due to us by nature. The want of baptism when it cannot be received may in adults be supplied by the *desire* of it, joined with contrition, as also by martyrdom. How grievous must be the crime of those who, by careless delays or wilful neglect, allow a child to die without baptism, when they could and ought to procure it!

Ceremonies of Baptism. — These ceremonies, which allude either to the state of the pagan before, or to the duties of the Christian after baptism, were originally performed, some of them, during the instruction of the catechumen, and some during the administration of the sacrament. They are all now joined together in *one* administration.

The child or the person to be baptized stops at the porch or door of the church, of which he is not yet a member, but into which he desires and asks to be admitted. The priest asks the name of the person, which ought to be some really Christian name, the name of some saint, and not a name that is foolish, worldly, or heathenish. He then breathes on the face of the child (as Christ breathed on the face of the apostles, when He said, "Receive ye the Holy Ghost"), and bids the evil spirit depart, and give place to the Holy Ghost. He signs the sign of the cross on the forehead, to signify the duty of outward profession, and on the breast to signify the duty of believing in the heart, the faith, and law of Christ. The priest puts a few grains of blessed salt into the mouth of the child, for salt is in Scripture an emblem of wisdom, as it is here of that spiritual wisdom to be given by the Holy Ghost, the spirit of wisdom, in this sacrament. He then places the stole which he wears (the emblem of priestly power and jurisdiction) upon the child, and leads him into the church; the sponsor recites the Lord's Prayer and the Apostles' Creed. Christ on one occasion cured a blind man by touching his eyes with spittle, and in a similar way He cured a man deaf and dumb. In imitation of this action of our Lord, the priest slightly touches the ears and nostrils of the child, to signify that by the grace of the sacrament, his ears are opened to the doctrines of Christ, and his mouth to confess His faith. Then, after the triple renouncing of Satan, the child is anointed with holy oil on the breast and between the shoulders, to signify that he is dedicated to God, as things in the old law (and also in the new law) were consecrated to God by being anointed with oil. Then after a more explicit profession of faith in the three persons of the Blessed Trinity and in the Incarnation, the child is baptized. He is then anointed on the crown of the head with the holy oil called chrism; a white garment is presented to him as an emblem of that purity he should carry before the throne of God, by preserving his baptismal innocence. A lighted taper is presented to the newly baptized, as an emblem of the light of faith, in which he should always walk and live here, until he comes to the eternal light of heaven.

Conditional Baptism.—Baptism sometimes given when there is a doubt about a former baptism is called *conditional* baptism. Converts to the faith receive this kind of baptism, unless there happen to be a certainty of a valid baptism already given. This baptism is given privately and without the ceremonies.

CONFIRMATION.

Scriptural Evidence.—Our Saviour, in order to console the apostles, who were grieved at the prospect of His leaving them, told them that it was necessary that He should go, otherwise the Paraclete, the Holy Ghost, would not come. The completion of what was begun for man by Christ, was reserved as the work of the Holy Ghost. The apostles went back from Mount Olivet to Jerusalem, after Christ's ascension into heaven, and waited in prayer and retirement the coming of the promised Comforter. We know in what manner the Holy Ghost came down, and what a wonderful change He effected in the apostles. But the graces of that Holy Spirit were to be given to all Christians in all times, and that by a positive ordinance and the imposition of the hands of the bishops, who have succeeded to the office of the apostles. (See Part I., chapter xix., Conversion of the Samaritans, page 73.) There is no positive evidence from the Gospels that the *giving the Holy Ghost* or *Confirmation*, as we call it, was instituted by Christ. But the silence of the Gospels is no proof to the contrary, as they are not a full and complete record of the words and actions of our Saviour. Let any one consider the text referred to above (Acts viii. 14, &c.), the nature, object, and circumstances of the ceremony, and the effect it produced, and he will at once see that the apostles adopted it, either in obedience to the express injunction of their Divine Master, or at the suggestion of that Holy Spirit whom Christ had sent "to teach them all things, and to bring all things to their mind, whatsoever He had said to them" (John xiv. 26). The apostles could not by that ceremony have given the Holy Ghost, if Christ had not ordained it for that end. A bishop only is the ordinary minister of this sacred rite, as may be seen from the general practice of the Church, founded on the example of the apostles. The Samaritans had been converted and baptized by Philip the Deacon; but to give them the Holy Ghost, that is, to *confirm* them, the apostles Peter and John were despatched to Samaria from Jerusalem.

Effects of Confirmation.—Confirmation comes next in order after baptism, because it is considered as the completion of baptism, inasmuch as it confirms and perfects that work of grace which baptism began in us. In the first ages, the new Christian was led immediately from the font to the bishop, to receive confirmation. But now that infant baptism has taken the place of adult baptism, confirmation is given to persons who have reached the use of reason, and are about old enough to make their first communion—that is, from about the age of ten to fourteen. As the devil tries to rob Christians of their baptismal graces, especially at the time when infancy and childhood are past, and corrupt nature begins to be stronger, it is necessary to be more and more secured in the possession of those graces. This is done, not only by the ordinary means of grace, but by a sacrament specially ordained for securing us, and strengthening us, that is, *confirming* us more and more in grace, and is therefore called the sacrament of confirmation. In this sacrament we receive the Holy Ghost, that we, who have been made Christians in baptism, may be made strong and perfect Christians. By baptism we were made subjects of Christ's kingdom, by confirmation we are made soldiers, His companions in arms; in baptism we are made children of God, in confirmation we receive the strength of full-grown men.

Chrism.—The chrism which is used in the administration of confirmation is significant, as water is in baptism, of the grace produced by the sacrament. It is made of oil of olives, mixed with a fragrant balsam. Oil is made use of to soothe and heal wounds. It gives activity, strength, and vigour to the body. The wrestlers rubbed it on their bodies in ancient times before entering into the combat. Oil also burns and gives light. It therefore admirably expresses the effects of the graces of the Holy Ghost, which *heal, strengthen,* and *enlighten.* Hence, in the hymn to the Holy Ghost, we invoke Him as "the Living Spring, the Living Fire, Sweet Unction, and True Love." And again we say,—

> "O guide our minds with Thy blest *light,*
> With love our hearts inflame ;
> And with Thy *strength,* which ne'er decays,
> *Confirm* our mortal frame."

And again,—

> "Come, Holy Ghost, send down those beams," &c.
> "Thrice blessed Light, shoot home Thy darts," &c.
> "Our wounds and bruises heal," &c.
> "Warm with Thy fire our hearts of snow," &c.

The balsam which is mixed with the oil sends forth a

sweet smell, and possesses qualities which enable it to preserve things from corruption, and is therefore emblematical of those virtues, by which " we become the sweet odour of Christ in all places," and are preserved from the corruption of sin. Being anointed signifies also our renewed consecration to the service of God. We are anointed also in baptism. Priests, and all things consecrated to God, such as altars and chalices, are anointed with holy oil.

Directions for Confirmation.—A sponsor is required as in baptism. A sponsor contracts the same affinity as in baptism. The sponsor should be of the same sex as the person confirmed, and should not be the same as the sponsors in baptism. Each person is brought up by the godfather or godmother, who lays his or her hand on the shoulder of the child, while the bishop anoints him on the forehead with chrism. The Christian and sirname of the sponsor should be given, so as to be entered in the confirmation register. Some take another name in confirmation, in addition to the baptismal name, but this is not necessary. It would be a grievous sin to neglect to receive confirmation when a proper opportunity offers itself, especially in a country such as England, where the faithful have often to suffer so much from the scoffs, ridicule, and malice of unbelievers.

Preparation for Confirmation.—He who is about to be confirmed should recollect, that at his baptism he was unconscious of the blessing which he then received, and was ignorant of the obligations he then entered upon. But now he is fully aware of the covenant he made with God, and by asking for confirmation, that he may be enabled to fulfil that covenant, he openly admits and accepts afresh his baptismal engagements at the foot of the altar, and in presence of the people. He who is to be confirmed should, if he has the opportunity, endeavour to *learn afresh*, and better than before, his religious duties and the principles of faith. As " the Spirit of God will not enter into a malicious soul, nor dwell in a body subject to sin," it is clear that the candidate for confirmation must strive to purify his soul from sin, and especially his body from any sin of impurity; for our bodies, as St. Paul says, are the very "temples" of the Holy Ghost. He must listen to what the Spirit of God will teach him, and know that the Holy Spirit always leads in a direction contrary to the spirit of the world. As "the Father will give His good Spirit to them that ask it," *prayer*, and often repeated hymns and invocations of the Holy Ghost for days beforehand, should be a part of the preparation for confirmation. What can be done only once should be done well. This is the case with confirmation.

Ceremonies of Confirmation.—Those who are to be confirmed are assembled together, and kneel in their places before the bishop, who turns to them, and solemnly extends his hands towards them, and over them. He, with his hands thus extended, prays that they may receive the sevenfold grace of the Holy Ghost. They then go and kneel (each attended by his sponsor), one by one, before the bishop, who dips the thumb of his right hand in the holy chrism, and laying that hand upon the head of the person kneeling before him, he anoints his forehead with the chrism in the form of a cross, saying at the same time, "N, I sign thee with the sign of the cross, I confirm thee with the chrism of salvation, in the name of the Father, and of the Son, and of the Holy Ghost." This being done, the bishop gives a slight blow with his fingers on the cheek of the person confirmed, which ceremony was originally instituted to warn the neophyte (the newly baptized Christian), that, like his Master, he must expect to be buffeted and scorned by the enemies of His holy religion. At the same time, the bishop says, "Peace be with you," to imply that trial and persecution for justice sake will bring true peace to the soul, which the favour of the world cannot give, nor its hatred ever take away.

The bishop closes the ceremony with a general prayer, that the Holy Ghost will always dwell in their hearts, as in His temple, and he concludes with his solemn blessing. Those who have received this sacrament should thank God for the blessing they have received; they should remember that henceforth they, as soldiers of Christ, must be willing to do and suffer more for Christ's kingdom, and not be ashamed of their Prince and Master. They should also remember the warning (Ephes. iv. 30), "Grieve not the Holy Spirit of God, by whom you are sealed." They would "grieve" the Spirit of God, by relapsing into accustomed sins, by being ashamed of Truth, resisting or denying it, and by allowing themselves to be led in their lives by the spirit of the world.

THE HOLY EUCHARIST.

The Holy Eucharist is the true body and blood of our Saviour Jesus Christ, under the outward appearances of bread and wine. Christ promised that He would give His flesh to eat and His blood to drink; and we read in the sixth chapter of St. John the effect which that extraordinary promise had on the minds of the Jews who heard Him. (Read Part I., chapter xviii., Christ feeds the multitudes, page 67; read also Part I., chapter xviii., Institution of the Holy Eucharist, page 70.) It is sometimes said, that in the words, "This is My body," "This is My blood," the word "is" only means "signifies;" that Christ at His last supper was speaking, not *literally*, but *figuratively*. But the most important in our Saviour's words on that occasion is the pronoun "This." "*This*" which I hold in My hand "is My body," says Christ. He has indeed said, "I am the door," "I am the vine;" but when did He lay His hand on a door or a vine, and say, "*This* door or *this* vine am I," or, "I am this door," "I am this vine"? And when Christ used those expressions, "I am the door," "I am the vine," the Gospel positively tells us, that the one was spoken as a *parable*, and the other as a *comparison*. Again, St. Paul, after relating the words of the institution of the Holy Eucharist, says, "Therefore, whosoever shall eat this bread, or drink the chalice of the Lord *unworthily*, shall be guilty of the body and blood of the Lord, for he that eateth and drinketh unworthily eateth and drinketh judgment (that is, damnation) to himself, not discerning the body of the Lord" (1 Cor. xi. 27, 29). How could any one be guilty of our Lord's body and blood by eating mere bread, if the body and blood were not there? Or how could any one bring judgment on himself, for "not discerning the body of the Lord," if it were not there to be discerned?

Communion under one kind.—The body and blood, soul and divinity of Christ are present under *one* kind only, just as much as under both. For Christ is present in the Holy Eucharist in a *living* body, having risen from the dead to die no more, and therefore where His body is, there must also be His blood, His soul, His divinity. From this it follows, that they who communicate under *one kind only*, receive Christ just as much as if they communicated under both; for, in either case, they receive Christ whole and entire, there being no difference except in the *appearances*. The priest, however, must consecrate and receive under *both* kinds, whenever he celebrates Mass—that is, whenever he does what Christ commanded when He said, "Do ye this in memory of Me." This is necessary, because one object of the mass is to "show forth Christ's death"—that is, to represent the sacrifice and death of Christ on the cross, and the shedding of His sacred blood, and this is shown by the separate consecration of the bread and the wine.

The effects of the Holy Communion are plain from the words of Christ: "He that eateth My flesh and drinketh My blood, abideth in Me, and I in him" (John vi. 57). If Christ, the author of all grace and holiness, *abides with us*, what more can we desire or need? We see the effects of communion from the words of the antiphon of the Church: "O sacred banquet, in which Christ is received, the memory of His passion is renewed, the soul is filled with grace, and a pledge is given us of future glory." If we receive Christ worthily now in the Holy Sacrament, we shall have no reason to fear to meet Him, when He will come to judgment.

Preparation for Communion.—He who prepares for communion, must carefully learn what the Church teaches upon so great a mystery. He must, in so important an undertaking, put away improper motives; he must not act through custom, vanity, through fear of being noticed, or from the consideration of what others expect of him. He must desire to communicate in order to sanctify his soul, to overcome temptations, to acquire virtue, or to obtain some spiritual good for others. He must have been *fasting* from the midnight before the day of communion, so that if even by accident he should have swallowed the smallest particle of food or drink, he cannot on that day receive communion. Christians, in the beginning, used to communicate in the evening, but on account of certain abuses this practice was soon changed, so that even before the end of the first century the Christians held their meetings in the morning before sunrise, and received the Blessed Sacrament fasting. This regulation of fasting is intended as a mark of reverence to Him whom we are to receive. Only persons in danger of death can receive communion *without* fasting, and this not only once during their sickness, but oftener, if they continue dangerously ill for any length of time. It is then called the "*viaticum*," which word means provision for a journey—that is, the journey out of this world into the next.

The soul must be in a *state of grace*—that is, free from *mortal sin*. He, therefore, who is conscious of mortal sin, must, as a matter of necessity, approach to the sacrament of penance before he goes to communion. He that receives in *mortal sin* is guilty of sacrilege by profaning the body and blood of Christ. By merely being free from mortal sin, we escape the guilt of sacrilege, but derive comparatively little good. In order to receive with greater profit and advantage, every one should try to be as much as possible free from *venial sin*, and especially from deliberate and habitual venial sins, in which too many indulge without wishing or endeavouring to amend. He who receives with this *affection* to venial sin deprives himself of the great graces which he might otherwise have gained. This explains why so many receive communion very often, but seem so little improved, and perhaps are not better than some who receive less frequently. The grace received depends on the purity of the soul and the preparation we make use of.

On the *eve of communion* a person should be more than usually retired and recollected, having his mind fixed on the great work he is about to perform. The more *immediate* preparation for communion consists in the actual devotion which a person should endeavour to have a little before communion, during the Mass; and for this purpose the devotions set down in prayer-books to be said "before communion" are very useful. A person also should be up in good time in the morning, and in his place in church, so as to have time for good thoughts, and not expose himself to be hurried and distracted.

At Communion.—When the time for communion has arrived (that is, at the "Domine non sum dignus"), those who are to communicate go slowly towards the altar, and there kneel down. Then the communicant should gather together all the devout acts which he has been making, and offer them and his whole soul to his Divine Redeemer. Persons in receiving communion should hold up their heads, open their mouths sufficiently, resting the tongue on the lower lip, in such a manner that the priest should not have the least difficulty in safely giving them communion. Many communicants fail in these particulars, and cause considerable difficulty and inconvenience to the priest who communicates them. After receiving they return to their places to perform their devotions after communion. Other more minute directions are often given by those who prepare children and others for their *first* communion.

After Communion.—No moments can be more precious to a Christian soul than those which follow a worthy communion; and upon the manner in which these are spent much of the fruit of communion depends. Every one, therefore, should spend as much time in devotion as he conveniently can, and no one without the *most urgent necessity* should spend less than a quarter of an hour. If a person could spend some time in recollection and prayer without the use of a book, it would be better, but for fear of wandering thoughts, a person can read the prayers set down for "after communion." Those who cannot read should sometimes have the prayers for "before and after communion" read to them, as these would show the spirit and the kind of devotion they should then aim at, and would assist them in their efforts. *During the day of communion* Christians should be more than usually thoughtful and careful, and not be ready to mingle too easily in their ordinary dissipations, for fear of losing any of the graces they may have gained.

THE SACRIFICE OF THE MASS.

The most solemn act of public worship is the sacrifice of the Mass. It is called a *sacrifice* (sacrifice means an offering made to God); and in the Mass there is made to God, the oblation of the body and blood of our Saviour, in remembrance of His death upon the cross. It was foretold that when the Jewish sacrifices should be abolished (being only figures and shadows of *One* to come), a pure oblation should be offered among the Gentiles, in every place, from the rising of the sun to the going down of the same (Mal. i. 11). Christ is that pure and holy victim, who was offered once in a bloody manner on Mount Calvary, and is offered daily, in an unbloody manner, on thousands of altars throughout the world, in the sacrifice of the Mass.

Scriptural Evidence.—The first Mass was celebrated by our blessed Lord, on the night before His passion, when He gave to His apostles to eat of His body, and drink of His blood. He was a Priest for ever, after the order of Melchisedec; and on that occasion, according to the language of all Christian antiquity, by the separate consecration of the bread and wine, He instituted the Christian sacrifice, offering to His Eternal Father, His body, which on the morrow would be given for us, and His blood, which on the same morrow would be shed for the remission of sins. Nor was this all; after the institution of the sacrifice He instituted also the Christian priesthood, commanding His apostles, and through them their successors in the ministry, to do what they had seen Him do, as a perpetual memorial and representation of His death upon the cross. "Christ," says St. Cyprian, "was the High Priest of God the Father, having first offered Himself a sacrifice to the Father, and ordered the same to be done in memory of Himself. The priest stands, therefore, in the place of Christ; and if he does what Christ did, he offers in the church a full and perfect sacrifice to God the Father." Similar language perpetually occurs in all the old Christian writers, even so far back as the first century. With all of them the Mass is a sacrifice, and Jesus Christ the victim.

Perhaps it may be asked, how then it happens that this sacred rite is not called a sacrifice, in the tracts of the New Testament. It should be remembered, as has been noticed before, that those tracts are not records of Christian doctrine, or worship. If they ever mention such matters, it is incidentally, and in covered language; for the writers had learned from their Master not to cast their pearls before swine (Matt. vii. 6); they practised the lesson which they taught also to their disciples, to conceal the mysteries of their worship from the knowledge and the derision of the profane. Yet they occasionally made allusions to the sacrifice, which were perfectly intelligible to those, for whose use they wrote. Thus St. Paul, having remarked that the eating of the Jewish sacrifices profited nothing, adds, "We have an altar, whereof they are not at liberty to eat, who serve the tabernacle" (Heb. xiii. 10), evidently intimating that Christians had a right to eat of the victim sacrificed on the Christian altar, as the Jews ate of the victims sacrificed on their altars.

Ceremonies of the Mass.—The *essence* of the Mass consists in the *consecration* of bread and wine into Christ's body and blood, and in the *communion* which takes place towards the end of the Mass. The other prayers and ceremonies which are used, though not *necessary* parts of the sacrifice, have been ordained, most of them, by the apostles themselves, or by their immediate successors, for the greater solemnity of the divine worship, and to assist and increase the devotion of the faithful. The Mass is the worship of the Christians of old ; if any of the ceremonies appear strange, it is because they had their origin ages ago, and are not of modern date. They continually remind, the learned especially (who are able to see the resemblance), of the habits and manners of nations which have long ceased to exist. This is the manner in which our fathers worshipped, when they first embraced the faith, and they received this manner of worship from men who had derived it from the apostles of Christ. A worship or a ritual made up in modern times may suit the ideas of the present age, but it cannot be the worship of the primitive Church. St. John in the Revelations, in a vision, saw a solemn worship, going on in heaven, the same which was in his time carried on upon earth, but the only worship now on earth which resembles that heavenly and primitive worship is the worship of the Catholic Church, which has brought down to these times the same rites which the holy evangelist beheld in the courts above.

Those things which to many seem strange, and which require some explanation, were first ordained by the Almighty in the Old Law, and were made use of in the divine worship in Jerusalem. The Church has adopted some of these usages and introduced them into Christian worship, especially into its most solemn act of worship, the sacrifice of the Mass. The Christian Church in arranging her ceremonial, certainly could not follow a better copy than that which was set by the Almighty Himself.

The Asperges.—The Jewish priests had to wash their hands and feet in a great vessel of water before they went in to minister at the altar, and the Jewish people washed their hands before they went to pray ; hence that word of the Psalmist (Ps. xxv.), " I will wash my hands among the innocent, and I will encompass thine altar, O Lord." The primitive Christians used to wash their hands before going to pray. For this purpose, fountains were made to spring up just before the door of the church to give an abundant supply of water. Besides this, in imitation of Christ, the early Christians used to wash their hands and feet also, before the celebration of the Eucharist. From all this it will be easy to understand that text of St. Paul (Heb. x. 12): "Let us draw near to the altar of holies; having our hearts *sprinkled* from an evil conscience, and *our bodies washed with clean water*." It is easy to see the Jewish custom and the ancient Christian usage still continued in the Catholic Church, in the vessel of water placed at the entrance of the church, and in the ceremony of sprinkling water on the people at the commencement of the solemn service. In allusion to this ritual observance of the Jewish Church, David prayed, and the Christian Church during this ceremony sings (*Asperges* me, Domine, &c.), "Thou shalt sprinkle me, O Lord, with hyssop and I shall be cleansed, Thou shalt wash me and I shall be made whiter than snow." Whether therefore we take water at the porch of the church, or are sprinkled with it at the ceremony of the "*Asperges*" before Mass, we are reminded of God's holiness and our own sinfulness; we pray that our sins may be washed away, and that we may worship at God's holy altar with the innocent in hand, and the clean of heart.

Incense.—God ordered that a certain kind of incense should be compounded and used in *His* service, and no one was ever to make or use the like; it was to be offered morning and evening at the golden altar. The use of incense was continued in the Christian Church, and is considered as an emblem of devout prayer, and is expressive of the desire which we have, that the sighs of our heart should ascend to God's throne in heaven, as the sweet perfume rises from the fragrant censer and envelopes His throne on earth. Therefore the Church prays, " May this incense ascend to Thee, O Lord, and may Thy mercy descend upon us;" and with David, " Let my prayer be directed, O Lord, as incense in Thy sight."

Lights.—A very remarkable object in the Jewish

sanctuary must have been the golden candlestick. Over the seven branches into which it was shaped, were suspended seven lamps of gold, and the oil to feed these lamps was of the purest oil of olives, and the high priest himself had to attend to them, that they should never be extinguished day or night. The Jews also had the custom of lighting many lamps to express their joy, and to show their religious devotion on their great festivals. This will account for the same custom having been introduced into Christianity, it will explain why lights are used in various parts of the Liturgy, in the administration of the sacraments, and why a lamp burns day and night before the blessed sacrament. Besides this, light is spoken of in Scripture as the emblem of all that is good and holy in heaven or earth. "God is light," says St. John, "and in Him there is no darkness." Christ is "the true light that enlighteneth every man that cometh into the world." Men were called upon to believe in the "light" that they may be the children of the light; the portion of the saints is in "light," the Gospel is called the admirable "light," and the "light" of our good works must shine before men. While "light" in Scripture is expressive of prosperity and joy, of every earthly and heavenly good; "darkness" is expressive of adversity and of every evil both in earth and hell. No wonder, then, that after what we read in Scripture of the use of lights in the temple, and of the beautiful images drawn from "light," that the Church, following the practice of the first ages, still continues to use symbolic lights in her services, to which are associated so many holy and cheerful thoughts.

Sacred Vestments.—God also ordained both the shape and material of the vestments to be worn by the priests and Levites. The ordinary Levite wore a linen garment, probably very much corresponding with the modern surplice, but we read that the high priest wore an ample vestment of the colour of hyacinth, which extended to his feet; to the extremity of this were attached pomegranates and bells intermixed to the number of seventy-two; then came the *ephod* of rich embroidery fastened on the breast with two clasps of precious stones; and over the ephod was the *pectoral*, covered with twelve precious stones; and around his forehead was a circlet of gold, on which was engraved " Holiness to the Lord." After such a precedent as this it cannot be a matter of surprise that in the Catholic Church *sacred vestments* should have been appointed and ordained for the use of bishops, priests, and the inferior ministers of the Church when they are ministering at God's altar.

Benediction.—These observances of incense, lights, &c., are used not only at Mass, but at other times when the Holy Sacrament is carried in solemn procession, as also at the rite of benediction or exposition of the Blessed Sacrament, when Christ at His earthly throne, the holy altar, like a king, receives the honour and the homage which His subjects have come to offer Him. On these occasions the altar is more than usually decorated with flowers and lights, a cloud of incense fills the sanctuary, and the priest lifts up the vessel called the " remonstrance," containing the sacred host, over the head of the people, to give them the blessing of Jesus Christ Himself. The ringing of the bell gives notice of this for the benefit of those who may not be able to see the altar; and the people bow down in silent adoration. A bell is rung occasionally at different parts of the Mass also, to awaken the attention of the faithful, and to give notice, especially in large churches where all cannot see the altar, or hear the voice of the priest, of certain portions of the sacred service, in which all should especially join.

At Benediction, hymns in honour of the Blessed Sacrament are sung with other suitable Litanies and Antiphons. What devotion at home can compare with the Mass and the benediction where we kneel in the very presence of Christ, and He is there Himself to bless His people who have come to visit and adore Him?

The Latin Language is used in the Mass and other services, because at the time Christianity was introduced into the western parts of Europe, Latin was the language most generally known and spoken; and in this language, therefore, the Liturgy began. For many reasons, too numerous to detail here, it has been thought wise not to alter the ancient language of the Church, either to suit the barbarous dialects of the middle ages, or to attempt to follow the changeable character of all modern languages. In the same way the Greek language was used in the eastern countries, and is continued to this day. When the Jews lost their original language in Babylon, it was still retained in their religious offices; they used a *dead language,* and an unknown tongue to the common people, and Christ must often have been present at such services. Notice also that the *striking of the breast* is an old scriptural practice, and is expressive of sorrow and contrition of heart. In going into a church, and especially in passing before the altar, we *genuflect*—that is, we bend the right knee to the ground in homage to Him who is there in His holy "tabernacle."

Parts of the Mass.—To comply with the obligation of hearing Mass, it is not necessary that a person should use any particular set of prayers, but it is sufficient if his mind be kept free from wilful distractions, and be engaged in *good thoughts of any kind* directed to the worship of God and the improvement of his own soul. An admirable way for a Christian to hear Mass is to follow the priest in the different parts, and to join his intention and his thoughts with the spirit of each part of the Mass as it proceeds. He should also notice the division of the Mass into four parts, and know the substance and general meaning of each part.

As to the *first* part, after the preparatory ceremony of the "Asperges," the priest goes to the foot of the altar, and, feeling his unworthiness, he in the "Confiteor" acknowledges his sins before heaven and earth. He then, having gone up to the altar (in a solemn Mass), *incenses* it, and when the "Kyrie eleison," which during this time is being sung by the choir, is finished, he intones the first words of the hymn which is then sung, "Gloria in excelsis Deo." Whilst the "Gloria," and also the "Credo," are being sung, all sit down, and every one may either devoutly listen to the singing, and follow the words, or he may employ himself with any good thoughts which suit the occasion. Music and singing are intended to be listened to, or joined in, in the hope that this may increase devotion, and not be a hindrance to it. After the "Gloria," &c., the "Epistle" is read, so called because generally taken from one of the Epistles of the New Testament, and the "Gospel" is solemnly sung by the deacon, accompanied with lights and incense, and all stand up to show respect to the holy words, and to express their willingness to do all that is enjoined. Then comes the sermon, or instruction to the people, after which is made the public profession of faith by the singing of the Nicene Creed. Thus ends the *first part* of the Mass, which is evidently a preparation for the more sacred parts that are to follow.

The *second part* of the Mass is called the *Offertory*. It is so called because the people then used to bring to the altar offerings of wine and bread, which were to be used in the Mass, and which the priest then offered to God. Besides these things, other offerings, wax lights and money, &c., used to be brought by the faithful, according to their means and their devotion, for the maintenance of the clergy, of the poor, and of the Church. After in ancient times receiving the various offerings, and again incensing the altar, the priest washes his hands, and concludes the *second part* of the Mass by a prayer said in secret, which was the prayer said *over* the various offerings, and therefore it often refers to them. At the Offertory now, the collection is made of money for the maintenance of the Church and its ministers.

After having prayed in secret, the priest chants the "Preface," which is an introduction to *the third* and most solemn part of the Mass, during which the consecration takes place. In the "Preface" he invites the faithful to lift up their hearts to God, to praise and bless Him, and to join with angels and archangels, who never cease their heavenly canticles. At the end of the "Preface," at the "Sanctus," the little bell rings to give notice that "the Canon"—that is, the words and prayers handed down from the apostles, and which have never been changed — is about to be said. The word "Canon" means a fixed *law* or *rule*. Again the bell rings to signify that the words of *consecration* are *about* to be pronounced, and again almost immediately to give notice that those mysterious words *have been* uttered. The priest kneels down, and the faithful bow down to adore Christ upon the altar, who by those sacred words of consecration, first uttered by Christ Himself, has become present. In the meantime, all throughout the church is hushed in silence.

The priest after a time chants the "Pater Noster," or Lord's Prayer, which is the beginning of the *fourth part* of the Mass, or the Communion. The priest receives communion, and the bell rings again to signify to the people that the time for communion has arrived. All who do not actually receive communion should make a *spiritual communion*—that is, a communion in spirit and desire. At the conclusion of the Mass, the priest dismisses the people, and gives them his blessing.

Penance.

In the 10th Article of the Creed (see page 123) we have seen that in the Church of God there is a "forgiveness of sins" through the power once given by Christ to the apostles. We have there seen the nature of mortal and venial sin, and that the sacrament of Penance is the ordained means by which forgiveness is conveyed to our souls. We have now to consider the parts of the sacrament of Penance.

Scriptural Evidence on Confession. — All the first Christians were converts from Judaism or Paganism, who, being instructed by the apostles, received the sacrament of Baptism, and in and by that sacrament the remission of their former sins. St. Paul, in his Epistles to such Christians, continually reminds them that they had been justified, not by the *works* which they had done, whilst they were Jews or Pagans, but by faith in Christ, which had brought them to the grace of Baptism.

These Christians had already obtained, in and by Baptism, the remission of their sins committed *before* Baptism; but how could they obtain the remission of sin committed *after* Baptism? To this the New Testament returns no very clear and decisive answer. As the several portions of it were written for persons who were living in the practice of the Christian religion, the practice of confession would only be referred to *incidentally*, and accordingly, though there is sufficient to *imply* that it was of divine institution, yet that doctrine is nowhere expressly recorded. It appears necessarily included in the power of "forgiving or retaining sins;" for how could any one exercise that power without a knowledge of the spiritual state of him that applied, or how obtain such knowledge, but from his own free *confession* of his sins? It may be said that the confession spoken of in Scripture may only mean a general acknowledgment of sinfulness, a private confession to God, or a public confession in presence of a congregation. To decide this we have only to consider what was the *practice* established by the apostles. Of this there can be no doubt, when we find in the most ancient Christian documents, that confession to priests, sometimes in private, sometimes in public, *universally* prevailed. Now a practice so humbling to human pride as that of confession could never have been introduced and propagated throughout the *whole* Church on any authority less than the authority of the apostles.

Examination of Conscience.—As he who applies to a physician is moved to do so in order to seek a remedy for the maladies which afflict his body, so also the troubles and the maladies of the soul—that is, our sins—oblige us to have recourse to a spiritual physician in the sacrament of Penance. But as it is not sufficient, in going to a physician, that the patient should merely make *general* complaints of bad health, but must say exactly where and in what manner he is afflicted, so also, in going to confession, a mere general accusation of sinfulness is of no use; but we must know ourselves what our sins are, and their circumstances, that we may be able to give an account of them, and so find a remedy, and seek "absolution" from them. No one can give any proper account of his sins to another without having first made up his own account of them, and having thoroughly considered them. The first step is called the *examination of conscience*. It is a spiritual exercise which should be done more or less *every day*, in the evening, with a view to find out the sins of the past day; but, however much it may have been omitted on ordinary days, it *must* be carefully done when any one is preparing for the confession of his sins. As we can do nothing of ourselves at any time, but always require the grace of God, this is especially the case when preparing for a sacrament. As we are so easily deceived in the opinion we have of ourselves, and as God's judgments are so different from man's, we must pray that our own self-love may not impose upon us, and that we may see and know our sins, as God sees and knows them, and as *we* shall know them in the hour of our judgment. This is the object of that prayer which is put down in prayer books, called a "Prayer to Implore the Divine Assistance in Order to make a Good Confession," and which is recommended to be said not merely once, but several times—that is, for some days before confession.

Directions for Examination of Conscience.—When a person has earnestly implored the light of God to know his sins, he should then begin his examination. Many sins will at once come into his mind as being the most grievous, and these he may at once specially consider, as to the number of times he may have committed them, and any circumstance that may make them worse. But a person should follow a *method* of self-examination (especially if it be for a general confession), and go through the commandments of God and the Church, the seven capital, or deadly sins, and the particular duties of his own state of life. For this purpose he may carefully read through the list of questions put down in the Prayer Book, as these may help to bring many things to his mind, both as to duties omitted and sins committed. Besides this, as a help to memory, persons should go through the general occupation of each day, the persons he is engaged with, the places he has to be in. A child may perhaps be helped in examination by considering his duties as chiefly threefold—namely, his *home* duties, *school* duties, and *holy* duties.

A person should take sufficient time for examination so as to feel tolerably clear as to the nature of his sins ; the *number of times* they have been committed, or (in confessions of a long period) *about* the number of times, or the length of time, the habit of a certain sin lasted. It is not sufficient to say, I have cursed,—I have stolen,—I have told lies,—I have been vexed, &c.; nor is it much use to add " a few times," or " a good many times." Sins of any consequence should be confessed with the *precise* number of times.

Again, to make a *useful* and very often a valid confession, a person should aim at confessing the *amount*, the *extent*, and the *greatness* of his sin ; therefore to confess the above-named sins, even with the exact number of times, still leaves the confession very incomplete. Thus, an act of disobedience may be trifling, or it may be most grievous ; a wilful distraction may be for a minute or two, or it may last the whole of a mass of obligation ; an evil thought may be for a few seconds, or it may have been entertained for days, and have led to other evil consequences ; anger may have been short, or it may have been violent, and lasted for hours and days. A Mass missed on a Sunday may have been, through positive idleness, or for the sake of pleasure, or it may have been through some difficulty, but that not quite sufficient to have excused a person's absence. A Mass omitted through a clearly sufficient cause is not to be confessed at all, as it is no sin. Only sin, and the amount of sin, is the subject-matter of confession. Sins, therefore, great and little, must not be confessed in the same form of words, as they would all sound alike, but an attempt must be made in the case of greater sins to convey to the mind of the confessor the extent and greatness of the sins committed. The use of some such words as " great " or " little," " grievous " or " trifling," will often express sufficiently the difference between one sin and another.

Doubtful sins should be confessed as doubtful, and, if necessary, advice should be asked as to future conduct. The only sins which we are absolutely bound to confess are those which we in our conscience *believe to be mortal.* But though this is sufficient to escape the guilt of sacrilege, of course it is by no means sufficient for any one who would confess with real profit, and with a view to his advancement in virtue.

Contrition.—After we have carefully examined our conscience, and discovered the sins of which we are guilty, the next great work, and the most important of all, is to be truly sorry for them. If we are sorry for sin, all the rest is sure to be well done. Confession may sometimes be impossible, or we may not be able to discover all our sins, or perhaps we may forget to confess some of them, but this, if not wilful, will not injure us, provided we are truly sorry for them all. *Contrition* is absolutely necessary, and without it, in no case will our sins be forgiven us. If, therefore, a person confesses his sins, *knowing* that he has not true sorrow for them, such a confession, followed by absolution, would be *sacrilegious.* But if a person comes to confession, really believing in his heart that he has sorrow for his sins, while in reality he has not, such a confession would be *without effect*; there would be no remission of sins, but there would be no sacrilege, and no new sin committed, because such a person had a sincere desire and intention of doing all that was required of him. It is important to notice that besides confessions positively good and bad, there may be confessions null and without effect.

Qualities of Contrition.—The word "contrition" means a *breaking to pieces,* and consequently by a "contrite heart" is meant a heart *broken with grief* for sin. The very meaning of the word, therefore, shows that sorrow for sin must not be a mere passing emotion of sorrow, but must be something deep and *earnest*, which really reaches the heart. 1. It should be a *predominant* or a *sovereign* sorrow — that is, a sorrow that rules and holds dominion in the soul; it must be stronger than anything else in the soul, so that we must have the *will* to do or suffer anything, rather than commit a grievous sin. The *feeling* of sorrow need not be stronger than any other feeling, because our *feelings* about natural things are *always* keener than our feelings are about things supernatural. But, for all that, our sorrow for sin may and must be sovereign and predominant in the soul, though it may not show itself by what we feel. 2. Sorrow for sin must also be *universal*—that is, it must extend to all our sins; it would not do to be sorry for one sin and to love another. 3. Our sorrow must not be natural, but *supernatural*. It would be a mere natural sorrow if it arose from the consideration that it had injured us in health, good name, or in some other temporal good. It is *supernatural* when it comes from motives and considerations of God and the next life. But there is a difference even in the value of supernatural motives. It is easy to see that the more our sorrow is referred to *God alone*, and the less it springs from *selfish* considerations, the higher and the more perfect it is. Thus, that sorrow which comes chiefly from the consideration that by sin we have offended a God infinitely good and great in Himself, is a more exalted sorrow than that which comes chiefly from the consideration, that by sin we lose heaven and deserve hell. The first is sometimes called *contrition*, or *perfect contrition*, the second is sometimes called *attrition*, or *imperfect contrition*. The first even remits sin without the sacrament of penance, when it cannot be had; the second requires the grace of the sacrament for forgiveness. It is clear, then, that in the prayers and meditations made use of by us to obtain contrition, we should always, more and more, with heart and mind, strive to base our sorrow on the thought of a good God offended, more than on the consideration of ourselves injured and ruined.

Firm Purpose of Amendment.—It is quite clear that a proper sorrow for sin, besides being founded on the right motives, will also be accompanied with a resolution of amendment. Sorrow could not be real, unless we were determined to abstain from doing that for which we are sorry. Any one who has such a resolution will at once avoid all places, persons, and occasions which are likely to lead him into sin again. But if any one, after he has professed to be sorry for sin, lives as carelessly as before, mixes with the same companions, goes to the same places which have been the scene of his former sins, he at once shows that his sorrow was very doubtful, and will probably fall again very quickly into his usual sins. A man is bound to quit those occasions which are continually leading him into grievous sin, even though it may be a great loss to him in worldly things, for it will not profit him to gain the whole world and yet lose his soul by offending God. Merely to go without necessity into the known occasion of sin, is itself a sin, more or less grievous, according to the nature of the danger; even if that sin which commonly follows is not committed. It is evidently sinful for any one wilfully to expose himself to the temptation of sinning and offending God.

Confession.—When a person has examined his conscience according to the directions given above, and has by prayer and by applying himself to various considerations, endeavoured to fill his heart with a true sorrow for sin, he is then ready to go to the confessional. The method of confession is set down in all prayer-books, and as every person who can read should have a prayer-book, and ought to be accustomed to make use of it, the method of confession is purposely omitted here. The confession should be made with the utmost *sincerity*, with no intention or desire to keep anything back, and then there will probably, in this point, be no defect of any consequence to be feared. However shameful or grievous any sin may be, a penitent knows that the confessor could not, to save his own life, reveal the smallest tittle of what he has been told in confession. The confession should be made in *few words*, but sufficient to make the *number* and the gravity of the sin known to the confessor. A person should not make mere *general* accusations or complaints of himself, such as "I have not loved God as much as I ought," "I have not been sufficiently charitable," "I have not prayed or prepared for the sacraments with proper devotion." Every one should *prepare* what he has to say, and not lose time by making long pauses, nor wait to find out his sins while in the confessional, nor expect the confessor to ask him a number of questions. *Ignorant* persons may have to be asked or instructed, but well-instructed persons ought not to require it. Having said all that he can remember, the penitent finishes with the words, "For these, and all my other sins," &c. If a person should have something to confess which he feels a special difficulty in mentioning, he may often relieve himself by saying that there is something that he feels it difficult to confess, that so the confessor may encourage or advise him.

Absolution.—After the penitent has to the best of his power confessed his sins, the confessor, unless he sees reason to the contrary, pronounces the words of absolution. These words, in substance, are: "I absolve thee from thy sins in the name of the Father and of the Son and of the Holy Ghost." If the confessor sees clear reason to doubt of the real sincerity of the penitent, or whether a due preparation has been made, he defers absolution in order that the penitent may, after putting himself in better dispositions, return to receive absolution validly or with more profit. If a penitent makes no improvement and amendment in sins that are grievous, and refuses to use all remedies; if he will not avoid the occasions of his usual sins, refuses to repair an injustice done to another, continues to bear malice in his heart to a neighbour; he is not fit for absolution, and such an absolution if deceitfully obtained, would only be a new sin added to the others. If any advice should be given to the penitent on some particular point of his confession, he must pay special attention to it, as such instruction given to the individual is of far more consequence to him than the general instructions addressed to a whole congregation can be. No special instruction or exhortation is necessary for persons in their ordinary confessions, who are in the habit of frequenting the sacraments, and often cannot be given when there is a crowd of penitents waiting.

The Penance.—When absolution is given, the confessor enjoins the penitent some good works to be performed, ordinarily a few prayers. This is called "the penance," as the *third* part of this sacrament is called "satisfaction." This easy "penance," which is given, is to signify to the penitent, that he must be willing not only to do this but other works of penance, in order to satisfy God for his sins, and to pay that debt of temporal punishment which often remains due to sin after the guilt or the eternal punishment has been remitted by the sacramental absolution. The penitent should speedily perform, in the manner prescribed, the penance which has been enjoined. Very easy penances are given now, for fear lest otherwise many should be kept from the use of the sacrament of penance, should continue in their sins, and perhaps die in the guilt of them and be lost. Other penitential works are left to the private devotion of the penitent, and he can also continually seek the spiritual benefit of the "indulgences" which the Church grants.

After Confession.—The penitent besides performing his "penance" or some part of it should after confession consider seriously the advice which has been given him, he should think over the good resolutions which he has made for the time to come, and *how* he is to put them into effect; *where* he may be most likely to fail, and in *what manner* he is to guard against any possible failure. He should not leave the church or chapel till he has begged of God, again and again, the grace of perseverance in virtue, and strength to save him from any relapse into sin. He should consider and fear the evils of relapse, and determine that if he should fall again into any such sins, which he has just confessed and repented of, he will *without delay* at once return to repentance and confession; and not allow the enemy to drive or tempt him to remain in sin. If some sin should come into his mind which he had forgotten to confess, it will be sufficient if it be mentioned in his next confession as a sin *forgotten* in the last.

Indulgences.—The doctrine of indulgences, the nature and benefit of them, requires a special explanation. It is a subject which requires explanation in this place, because an indulgence is connected with the satisfaction which we have to make to God for our sins, and also because an indulgence is a *supplement* to the sacrament of penance, inasmuch as it completes what had before been left unfinished, by removing the temporal punishment which might still remain due to us after absolution had been given. According to the doctrine of the ancient Church, the convert to Christianity was freed at once from all sin, and all punishment of sin, and this is that gratuitous justification given in baptism which the Scripture speaks of. But if the convert afterwards relapsed into the sins he had renounced, he was subjected to a course of penance, partly in satisfaction to God, partly in satisfaction to the Church for the scandal he had given to it. This discipline prevailed for some centuries, but in course of time it was thought advisable to abandon it, and only a small portion of it remains in the "satisfaction" still enjoined by the priest in the sacrament of penance. No satisfaction which the sinner offers to God for sin can be an injury to Christ, while he knows that his satisfaction can be of no avail, except through the satisfaction of Christ; otherwise prayer itself would be injurious to the mercy of God, and to the atonement offered by our Saviour. "Indulgences" grew out of the discipline just mentioned; that is, the bishops used to shorten the time or lessen the severity of the penitential course, as circumstances seemed to require. But in the imposition, as well as in the relaxation of such penance, they had the same object in view, namely, the *spiritual* benefit of the repentant sinner, and this benefit consisted in the relaxation of that punishment which the justice of God would have inflicted upon the sinner in this life or the next. In the exercise of both these powers, they were justified by the promise of our Saviour, " Whatsoever you shall bind on earth shall be bound also in heaven, and whatsoever you shall loose on earth shall be loosed also in heaven" (Matt. xviii. 18). Such a power has always been exercised in the Church, and therefore must exist, otherwise the Church would have fallen into grievous error. This consideration is sufficient for a Catholic who believes in the Church of Christ, though he may often be perplexed how to answer many questions that may arise upon this subject. This power which is lodged in the Church seems like a *sacramental* power, and in a manner the perfection and completion of the sacrament of penance. If non-Catholics believe that any one by a mere private repentance is at once saved from hell, and capable of being admitted into heaven, they need have no difficulty in believing in the Catholic system of repentance and salvation. It requires all their system requires, and in addition to that, the humbling confession of sin and a twofold exercise of power on the part of the Church, the one to remove the eternal, and another to remove the temporal punishment.

The effect of absolution validly received is to free us from the eternal punishment of hell, but commonly there remains some expiation to be made by our own voluntary acts of atonement here, or else hereafter in purgatory. In proportion to the fervour of our repentance, more or less temporal punishment remains; but whatever that unknown amount of debt may be, it is removed by the faithful performance of the penance enjoined by the priest in confession, by prayer, fasting, and alms-deeds, and by all other meritorious works. The other means of lessening or totally removing that temporal punishment, is by the use of indulgences which attaches to our works of piety the treasures of the satisfaction of our Lord and His saints. The practical duty, then, of an earnest Catholic is to strive to gain as many indulgences as possible, being fully assured that he is thereby availing himself of the benefit of all the power which the Church possesses, to remove everything from the soul that can hinder his speedy entrance into heaven. Though no one can ever be sure that he gains a *plenary* indulgence, every one may feel sure that he can gain many partial indulgences, and that his efforts will be far more abundantly rewarded than they deserve. It is sufficient to know that a *partial* indulgence is not of so much advantage as a *plenary* indulgence, for the last, if gained, would cause a person immediately after death to pass directly into heaven, without the delay of purgatory. The most important plenary indulgence is that which is given to us on our deathbed by the attendant priest, after the Holy Viaticum and Extreme Unction have been received, and is called the " Last Blessing."

Extreme Unction.

The name Extreme Unction, or " Last Anointing," has been given to this sacrament. We have been anointed in baptism, in confirmation, and priests in holy orders also, but this sacrament being for persons dangerously ill, it is called " Extreme Unction," or the " Last Anointing." It is mentioned in St. James (v. 14)—" Is any man sick among you? let him bring in the priests of the church, and let them pray over him, anointing him with oil, in the name of the Lord." This sacrament must be received by a person in the state of grace, and, therefore, if necessary, he must make his confession and be absolved. Then, if judged convenient, he should receive the Holy Communion, called in this case, the *Holy Viaticum*.

Ceremonies of Extreme Unction.—At a convenient time before the viaticum, or more commonly after it, extreme unction is administered. The priest, after sprinkling the sick person and the attendants with holy water, says the " Confiteor," and another preparatory prayer, and then administers the sacrament. He anoints in the form of a cross the different senses of the body—namely, the eyes, ears, nostrils, mouth, hands, and feet. At each anointing he says this prayer: " May our Lord, by this holy anointing and His own most tender mercy, pardon thee, whatever sin thou hast committed, by thy sight," or "by thy hearing," &c., according to the particular sense which is anointed. During this time the sick person should unite with him in spirit, by begging with deep contrition that same pardon for himself. The priest concludes by imploring Divine blessings for the sick person, the remission of his sins, spiritual consolation, corporal relief, &c.

Effects of Extreme Unction.—The effects of extreme unction are declared by St. James,—"The prayer of faith shall save the sick man, and the Lord will raise him up, and if he be in sins, they shall be forgiven him." Extreme unction strengthens the soul against the temptations of the enemy, who knowing now that his time is short, tries more than ever to prevail against us. It cleanses the soul from the remains of sin, gives us patience and resignation in the trials of sickness and death; and (when it is expedient for the good of the soul) it restores the sick person to health, of which last effect many singular instances have been often observed.

Directions for the time of Sickness and Death.—All Christians are bound during the days of health to keep in order their affairs, both temporal and spiritual; but this duty is still more urgent, if any one is overtaken with a dangerous sickness. A man who dies with his worldly affairs not put in order, may leave many injustices behind him, which will never be set right, and many causes of quarrel among his relatives and his family. Those who have neglected too much the claims of charity and of religion in life and health, would do well, on coming to the end of life, to make up even by their last will and testament, if necessary, for their past deficiencies. It is not wise to trust that surviving relatives will execute their dying *wishes* notwithstanding the most positive promises. They who intend any good to charity or religion should, by guarding against *legal* informality, put it out of the power of needy or greedy relatives to get possession of what was never intended for them. Those especially who have neglected their salvation in time of health, must lose no time in severe sickness. The friends of a person who is dangerously ill may and ought to feel that the precise time and manner of acquainting a person with his danger, is a question of prudence; but one thing is unpardonable, that they should ever, by all manner of lies, assure the person of coming health, when there is not the remotest chance of recovery, and thus, by deceit, prevent the dying man from making any proper preparation to appear before God. Though extreme unction may alarm some very timid persons, yet there can be no difficulty in urging a person to *confess* and *receive the Holy Communion in any case;* as this is desirable whether in health or sickness.

A person, therefore, who is dangerously ill should make ready to confess his sins; he should send for a priest early in the day, that he may be visited that day or the day following, and not send at late and unseasonable hours, or expect to be visited at a moment's notice. A person should commonly have been first visited by a medical man, and a priest should not be hurriedly sent for on the idle fancy of any one that every ache or pain is likely to prove fatal. Persons should, if possible, receive the last sacraments while they are in the *full* use of their senses, which is too seldom the case. The room should be prepared in a suitable manner; especially there should be a table covered with a white cloth, on which to place the holy oils and the Blessed Sacrament. The sick person should have the parts to be anointed washed and clean, as a matter of common propriety as well as of religious respect. Prayers set down in prayer-books should be occasionally read to the sick person by some friend or charitable visitor, in a very gentle tone of voice, and not much at a time, for fear of causing weariness. Too often the room of sick and dying persons is crowded with visitors who come to satisfy an idle curiosity, but seldom attempt to read a few prayers, or give any spiritual consolation or help, at a time when it is most needed. The last act of the priest's ministry to the dying, is to give a plenary indulgence, called the "last blessing," which he is empowered to do by a form prescribed in the ritual. The living should not spend their time in unavailing sorrow, and merely in making funeral preparations, but should be earnest in their prayers, and, if they can, should procure masses for the deceased. Whatever can be done for the dead should be done as early as possible, that they may *at once* receive the benefit of the prayers of the living in their behalf, rather than have to wait in purgatory the slow return of many anniversary masses.

Holy Orders.

From a few scattered notices in the inspired writers, we gather that our Blessed Lord appointed His apostles to spread His religion and worship throughout the world; that they appointed others to aid them in the great work, ordaining such persons with fasting, prayer, and imposition of hands; and this *ordination* conferred on the ordained certain spiritual graces adapted to their respective duties. But of the constitution of the Christian hierarchy, or of the exact form of ordination, not one of the books of the New Testament contains any detailed account. For information on this subject, we must have recourse to the most ancient Church historians; and when we find in their pages, described as existing everywhere, the same gradation of office and authority in the sacred ministry which still prevails in the Catholic Church, the only conclusion from such antiquity and universality is, that it was established by the apostles themselves, in conformity with the teaching of their Divine Master. No other authority could have established it *everywhere*.

As in political States there are governors to preserve order and to prevent confusion, so in the Church there are some who exercise power to preserve the body of the faithful in peace and unity, and conduct them in the way of eternal life. Under the law of nature, the priesthood belonged as a right to the first-born. Thus, the ancient patriarchs were priests, and offered sacrifices, as we read of Abel, Noe, Abraham, Melchisedech, Job, &c. Under the written law, the priesthood was confined to Aaron and his family; but under the new law, Christ being our

High Priest, all spiritual power must be derived from Him. This power He first conferred on the apostles, and instituted the sacrament of Holy Orders, by which they ordained bishops and priests, who were also to be succeeded by others, receiving the like appointment. No one can have power to officiate as a bishop or priest, but such only as are lawfully ordained by the hands of those who had received lawful ordination before them. The apostles could have exercised no power till Christ had commissioned them, in the first place, to *consecrate*, as He did at the Last Supper; afterwards to *forgive sins*; and finally to *preach the Gospel and baptize*. So none can exercise such power until they have by ordination received such a commission in the sacrament of Holy Orders.

Various Orders of Ministers.—They who are preparing to enter holy orders, receive the tonsure (a ceremony performed by the bishop), in which the hair is cut off the top of the head, to signify that they henceforth renounce the world, and choose the Lord and His Church for their lot (cleros) and inheritance. Persons thus tonsured are henceforth called *clerics*. The four *minor* orders of porter, reader, exorcist, and acolyte, were for the appointment of persons to fill certain inferior offices in the Church. Of the greater, or the holy orders, the subdeacon assists the deacon, and the deacon's principal office at present is to assist the priest during the solemn Mass. The priest has to preach the Word of God, to administer the sacraments, to offer sacrifice, and to direct in the way of salvation those who are committed to his care. He is subject to his bishop, and receives from him mission or jurisdiction. Each bishop has jurisdiction over the particular district assigned to him, called a *diocese*, wherein he governs the priests and the faithful. The Bishop of Rome, by Divine appointment, is the head of the whole Church; he has the charge first given to Peter, to feed the whole flock, both lambs and sheep.

Celibacy.—From very early times, the Western Church has required her bishops, priests, and deacons to be unmarried men—that is, to lead a single life, called a life of celibacy; and for some centuries has included subdeacons under the same law. She will not ordain married men, much less will she suffer them to marry *after* ordination. It is not asserted that this practice is of Divine precept. There are, however, the strongest reasons for this law of the Church. 1. Because celibacy is a more perfect state than that of marriage; and the clergy ought to be examples of that which is most perfect. 2. Because the distractions and cares of a married state would sadly interfere with the duties of the priest, and prevent his giving himself wholly to the service of God. "He that is without a wife is solicitous for the things that belong to the Lord, how he may please God; but he that is with a wife is solicitous for the things of the world, how he may please his wife, and is divided" (1 Cor. vii. 27).

It is a duty of the faithful to pray, especially at the Ember Weeks (the appointed times of ordinations), for those who are to be made priests, to pray that the Church may always abound with good and zealous ministers, and to contribute, as far as they can, to the maintenance and education of those who are reared up to the priesthood from their early youth, and who have to go through a long course of preparation for the sacred ministry separated from the world.

MATRIMONY.

At first marriage was a natural contract by which a man and woman, being at full liberty, agreed to live together as man and wife. In every country which has laws, it is moreover a *civil* contract, which to have any civil effect must be entered upon after the manner prescribed by the law. Lastly, our Blessed Lord made it a sacramental contract, which, to have any sacramental effect, must be made after the manner prescribed by the laws of the Church. Marriage, being the great source of happiness or misery, has been the especial object of ecclesiastical and civil regulations, in order to prevent, as far as possible, the evils which may arise to society and to individuals, from thoughtlessness, deceit, imprudence, or wickedness. Reason, religion, the law of the land, the usage of good Christian and Catholic society, worldly prudence, must all be consulted and attended to in a matter of so much importance.

Marriage Indissoluble.—Marriage, as at first instituted in Paradise, was the union of one man with one woman. Men in time went contrary to this first institution by taking a *plurality* of wives, and divorcing themselves from those whom they had married, but our Saviour brought marriage back to what it was at first, making it the *indissoluble* union of *one* with *one*. Our Lord has indeed allowed divorce, so that they are not obliged to live together, in the case of adultery by either party (Matt. v. 23, and xix. 9), but the *bond* of marriage still exists, and will exist, till an end be put to it by death. Therefore, when parties have from whatever cause been separated, without hearing of each other, no length of absence can entitle either of them to marry again, without a *certainty* based upon undeniable evidence, and not on mere suspicion or vague report, of the death of the other party. For a century back the Legislature in this country had occasionally passed bills of divorce in particular cases, pretending to separate man and wife, so that they could marry again. By more recent laws such divorces have become matters of every-day occurrence. Nevertheless, it must always be borne in mind that the effect of these *civil* divorces, is not to dissolve the bond of matrimony in the *sight of God*—for that is beyond the power of any human authority—but to deprive the existing contract of all *civil* effect, and to place the persons so divorced, with respect to *civil* consequences, in the same situation as if they were actually unmarried. But they are still married in *conscience*, and cannot in that respect avail themselves of the liberty which the *law* of men may allow them.

Impediments to Marriage.—Besides those impediments spoken of under the sixth commandment of the Church in the way of affinity and consanguinity, which make a marriage null (that is no marriage at all), there are also some others of less common occurrence. Again, a promise of marriage to another person (that promise still existing), also a *simple* vow of chastity, render a marriage *sinful*, though valid. Those who marry in ignorance of such impediment which renders their marriage null, must, on becoming acquainted with it, have immediate recourse to their pastor, and seek for a dispensation, in order to give validity to their marriage. Good Catholics should guard against anything which may require a dispensation.

Mixed Marriages—that is, marriages between Catholics and non-Catholics—are also forbidden. The Church has always disapproved of such marriages, in consequence of the danger to the Catholic party of either losing the faith or becoming indifferent to it, and of the difficulty and almost impossibility of bringing up the children in the true faith. Besides this, the non-Catholic, perhaps not looking upon marriage as *indissoluble*, may, according to his or her principles, separate and marry again, which the Catholic party can never do. This is quite sufficient to make a Catholic fear such marriages. A dispensation now is necessary, and must be obtained from the Pope through the bishop, for a mixed marriage. The Church grants it, but only in order to prevent perhaps greater evils. It is granted only on condition:— 1. That the Catholic party have the free exercise of religion. 2. That all the children be brought up in the Catholic religion. 3. That the Catholic take all pains to convert the non-Catholic party.

In a recent Pastoral (1863) of one of the bishops, we read the following passage upon the subject of mixed marriages:—" Early marriages are a much less evil than *mixed* marriages, yet most parents seem to be unconcerned about the latter. And yet the evil consequences of such marriages are often felt through a long life, and for generations afterwards. They are seldom happy under the most favourable circumstances, and are often miserable beyond the idea of those who engage in them. The Church may allow them on condition that the children are brought up Catholics, but how often is such condition violated, and the poor wife, the victim of her trustfulness, is made miserable for life, and suffers a death at the birth of every child. Even if the condition is fulfilled, the children are often lukewarm in their duties, indifferent to the practices of devotion, neglect the sacraments, and at last fall away from the faith."

Ceremonies of Marriage.—The parties having been questioned as to their consent, each takes the other by the right hand, and first the bridegroom, then the bride, repeats this form of words: "I, N, take thee, N, to my wedded wife [or husband], to have and to hold, from this day forward, for better, for worse, for richer, for poorer, in sickness and in health, till death do us part, if holy Church will it permit, and thereto I plight thee my troth." After they have in this manner solemnly given and accepted each other, whilst their right hands are still joined together, the priest standing before them says—"I join you together in matrimony, in the name of the Father, and of the Son, and of the Holy Ghost—Amen;" and sprinkles them with holy water. The priest then blesses the ring, which he returns to the bridegroom, who puts some money into the hand of the bride, and puts the ring on the third finger of her left hand, saying—"With this ring I thee wed, this gold and silver I thee give, with my body I thee worship, and with all my worldly goods I thee endow, in the name of the Father, and of the Son, and of the Holy Ghost." The ring is everywhere recognized as a symbol of the mutual fidelity they have promised to each other. Then (if the marriage is *solemnized*) follows the Nuptial Mass, or at least certain prayers from the Missal, which are called the Nuptial Blessing. This blessing is not given within the forbidden times, nor in mixed marriages, nor on the marrying of a widow. It may not be without its use to know the form of words which have to be said in presence of the legal official called the Registrar, for the *legal* validity of the marriage. The words are as follows—" I do solemnly declare that I know not of any lawful impediment why I, N, may not be joined in matrimony to thee, N." The bridegroom first says them, then the bride. Also, " I call upon these persons here present to witness that I, N, do take thee, N, to my lawful wedded wife " [husband]. The bride repeats the same after the bridegroom has said them.

Holiness of Marriage.—The first miracle of Christ was on the occasion of a marriage feast: we must therefore conclude that in the judgment of Christ marriage must be a very solemn and holy thing to have been thus ennobled by His presence and glorified by His power. Marriage was raised to the dignity of a sacrament of the new law, so that a supernatural grace was henceforth by the appointment of Christ to be given to those who contract marriage with due dispositions. Thus Christ, who once in His humanity blessed the marriage feast with His presence, does in every age promise to bless by a *sacramental* grace those who in their marriage will have Him, and will not shut Him out.

Bad Marriages.—But what has Christ to do with the marriages of most *Christians* of these times, any more than He has to do with the marriages of heathens or of Turks? What has Christ to do with the marriages of too many *Catholics*, who even profess to believe that marriage is one of the seven sacraments, and that persons contracting it ought to be in a state of grace ? While it is so sacred, and the salvation of the contracting parties and of their children depends so much upon its having the blessing of Heaven, that blessing is little thought of, and often, it is to be feared, never obtained. *One* Catholic enters into an alliance with a party who does not believe in Christianity, or who hates the Catholic religion, and will never hear it named, who perhaps, though promising liberty of conscience to the wife, and a Catholic education to the children, is very likely soon to think that he did wrong in making such promises; he perhaps turns persecutor, or at best, being totally ignorant of the faith, and not knowing its necessity, can be of no use in the religious education of the children, and often, even unintentionally, will do, and require to be done, things that grievously afflict the conscience. *Another* pair of

Catholics, who believe that marriage is a sacrament, go for their sacramental blessing to some man in whose ministry they no more believe than they do in the mission of Mahomet. *Another* pair of Catholics having lived a course of sin for months or years, intend (now they have found a suitable house, and bought a little furniture, and have completed their little worldly arrangements), that their past manner of life shall become marriage, and having settled the day, without a pretence of shame or sorrow for sin, they expect the Church to bless, and Christ by His grace to be present at an alliance long ago contracted in spite of Christ and of His Church. What can be expected from such unchristian doings as these, but spiritual ruin and very often temporal misery both to parents and their children?

Cautions and Directions for a good Marriage.—Religion and the usages of good society require that young persons should not make or entertain proposals of marriage, or keep up any intimacy which, according to the common sense of the world, is likely to lead to any such proposals, without the knowledge, consent, and approbation of parents or guardians. Religion warns a Christian that he should in the first place seriously consider *whether* he should be married at all—that is, whether marriage is likely to enable him to save his soul, or whether, all things considered, it is likely to act as a hindrance. He who in the latter case marries against his conscience will run a risk of his salvation. It is absolutely necessary that a man should save his soul, but not by any means necessary for every one to marry; and the Scripture tells us also that the unmarried is the better state. The salvation of the soul having settled the question of marriage or no marriage, should also determine a number of other questions which commonly arise, as to the suitableness of the person who is to be chosen as a partner for life. Wealth, station, beauty of person, family connection, mental accomplishments, and other things usually studied in the world, may be considered and have their value, but though valuable they are not the most essential points on which to base a marriage contract. The faith, the *religious* dispositions of the person to be chosen are the more essential conditions, and if these, so far from being chiefly considered and required, are perhaps not even thought of at all, such a marriage will prove, in all probability, the ruin of both parents and children.

In the choice of a partner who is to be the happiness or misery of another, there is a necessity for *all manner* of caution and investigation that no error may be committed and have to be discovered when it is too late to be remedied. In this let no one trust his own judgment; let wise, virtuous, disinterested, and experienced persons be consulted, who may say whether such a choice is likely to be conducive both to present and future happiness, to the temporal and the eternal welfare of the parties concerned. When persons have been judged proper and suitable for one another according to the dictates of reason and religion, something of a more intimate acquaintance may begin, but must be conducted *with reserve* and in the fear of God; it should be so managed as to be above any suspicion of evil, nor should such persons, notwithstanding the boundless licentiousness of practice to the contrary, be accustomed to be much *alone* with each other. When after due consideration parties have been in a manner *engaged*, or are supposed to be so, the sooner they are married the safer and the better. Moreover, religion requires that persons should not engage in marriage without learning the *duties* of their state, which are often very grievous, difficult, and burdensome. They accept each other for better or worse; they should often consider what they are pledged to before God's altar; they must be resigned to the trials of their condition; and St. Paul warns us that married persons shall have "tribulation of the flesh."

Finally, religion teaches Christians that they should so marry as to have the blessing of the Church, that on the day of their marriage their minds should be filled with such good thoughts that they may be fit to receive the Holy Communion; that Christian modesty and decorum should be seen throughout, and not extravagance, vanity, or licentiousness. How different would be the condition of thousands and millions of the human race if marriages were more regulated by religion and Christian prudence, and not so much by caprice, chance, or brutal sensuality! What but ill-assorted marriages of old led to the total corruption of the world and the coming of the universal deluge? and what else is it that now deluges the world with so many evils which men complain of? This is the great cause of vice, of irreligion, of beggary, of destitution, and of misery of every kind.

CHAPTER VII.

VIRTUES AND VICES.

Theological Virtues.

Faith, Hope, and Charity are called *theological* virtues, because they relate immediately to God Himself; others are called *moral* virtues, because they regard in general our *moral* conduct and dealings chiefly with our neighbour.

Faith.—What we believe on the evidence of our senses is called *knowledge* or *experience;* what we believe from the exercise of our mind is called *reason;* what we believe from the testimony of men is called "*belief*" in mere human things and "faith" in things divine. Our faith rests on the Word of God, who has revealed to us His truths; but those truths are proposed and become known to us by the infallible teaching of the Church, "which is the pillar and ground of truth" (1 Tim. iii. 15). The merit of faith consists in believing what we do not see. "Faith is the substance of things to be hoped for, the evidence of things that appear not" (Heb. xi. 1).

Faith should be *firm*, without the least doubt or misgiving. Doubts when they are voluntary, or wilfully consented to, are very sinful. When they *first* arise in the mind they should be immediately rejected, without stopping to reason with them; they should be opposed by acts of faith and by prayer. If they proceed from ignorance it is necessary to get instruction; if from the enemies of our religion, by giving ear to their irreligious conversation or by reading heretical books, then these things must be avoided; for thus to expose our faith, knowingly and unnecessarily, is a sin. Faith should be *entire*, comprehending all revealed truths, both those which seem more difficult as well as those which seem less mysterious. Faith is called *explicit* when, knowing that a certain truth is revealed, we believe it distinctly and in particular. Faith is called *implicit* when we believe all revealed truths in *general*, whether we know them or not; as, for instance, when we believe in general *all* that the Church believes and teaches. An *explicit* faith is necessary as a means of salvation, in one God, in the Trinity, in the incarnation and death of Christ. It is necessary to become acquainted with other doctrines which immediately concern *practical* duties, such as penance and the Holy Eucharist. All should make diligent use of the means which are afforded them of not merely knowing the essentials, but of becoming *thoroughly* instructed in religion so as to be able to help others. Faith is a precious gift of God, which we should use every means to increase, and endeavour every day to put in practice.

Hope is a gift of God, whereby our souls are raised to the expectation of eternal glory. This is founded on the power of God, and the merits of Christ, who has promised heaven to such as do good works, and grace whereby to do them. Hope encourages us in the practice of virtue, strengthens us in afflictions, and cheers us in the hour of death. The sins against hope are despair and presumption. *Despair* is a distrust of the power of God, or the promises of Christ, which leads a person to think he will never be saved, and therefore to give up all attempts at salvation. Those persons are guilty of it who give up all hopes of salvation on account of its difficulties, or of pardon on account of the number and grievousness of their sins, who despair of amendment on account of the violence of their evil inclinations, the force of bad habits, or the experience which they have had of their weakness; those also who despair of obtaining what they ask for in prayer, because it is deferred; or of receiving relief or support in distress or sickness, and so wish for death when they are not ready. *Presumption* is a vain expectation of salvation, and of the necessary helps without performing the conditions required. Those persons are guilty of presumption — 1, who continue in sin with the intention of repenting before death, deferring their repentance because God is merciful; 2, those who expose themselves without necessity to the immediate occasion of sin, depending on their own strength; 3, who in temporal or spiritual affairs trust to their own power, prudence, or endeavours, independently of God. God is merciful, therefore no one should despair; He is just, therefore let no one presume.

Charity teaches us to love God above all things, for His own sake; and our neighbour as ourselves, for God's sake. The more we love God, in consideration of His own infinite greatness, glory, and perfections, rather than from the hope of reward or fear of punishment, the more perfect our charity becomes. No one of the moral virtues, nor all of them together, will be of any avail to salvation without charity, which alone can give life and merit to all our works. We must love God " with our whole heart and soul," by giving Him the preference in our affections before all that is dearest in this world; " with our whole mind," by employing the natural powers and faculties of our minds upon Him; and " with our whole strength," by employing also the whole outward man, the body with all its powers, in doing His service.

Charity teaches us also to love our neighbour as ourselves. All mankind, without exception, are our neighbours, especially Catholics. All men were made to the image of God, and Christ came to redeem and save *all men;* but Catholics are especially our neighbours, because they are members, like ourselves, of that mystical body the Church, of which Christ is the head. To love God above all things, is to be willing to wish our neighbour the same good as we do ourselves, and to do him no wrong. This charity to our neighbour must be extended even to our *greatest enemies.* We cannot for a moment wilfully entertain sentiments of hatred or desire of revenge, even against an enemy, much less do him an uncharitable action, without incurring the guilt of sin; and when either hatred, the desire of revenge, or uncharitableness, is considerable, the sin becomes mortal. "I say to you," says Christ, "love your *enemies*, do good to them that hate you," &c. Christ prayed for His enemies, and died for them.

Cardinal Virtues.

Four of the moral virtues are called "cardinal" virtues (from the Latin word "cardo," which means a "hinge"), because they are, as it were, the hinges on which all the other virtues hang, and by which they must move and be regulated. The *first* is *Prudence.* This leads us to caution and thoughtfulness in things which concern our temporal or eternal well-being. Prudence teaches us to examine well before we determine; to suspend our own judgments, and willingly to learn from those who have had more experience, to lay up in the memory what has happened to others; to be cautious in considering what difficulties we are likely to meet with. By this great virtue, kings and magistrates should rule, and people obey; by this, armies should be commanded, families governed, and the life and actions of each individual be directed to all good.

2. *Justice* is a virtue which teaches us to give every one his due. There is a justice we owe to God, in giving to Him, as our Creator, all that love, fear, and homage, which is due to Him from His creatures. Justice to our

neighbour teaches us to wrong no man. It is a virtue which must run through the whole course of a man's life, as we continually have dealings with others, so that of all the moral virtues this is the most beneficial to society. There is a justice in honouring our parents next to God; there is a justice in loving our country in which we have received our birth and education; a justice in being grateful to our benefactors. The just man gives glory to God, obedience to his superiors, love to his equals, and assistance to his inferiors. He does no injury to another, in word or deed, nor even in thought; neither in his goods, or in his honour, or in his person. God is just, and with Him the just shall live for ever.

3. *Fortitude* is a virtue which gives us courage to face all the evils of life, and to withstand even death itself, rather than abandon duty. It is fortitude to face death in a just war in defence of one's country— this even the heathens did; to die voluntarily for the cause of God in defence of the true faith, or to avoid sin, is martyrdom. If fortitude keeps the soul steady and firm in the midst of the greatest dangers, nay, even in death itself, it cannot fail to fortify us against lesser dangers, so that we should never abandon any duty through fear. Fortitude teaches us *patience* to support the evils of life with cheerfulness rather than forfeit the friendship of God; it teaches us *constancy* to persist in virtue against all difficulties, from whatever source they proceed; it teaches *perseverance* to remain firm to the end of life amidst those persecutions and sufferings which cause so many to abandon virtue and religion.

Temperance, in its ordinary use and in a limited sense, means *moderation in eating and drinking;* but, as a cardinal virtue, it means moderation in *all* things; and it enables us to restrain *every* desire of the heart according to the dictates of reason and religion. Even virtues may be injured by *excess*, as well as by deficiency. Virtue has two powerful enemies to contend with — fear of pain on the one hand, and love of pleasure on the other. The first would *frighten* us from the practice of virtue; the second would *allure* and entice us to the practice of vice.

Against the first, *fortitude* is necessary, and against the second, *temperance*. Now, as amongst all sensual gratifications, those of *lust and gluttony* are the most violent, we stand in especial need of temperance to guard us against these propensities, so as to keep them within the bounds of reason and religion, lest otherwise they offend God. But besides that temperance which moderates the violence of our appetites towards lust and gluttony, there is a temperance or moderation to be observed in many other things—in dress, in furniture, in mirth, discourse, recreation. Moreover, clemency, mildness, abstemiousness, fasting, sobriety, continency, or chastity, all originate in *temperance*. Every Christian, then, should keep watch over his appetites and desires. He should use the blessings bestowed upon him with moderation; he should follow necessity, not excess and superfluity; for whatever goes beyond necessity becomes luxury, and feeds the passions. Let moderation regulate the whole outward and the inward man. We should use all things in this world with the recollection that we shall have to part with them, and perhaps soon. Such is the lesson of St. Paul (1 Cor. vii. 29)—"The time is short: it remaineth that they who have wives be as if they had none; and they that weep, as though they wept not; and they that rejoice, as if they rejoiced not; and they that buy, as though they possessed not; and they that use the world, as though they used it not; for the fashion of this world passeth away." We must live "soberly"— that is, in the practice of universal temperance in this world, keeping free from all forbidden pleasures here, that we may hope to enjoy eternal pleasures hereafter.

The corporal works of mercy are those different ways by which we may relieve the various bodily wants of our neighbour, whether it be by procuring for them food, clothing, lodging, medicine, giving assistance towards a decent and Christian burial, or by any other means which charity can find out. All these different things are highly commended in Scripture, so that not even the giving a cup of cold water for Christ's sake will lose its reward. In some countries, the poor are entirely dependent on charity; in others, a *legal* provision is made for them, so that no one should perish for want. In this latter case, persons have to pay out of their property for the maintenance of the poor, and therefore he who pays in this manner must be considered to have done something towards the fulfilment of obligations which charity would have otherwise more strictly imposed upon him. He cannot be obliged in conscience to do in charity as much as if he had to pay nothing from his property for the maintenance of the poor. But in spite of all legal provisions, which, like all human laws, must be imperfect, what a multitude of cases continually occur, especially of persons advanced in years, sick and disabled, or who have come to sudden and unforeseen distress, which deserve the utmost sympathy and the most generous charity. As long as the world lasts, there will be abundance of poor, not only of those who have brought their poverty on themselves by vice and irreligion, by drunkenness, imprudent marriages, &c., but of those who are poor without fault or sin of theirs, but by the ordinary course of human things, and the permission of a mysterious Providence. The words of promise to those who do works of charity still remain, and will never fail; and though we forget them now, they will be heard both by good and bad on the day of judgment; and it is expressly declared that the doing works of charity, or the neglect of them, will be one principal cause of acquittal or condemnation on that great day.

The Spiritual Works of Mercy.—As the corporal works of mercy relate to the body, so the spiritual works of mercy relate to the *soul;* and as the soul is more excellent than the body, so the spiritual works of mercy by far surpass the corporal, and ought therefore to be more diligently practised. If so great a reward is promised to those who do the least corporal work of mercy, how great must be the reward for works that are spiritual? Next to the salvation of our own soul, the best thing we can do is to help in the salvation of others. The seven spiritual works of mercy are these: 1. "To convert the sinner." The most necessary good that we can procure for any one who is living in habits of sin is to convert him from his evil ways. "He who causeth a sinner to be converted from the error of his way shall save his soul from death, and shall cover a multitude of sins" (St. James v. 20). To admonish sinners with a view to their amendment, though a delicate point, is often a strict duty; but it is a duty in the performance of which great prudence is required. We should not neglect to give charitable admonitions when there is a prospect of doing good. 2. "To instruct the ignorant." Lose no opportunity of doing this good work. "They that instruct many to justice shall shine as stars for all eternity" (Dan. xii. 3). 3. "To counsel the doubtful." When doubts are floating in the mind of any one in regard of duty, and he knows not how to act in consequence of there being difficulties on every side, it is a great charity to give him, or to procure for him, suitable advice, to relieve his anxious waverings, to clear up his doubts, and perhaps save him from some dangerous or fatal error. 4. "To comfort the sorrowful." Endeavour to soothe the afflicted heart with words of consolation, to suggest motives of patience and resignation. Show to the distressed a compassionate and kind treatment—that is, in the words of St. Paul, "Weep with them that weep" (Rom. xii. 15). As there is so much trouble and affliction in the world, what can be a nobler work of charity than to bind up the wounds of sorrow, and to pour into the heart the soothing oil of consolation? 5. "To bear wrongs patiently." The humours, ill-tempers, and failings of others, their ingratitude for kindnesses received, are often so tiresome and provoking, that it requires no little patience to bear with them. But this patience will not only be a benefit to our own souls, but will be more likely than anything else to remove the evils we complain of in others. 6. "To forgive injuries." It is difficult to forgive an enemy; but, though difficult, it is absolutely required of us. Our forgiveness of others is to be the measure of the forgiveness we shall receive ourselves. 7. "To pray for the living and the dead." We should pray for all mankind, for both friends and enemies. The latter, indeed, have more need of our prayers, and our praying for them shows a more disinterested charity. "Pray for one another, that you may be saved" (St. James v. 15). "Pray for them that persecute and calumniate you." Pray for those whom you know to be in great need of prayers. We should pray also for the dead, for our deceased relatives, friends, and benefactors, and for *all* the faithful departed: this is the last act of charity we can do for them. "It is a holy and wholesome thought to pray for the dead, that they may be loosed from their sins" (2 Macc. xii. 46).

The Eight Beatitudes.

The word "beatitude" means blessedness or happiness. Before Christ came, the wisest of men disputed with each other, and were unable to decide in what man's greatest good ("summum bonum") consisted. They sought happiness in all manner of things which could not satisfy them. So it has been since. But Christ in His sermon on the Mount lays down eight maxims which must be the foundation of all true happiness, both here and hereafter. These are called the eight beatitudes; that is, there are eight classes of persons who are pronounced by Christ Himself to be truly happy, and they are these:—1. The "poor in spirit" are those who being poor bear their privations in a spirit of patience, resignation, and humility, and are content with their condition. The "poor in spirit" means those also who being rich have their hearts and affections free from riches, who do not love them overmuch, but employ them in doing good. 2. The "meek" are they who show a mildness and gentleness at all times, who even practise patience under insults, violence, oppression, injuries, and ill-treatment. Such are pleasing to God, and well-beloved by men. 3. "Mourners" are they who thinking little of the pleasures and dissipations of the world, and shunning them as much as possible, often bewail their own sins and the sins of others, who sigh over the dangers to which their salvation is continually exposed, and look upon this life as a place of banishment and a valley of tears. They lead a penitential life, and suffer patiently, perhaps cheerfully, for the love of God, all temporal afflictions. These sow in tears but reap in joy. 4. They "hunger and thirst after justice" who ardently desire and earnestly seek to become *just;* that is, to become every day more and more virtuous. This disposition of the soul is a great grace, enabling us to advance rapidly and with great ease in the practice of virtue, and to arrive in a short time at a high state of perfection. 5. The "merciful" are those who, being full of mercy and compassion to others, do what they can to assist their neighbour in all his spiritual and corporal necessities. 6. The "clean of heart" are they who are free from earthly, carnal, impure affections which defile the heart. It is from the "heart" that there come forth evil actions, as well as evil thoughts and desires. The fountain must be pure or the waters that issue forth will be defiled. 7. "Peace-makers" are such as live at peace with themselves in their own interior, at peace with all their neighbours, and at peace with God. These are especially the followers of Him whose title is "the Prince of Peace," and who gave His peace as a legacy to His followers. Such will also endeavour to reconcile persons who are at variance by making peace between them, and will never be of the number of those who, by tale-bearing and imprudent speeches, are ever sowing discord amongst brethren. 8. They that "suffer persecution for justice sake" are those who are ill-treated, calumniated, and despised, because they support truth and justice. All must expect to taste of persecution occasionally, sometimes from enemies, sometimes from friends. "All that will live godly in Christ Jesus shall suffer persecution."

The Seven Deadly Sins.

They are called *deadly* because they bring death to the soul which yields to them. They are also called the *capital* sins ("capita" means "heads"), because they are the *heads* or *sources* from which all other sins proceed. In each person there is generally *one* passion which is stronger than the rest, and which, because it rules more strongly in the breast than the others, is called the *predominant* passion. Every one should endeavour to discover his ruling or predominant passion, because if he can conquer the leader the rest will give him no trouble; and that leading passion in each individual is the great cause of nearly all his sins. On these vices there will be found in the "Garden of the Soul" some excellent instructions entitled "Remedies against Vices," which it would be well to read occasionally with attention.

1. *Pride* is an inordinate, that is an excessive and unreasonable, esteem of ourselves and of what we have; as for example, of personal appearance, furniture, fine clothes, ability, judgment, &c. As people wish others to think as they do themselves, the proud often become *vain*—that is, they have an immoderate desire of the praise and esteem of others. To secure that good opinion of others they fall into *hypocrisy*, which consists in a pretence of more piety, virtue, riches, or learning than they really possess. They become *ambitious*, desiring and seeking by any means, lawful or unlawful, and at any cost, honours, preferments, dignities, and to sit down in the highest places. They are full of *presumption* in their own opinion, and of *disdain* and contempt of others. They are full of *obstinacy* in keeping to their own judgment, so that rather than yield, they will resist the known truth even in questions of faith or morals; they are filled with the spirit of contention, discord, and wrangling, in defending their opinion with noise, confidence, and violent language. The proud are the most disobedient, and are often full

of singularity and affectation in opinion, dress, and behaviour. It may, then, well be said, that pride is the root of all evil, and that from "pride all perdition took its beginning" (Tob. iv. 14).

Humility is the exact opposite of pride, and is the remedy of all those evils which pride brings along with it. Humility is the distinguishing virtue of a Christian. Christ told His followers to learn humility of Him. "He that humbleth himself shall be exalted," says our Saviour.

2. *Covetousness*, sometimes called *avarice*, is an excessive love or greediness of riches and earthly possessions. The more this love is gratified the stronger it becomes. As the possessions of a covetous man increase, his want of still greater possessions increases also; and therefore covetousness makes a man *wretchedly poor* even in the midst of plenty. It makes him deaf to the cry of the needy, unmercifully sparing, sometimes even to his own individual necessities, and it naturally leads to many other sins, in order to get money; for example, to extortion, cheating, stealing, and lying. What with the desire of getting more, and the fear of losing what he has, the covetous man is always restless and unhappy. A man who grasps at everything and hoards it up without using it is called a *miser*, which means a *miserable* man. *Liberality* is the opposite virtue, which prompts a man not to be too eager after worldly things; to use them (though without extravagance) in a generous manner for the purposes for which they were intended, and not to forget the claims of religion and the calls of charity. To put by a sufficient and reasonable provision for coming wants, and for those who may depend upon us, and would otherwise become perhaps destitute, is not covetousness but Christian *prudence*. A man who possesses riches should take care not to be possessed *by* them; but both in acquiring and in possessing them should never put too much confidence in them, nor allow them to be a hindrance to his salvation. We are warned in the Gospel against pleasures, cares, and "*riches*" as three great enemies of our souls.

3. *Lust*, or an irregular desire of carnal pleasures, has already been spoken of under the sixth and ninth commandments.

4. *Anger*, which has already been spoken of under the fifth commandment, is a vice directly contrary to the spirit of the Gospel, which breathes everywhere meekness and patience. Anger hurries a person into many other sins, as contentions, enmity, hatred, revenge, fighting, &c. How many oaths, curses, and blasphemies proceed from it! How many a man has ruined his worldly prospects by the imprudences he has committed in *one* fit of anger. "Therefore let all bitterness and anger be put away from you." *Meekness* is the virtue opposed to anger. It shows itself in mildness of words and conduct, in gentleness of temper, in patient forbearance with the faults of others. It is a most amiable virtue, which not only corrects our own anger, but also disarms that of others. "Learn of me, because I am meek and humble of heart, and you shall find rest to your souls" (Matt. xi. 29).

5. *Gluttony* is an inordinate love of eating and drinking, though the latter is generally called *drunkenness*. Gluttony may be committed either by eating or drinking to excess in quantity, so as to injure the health of the body, or by going to extravagant expense in meat or drink to procure luxuries. Those who are addicted to this sin, especially to drunkenness, expose themselves to all manner of disorders. They ruin their families, destroy their reason, and hasten death; and they are generally addicted to every species of impurity. Gluttony has killed more than the sword or the plague. Gluttony has killed more than famine. Gluttony brings and aggravates diseases, beyond all the skill of physicians to cure. *Temperance* is the virtue opposed to gluttony. It is a virtue which few practise, and those who are temperate in their diet are careful more for the health of the body than of the soul; whereas, when practised from the true spirit of Christian mortification, it becomes conducive to both, especially to the latter. The Church commands us to fast and abstain, in order to promote this virtue, and to subdue the vice of gluttony, as a preservative against

excess, and an atonement for past sins and excesses. It should be remembered that we do not live in order to eat and drink, but we eat and drink in order to live. Eat then to live, to support nature, to preserve health, to prolong life, not to destroy it. Drink to quench your thirst, not to drown your reason. We are never more in the power of the devil than when we are overcome by excess in eating and drinking. It is the duty of a Christian to live "soberly" as well as piously.

6. *Envy* is a sadness or repining at another's good, because it seems to lessen our own. An envious man, though he has received no injury from another, often shows as much enmity, anger, and malice to the person envied, as though he had actually been injured by him. It is directly contrary to Christian charity, which, as St. Paul says, " envieth not, but rejoiceth in good." If we sincerely wished well to everybody as we profess to do, we ought to rejoice when we see others doing well, because our own desires and wishes are being fulfilled. But instead of this, we envy those above us; we are jealous of our equals lest they should get before us, and are afraid of our inferiors lest they should become our equals. Envy seems the most unreasonable of all vices. It has been the cause of some of the greatest crimes which were ever committed in the world. *Brotherly love,* which is only another name for charity, teaches us really to wish another all the good we wish ourselves, and will never lead any one to get an advantage over a rival by anything sinful, dishonest, or dishonourable.

7. *Sloth* is a laziness of mind in neglecting to begin or to prosecute such things as relate to the service of God and our salvation. Those are guilty of sloth who neglect prayer, who never use their minds about religion, who are too idle to make any effort to curb their passions, or to acquire virtue. This sloth is opposed to all virtues; it makes people faint-hearted in every undertaking; it causes an aversion to all good; it produces despair of all improvement. Then there commonly follows a dissipation of mind in pleasure and amusements, curiosity, idle conversation, and company. There are Christians who seem

free from the grosser vices of sensuality and intemperance, who seem to have no vices, to commit no positive acts of sin, and yet who by sloth, or some want of faith, are as negligent and cold about all religious duties as though they were the slaves of the worst passions. *Diligence* or *devotion* is the virtue which we must aim at, as opposed to sloth. We are sent into this world, not to live at our ease, but to *work* out our salvation; and to succeed in this work, we must not only be resolute " in declining from evil," but diligent also " in doing good." The "*night*" is approaching in which no man can work. Men labour earnestly for riches which may be taken from them by death at any hour; how much more diligently should they labour for those riches that will endure for ever. As the idle man can expect nothing but poverty and want, so a Christian who has done nothing for the life to come can expect nothing but eternal poverty and misery.

Sins against the Holy Ghost.—There are many sins which we commit through human weakness, or through ignorance and want of thought. Though weakness and ignorance do not justify us in the midst of our sins, yet they will, in some degree, plead in excuse for us; for God knows that even the best disposed to keep His law are very frail and erring. But such sins of frailty are very different from sins of *malice*, when men sin with full knowledge, and often with contempt of the law. A man who commits such sins as these must have brought himself to them by continually hardening his heart, and resisting the good thoughts that were given him—that is, by shutting his heart against the inspirations of the Holy Ghost. The sins of this description are therefore called " sins against the Holy Ghost," and being so full of wilfulness and malice, are far more grievous than ordinary sins. There are commonly said to be six sins of this class. As " final impenitence " and " obstinacy in sin," year after year, oppose the inspirations of the grace of God, calling us to repentance, so " envy at another's spiritual good " is opposed to charity, without which no one can be in a state of grace and salvation. " Resisting the known truth" opposes that which is to convert us from our errors and evil ways. "Presumption" sets itself in opposition to good works, without which faith cannot save us; and "despair" shuts us out from even the hope of mercy. Those who are guilty of these sins are seldom pardoned, because they seldom repent; but there is no sin which the mercy of God does not reach, except "final impenitence."

The four sins which cry to Heaven for vengeance are four crimes against which Almighty God expresses His anger in the strongest terms. The consideration of them belongs properly to the explanation of the commandments; for "wilful murder" is forbidden by the fifth commandment; "sodomy" (which is an unnatural sin of impurity) by the sixth; "oppression of the poor" and "defrauding labourers of their wages" by the seventh. These sins are said "to cry to Heaven for vengeance," because such is the expression used in Scripture concerning them.

Partaking of the Sins of Others.—We become answerable for the sins of others whenever we are the cause of their sins through our own fault. There are some persons who concern themselves very little about the sins which they cause their neighbour to commit, although they are as guilty before God as if they committed the sinful acts themselves. We may cause others to sin (and so be guilty ourselves) in these *nine ways*, namely—

1. "By counsel"—that is, by advising or directing the commission of an evil.

2. "By command," by forcing or obliging any one to sin.

3. "By consent," by permitting any one of those under our control to commit sin.

4. "By provocation," by exciting any one to passion, to cursing, to impurity, &c.

5. "By praise or flattery" for the evil which a person has done, and thereby encouraging him to do it again.

6. "By concealment," by hiding the crime, or the criminal, or things that have been stolen, and thereby encouraging the evil to go on, or by harbouring thieves,

or lewd persons, &c., thereby favouring their criminal practices.

7. "By partaking," by sharing in ill-gotten goods, or in any other fruits of wickedness, whereby we encourage the transgressions.

8. "By silence," by not speaking to prevent an evil, when we *should* and *could* have prevented it.

9. "By defence of the ill done," by justifying the evil-doers, or their evil actions.

When an injury has been done to our neighbour by any of these sins, he who has *caused* the injury to be done is bound to repair it, just as much as if he *had done it himself*. When you commit a sin yourself, you know where it stops, and may have the comfort to know that you have confessed and done penance for it; but when you have been the cause of another's sin, you know not where it will end, or whether he will ever repent; perhaps you have made a wound which will never more be cured, the thought of which must necessarily torture your soul with remorse as long as you live. Do not make your own account heavier by adding to it the sins of others; you will find the debt of your own sins heavy enough of itself.

Prayer, fasting, and almsdeeds are called the three *eminent good works*, because they are *eminently* and especially pleasing to God, and because by them we devote to God all that we are and all that we have. They signify a certain *class* rather than any one kind of good works. By "prayer" we make to God an offering of our *soul* with all its powers, and of our heart with all its affections; employing them not only in acts of petition but in acts of adoration, praise, and thanksgiving, as also in the practice of daily or frequent meditation on eternal truths. By "fasting" we devote to Him our *body* with all its senses, offering it to Him as a living sacrifice. This good work extends not only to a faithful observance of the fasts and abstinences commanded by the Church, but to every species of mortification and self-denial so necessary for leading a *spiritual* life; for the stronger the *flesh* the weaker the *spirit*. By "almsdeeds" we dedicate to Him our earthly possessions, with all our means of assisting others, employing them in all *kinds of charities*, both corporal and spiritual, which we can render to our neighbour. By these *three eminent good works* we offer to God, like the three wise men, our frankincense (by prayer), our myrrh (by fasting), and our gold (by almsdeeds). The archangel Raphael said to Tobias (xii. 8), "*Prayer* is good with *fasting* and *alms* more than to lay up treasures of gold."

The Three Evangelical Counsels.—They are called "*counsels*," because they are not commanded, but recommended as means of greater perfection; they are called "*evangelical*" or Gospel counsels, as contained in the Gospel, or the Word of God. 1. "Voluntary poverty" is the leaving all things of our own free will, and becoming poor in order to be able the better to follow Christ. The practice of this counsel uproots a most *dangerous* passion—namely, the love of riches and earthly things. The apostles left all to follow Christ, and many in every age of the Church have done the same. If we are not obliged to embrace this poverty, we ought to admire those who, for the sake of Christ, have done so, and always to remember the duty of moderating any undue love we have, or may have, to the things of this life. 2. "Perpetual chastity" is a voluntary abstaining from marriage and all carnal pleasures, in order to be more free to dedicate oneself to the love and service of God. This helps us to observe the whole law of God with more purity and sanctity, by deadening within us all thought and desire of carnal pleasures. This counsel many multitudes of both sexes have followed, and it must be observed by all who take the orders of priest, deacon, or subdeacon, according to the command of the Church. Jovinian, an old condemned heretic, was the first who taught marriage to be preferable to virginity, for which he was called by St. Augustine "a monster." 3. "Entire obedience" is a total subjection of one's own will to that of a lawful superior in all that is not sin. The life of Christ was one continual model of obedience. It is a most effectual means of subduing *self-will* and self-love, which are our most fatal enemies. By breaking our stubborn wills and making them subject to the will of another, this counsel helps us the more readily to obey the will and the commandments of God.

They who bind themselves to these three Gospel counsels by vow, and who commonly live together in communities, that is in convents or monasteries, are called monks and nuns. Their state is called the "religious state," and the followers of it are called "religious." Other devout persons sometimes observe these counsels in a less perfect manner while living in the world. The observance of these counsels is often much ridiculed even by persons who profess to believe in Christianity, notwithstanding the words of Christ and of St. Paul upon this subject. All *religious* orders observe these counsels, some with more severity than others, but they differ from each other in their manner of spending the day, and in the proportion of time they give to prayer, study, silence, manual labour, or works of charity; and are called by different names, generally from the name of the holy founder of their order or institute: as Benedictines, Franciscans, Dominicans.

The Four Last Things.—Death, judgment, hell, and heaven, ought every day of our lives to be in our minds. If we reflected seriously on these awful truths, how deeply we should fear the great evil of sin, and how carefully we should avoid it; how diligent we should be in making use of the means proper for obtaining God's grace, and for persevering in our duty to Him. Reflect, therefore, frequently and seriously on these truths, on these four last things; keep them constantly in mind, and you will find them a powerful preservative against falling into sin in time of temptation. "In all thy works remember thy last end; and thou shalt never sin" (Eccl. vii. 40).

Conclusion.

In the eighth chapter of the Catechism, called the "Christian's Rule of Life," will be found mentioned the great principles of religion by which a Christian must regulate his whole life if he hopes to be saved. These principles are, to hate sin above all other evils, to love God with our whole heart, and continually to use the means to acquire and increase that love; to love all mankind, even our enemies, for God's sake; to deny our own inclinations, which are continually prone to evil; "to take up our cross," by patient submission to trials and afflictions; also, "to follow Christ," by walking in His footsteps, and by imitating all His virtues, especially His meekness, humility, and obedience. Besides this, we have continually all the days of our life to fight against those three great enemies of our salvation, the devil, the world, and the flesh, relying on God's grace, and not on our own strength. All these important principles of practical religion have been more or less already treated of, and perhaps sufficiently, in this little book; but they are subjects which are so important that one or other of them will be found to be, in a great measure, the real object of all that we shall read elsewhere in spiritual books, and of all the sermons we shall hear. That admirable prayer called the "Universal Prayer" reminds us also of all the great principles of religion, and the virtues which we should cultivate. It is worthy of being said every day, or even any *one* petition of it would be abundantly sufficient for each day, if we often repeated it, and thought of it during the course of the day. Happy will they be who strive to put in practice every day what they have already learnt, and endeavour year after year, by reading, meditation, and hearing sermons and instructions, to *add* to their spiritual knowledge. Alas! how often are the duties of religion, which have been practised for a short time in early youth, speedily abandoned, and even the truths and principles of religion almost entirely forgotten!

The ninth chapter of the Catechism, called the "Christian's Daily Exercise," teaches how every one should begin, and spend, and end each day, in order to make it truly holy and acceptable to God. If we knew how to spend any one day well, we should know how to spend the *three hundred and sixty-five* days well; and if one year, then all the years, few or many, that we shall have to live. If to the instructions given in the Catechism be added certain *instructions* contained in the "Garden of the Soul," on the manner of spending the day well, nothing more need be added here.

THE END.

COX AND WYMAN, PRINTERS, GREAT QUEEN STREET, LONDON.